EATS
A Folk History of Texas Foods

EATS

A Folk History of Texas Foods

by Ernestine Sewell Linck *and* Joyce Gibson Roach

with a foreword by James Ward Lee

Texas Christian University Press
Fort Worth

Library of Congress Cataloging-in-Publication Data

Sewell, Ernestine P.
Eats : a folk history of Texas food / by Ernestine Sewell Linck
and Joyce Gibson Roach ; with a foreword by James Ward Lee.
p.   cm.
Bibliography: p.
Includes index.
ISBN 0-87565-032-5. ISBN 0-87565-035-X (pbk.)
1. Cookery, American—Southwestern style.   2. Cookery—Texas.
3. Folklore—Texas.   I. Roach, Joyce Gibson.   II. Title.
TX715.2.S69S48   1989
394.1′2′09764—dc19   88-20158
CIP

The endsheets, *Food Plants in Cherokee* and *Months in Cherokee*, 1987,
pen and ink drawings, are the work of Native American artist
Murv Jacob, Peggs, Oklahoma. Printed with permission of the artist.

Drawings by Barbara Mathews Whitehead
Book design by Whitehead & Whitehead

Contents

to the memory of my mother,
NELL GREENROOS PORCHER,
whose recipe for rice custard, the family favorite,
is not in this book because we
have never figured out
how she made it so good.
E. S. L.

to my Texas mother,
ANN GIBSON,
in whose presence none have ever
hungered and thirsted.
J. G. R.

Preface

Elmer Kelton says it's well known when you are driving along Texas highways and see a food joint with a sign out front saying "Eats," *don't stop!*

Paul Patterson advises that you can be sure of the chuck if you stop at a cafe. When his father first took him to such a place, he looked at the words and thought c-a-f-e must rhyme with s-a-f-e.

We trust the title *Eats* does not stop you from tasting our book. You'll find foods overcooked and drenched in grease, foods that will make you say, "Lord, what foods these mortals et." You could look for calf fries, barbecued cicadas, roast possum, pickled kidneys, and fried rattlesnake—but we do not presume to give "receets" for everything Texans have found to their taste. We do offer a sampler as *safe* as what you'd get at Paul's *cafe*.

The foreword concludes with James Ward Lee's comment: "Eats. I am a monument to them. We all are. And they are a monument to us."

That is what this book is: a monument to Texas foods. We begin with early travellers to Texas and what they found the folk eating. Their reports show us some more-or-less-defined geographic areas distinct for the foods those stalwart settlers fed on and thrived on.

We also include stories of Texans when they celebrate, for at holiday times the folk return to their traditions and inadvertently reveal the remnants of their folk heritage and the changes time and place have brought.

Finally, this is a folklore book. It has all sorts of odd lore that reflects reality as well as the made-up. It could be a companion piece to *Texas Augustus*, a work in progress by Clay Reynolds, which has a humorous subplot about a "fellow who goes off the deep end and develops a tooth for chicken-fried steak, Tex-Mex, and other curiosities of Texas kitchens while his long-suffering New

York wife tries to cope." And with that invitation to find something to make you laugh, we turn to a more serious vein.

The pages are a memory and preservation of the richest of our Texas traditions—its incomparable food and folk indivisible. Read, rejoice, and remember! And in the remembering may you recreate one special time and place when you were content and didn't hunger for either food or love. For Joyce, "It was in Ann's bright yellow kitchen, black cookbook on the table, when 'armies clashed by night' in 1944 and I waited for my birthday cake and the storyteller to come home from the war. How about you?"

We are indebted to the host of friends who invited us to their celebrations, shared their stories with us, gave us their recipes, and endowed this manuscript with folksiness by their random remarks. We have printed the recipes as they were given to us. Some of the frontier food recipes will require the imagination of the cook. Some of the Southern recipes may seem a little sweet. Some recipes specify a brand name, but the use of the brand name does not necessarily carry our endorsement.

To photography archivists at the Amon Carter Museum, Fort Worth; the Southwest Collection at Texas Tech University, Lubbock; East Texas State University, Commerce; and to Sarah Greene, Gilmer; Elly Hutcheson, Fort Worth; Otha Spencer, Commerce; and Charles Linck, Commerce, go our thanks for photographs. Also we appreciate permissions to photograph Old City Park, Dallas, from Pam Brewster, and Log Cabin Village, Fort Worth, from Bettie Regester. And we are grateful for permission to use aphorisms, proverbs and riddles from the John O. West Collection of Texas Folklore at El Paso, from *Mirrors, Mice and Mustaches* by George Hendricks, and from the Carl Coke Rister Collection at Texas Tech University in Lubbock. Finally, to Chris Elliott goes a special vote of thanks for her editorial advice and expert typing.

I, Ernestine Sewell Linck, acknowledge the enthusiastic support of my family, who gave me the idea for the book to begin with and then helped with their reminiscences.

I, Joyce Roach, acknowledge my kinfolks, the Fines and the Hartmans, who had as many wonderful places to offer food as they had ways to fix it; my deep roots in Jacksboro, Jack County, Texas, where I was nurtured on history and lore and friendship along with my victuals; and my associates in the Texas Folklore Society from whom I have drunk deeply and fed generously for many years.

E. S. L. and J. G. R.

Foreword

Eats. At two hundred twenty-five pounds, I am a monument to them. Eats—meals, grub, chuck (when you pointed them north up the Great Western Trail), chow, groceries, bites, vittles, victuals (to social historians), snacks, mess (for soldiers), provisions, refreshment and sustenance (when preachers are thanking the Lord), gut-waddin', viands, foodstuffs, refection (if you take your meals in a monastery), meals, meat (as in Yeats's "It's certain that fine women eat/A crazy salad with their meat").

And when we are ingurgitating our eats we are dining, breakfasting, brunching, snacking, lunching, nooning, supping (after the theatre, of course), feasting, eating, victualling. We may be scarfing them up—or down—hogging them, pigging out (a vile new phrase), slopping, chowing down, wolfing, gobbling, cramming, inhaling, stuffing, picking-at-like-a-bird, chomping, gnawing, gumming, swallowing whole, masticating, swilling down.

And the places for eats. Restaurants, bistros, mess halls, cafes, chuck wagons, refectories (meanwhile, back at the monastery), greasy spoons, chop houses, cook shops, chow halls, cafeterias, dining rooms, kountry kitchens, snack bars, DQs, grills, eateries, pits (as in barbecue), pubs, delis, diners, pizzerias, steak houses, hotdog stands, gedunk wagons, lunch wagons, and ten thousand "Rooms" ranging from the Pump Room to the Venetian Room to the Farmer's Elbow Room in Santa Cruz, California. Ill-built grammar schools even have cafetoriums.

> Eats. Some give thanks for them in advance—a sign of faith:
> Bless us, O Lord, in these thy gifts,
> Which through thy bounty we are about to partake.

> Instead of blessing some merely anticipate the eats:
> > Over the lips and past the gums
> > Look out, stomach, here it comes.

But it is most common to bless *and* anticipate:

> For what we are about to receive
> Lord, make us truly thankful,

or

> Bless the meat and damn the skin,
> Back your ears and cram it in.

Eats. I am a monument to eats. But not nearly so monumental as Diamond Jim Brady, who at an evening sitting would eat five dozen oysters as prelude. That would be followed by five pounds of Delmonico steak, a peck or two of vegetables, various desserts, all washed down with four gallons of orange juice. The great eaters have been called gourmets, gourmands, trenchermen, gluttons, hogs, tubs of guts. Some pussell-gutted heroes have been immortalized for their exploits with knife and fork—or with bare hands. Here are a few of the real and fictional: Henry VIII, Falstaff, Nero Wolfe of West Thirty-Fifth Street, the Big Bad Wolf, William Howard Taft, J. Edgar Hoover, the King of France in *Winnie the Pooh*—he is called "King Louis So and So" and is "handsome, if a trifle fat."

Eats. Some have become immortal in the preparation and propagation of eats. Escoffier, for one. Julia Child, for another. And the late James Beard could qualify as both propagandist and trencherman. And who has not heard of Craig Claiborne, Helen Corbitt, Betty Crocker, the Galloping Gourmet, the Frugal Gourmet, Justin Wilson the Cajun chef, and the Junior League of Baton Rouge, Louisiana? Not to mention Paul Prudhomme, Chef Tell, and the famous Lobell Brothers who purveyed fish, flesh and fowl to the rich and famous of New York's Upper East Side. Their famous book bore a starkly simple (but succulent) title: *Meat*.

Eats. There are storied eateries—Maxim's of Paris, Claridge's of London, 21 of New York, Ernie's of San Francisco. Less famous to the world, but of note in the Lone Star State are Jean Claude's and the French Room of the Adolphus Hotel in Dallas; Maxim's and Tony's and Ruth's Chris Steak House in Houston; San Antonio's Paesano's and La Louisiane. And these names only cover continental eats. What about Joe T. Garcia's Mexican Dishes in Fort Worth, Chiquita in Dallas, El Rancho in Austin, or Mrs. Crosby's in Ciudad Acuna across from Del Rio, Texas, in the State of Coahuila? And the thousands of paper napkin cafes that have made the succulent chicken fried steak the national food of Texas—not chili, as some misguided propagandists like the late Francis X. Tolbert have asserted. The following list of great Texas grease joints barely suffices: the lamented Gude and Iola's in Denton (in 1958 they offered "three vegetables, a meat, one roll, one corn muffin, and tea for 45 cents." *Où sont les neiges d'antan?*), the City Cafe in Elgin, Chef Latin's in Nacogdoches, Tusa's Cafe at 8th and Franklin in Waco ("Grub four bits a plate; Tums free"), the Dew Drop Inn at Oenaville, Jake and Dorothy's in Stephenville, and a myriad of others that dot the state—offering the breaded and dreaded chicken fried steak: a piece of commercial-grade round hammered into tenderness, covered with a crust the thickness of a Florsheim sole and slathered all over with a pale cream gravy. All this comes with fries (or, after five, a dried, shriveled, aluminum-wrapped, unflavored baked potato to teach you to order fries next time), canned green beans, enough whole kernel corn to set your diverticulitus in motion until St. Swithin's Day, some rolls by Rainbow or Mrs. Baird steamed to a sweat, and a truck-driver sized glass of tea tasting faintly of chlorine. *These are eats.* And I am a monument to them.

Eats. More words have been written on how to get vittles from stove to table than on ways to achieve peace, solve the world's hunger problems, or win friends and influence people. There are enough recipe books in this state to fill the Cuero, Texas, Public Library. And two walls of that building could be taken up with recipe books dreamed up by the various Junior Leagues that infest the United States. The oldest and proudest of those Junior League productions is the *River Road Cookbook*, Southern dishes concocted by the maids of the rich women of Baton Rouge, Louisiana.

And church cookbooks. Publishers all over the country will do a cut-and-paste of good Baptist recipes from your hometown. Even Neiman-Marcus, the famous dry goods store, puts out cookbooks from some of their local stores. Ann Owens, wife of Texas folklorist William A. Owens, edited the recipes submitted by employees of the Westchester County, New York, Neiman-Marcus. Some of the great quiche and caviar recipes of the world are probably in that volume. I would not, however, look for ways to boil collards or bake a possum.

Eats. Think about some of the names that we attach to the books that tell us how to be gourmets. ("Gourmet" is probably a verb nowadays—like "parent" and "party.") One of the best is *How to Cook a Wolf* by M. F. K. Fisher. But there is also *The I-Can't-Cook Cookbook, Recipes for Lovers, Helpful Cooking Hints for Househusbands of Uppity Women,* and *The Divorced Man's Guide to Culinary Pleasures.* And don't forget the classic *Jim Lee's Chinese Cookbook.* In addition to books of recipes, there are books about the pleasures and pastimes of eating. Calvin Trillin's *American Fried* and *Alice, Let's Eat* are among the best. Trillin can become orgasmic arguing that the best barbecue in the world is to be found at Arthur Bryant's in Kansas City. Dallasites favor Sonny Bryan's. But Fort Worthians stick with Angelo's and Central Texans divide evenly between Kreutz's in Lockhart and Clem Miskesa's in Temple.

Once we have eaten and dined and gourmeted to excess, there are almost as many diet books as recipe books. And as many fads—diets of nothing but grapefruit and eggs, cottage cheese and chunks of pineapple, marshmallows and hominy, kumquats and clotted cream.

Eats. You may wonder what mountains of mashed potatoes, steaming bowls of fried corn, half-bushel pots of collards and rape, great stewers of Kentucky Wonders floating in hog grease, platters of fried chicken marinated in butter-milk and then fried in bacon drippings or pure lard, massy wheels of corn bread cut into wedges, molds of butter with shocks of wheat or images of Jersey cows standing high in bas-relief on the tops, small cups of chow-chow and relish and tomato Jerusha shouldered up against plates of radishes, celery, and pick-led okra have to do with folklore.

Simply this: folklore, which delves into the culture of peoples, may be a more important study about real life—private life—than standard, formal his-tory. History is mostly concerned with the mere events that took place among rulers and armies. The real history of the world—cultural and social his-tory—has been hidden because the historians have been either in the pay of the rulers or bedazzled by them. Consequently, the history of the mass of mankind lay hidden until about two hundred years ago when folklore began to be taken seriously and written down. One of the lessons that we have learned—or are beginning to learn—from the study of folklore is the impor-tance of food and eating customs in unravelling the history of a people.

Robert Darnton in his excellent book of cultural history called *The Great Cat Massacre and Other Episodes in French Cultural History* shows, in his first chapter, the importance of food in the French peasants' tales, mostly those collected as *Tales of My Mother Goose*. Darnton, after surveying a number of the best-known tales—"Puss 'n Boots," "Cinderella," "Tom Thumb," "The Ridiculous Wishes"—concludes by saying, "the full belly came first among the wishes of the French peasant heroes. It was all the peasant Cinderella aspired to, even though she got a prince. . . . To eat one's fill, eat until the exhaus-tion of the appetite . . . was the principal pleasure that the peasants dangled before their imaginations, and the one they rarely realized in their lives" (34). In times of dearth, tales and customs of the folk show the intensity of their desire for food. In times of plenty, food is a signal of our prosperity. Power eating. Intimidation by food.

A column in the *Dallas Times Herald's* Living section for Monday, March 17, 1986, tells of food groupies who pay forty dollars to watch well-known Dallas chefs prepare their viands. "Chefs are the adored designers, gourmet food the drug of choice of the mid-80s. What with pot passé and coke low class, the truly trendy are eating."

The article goes on to quote a food groupie who, after a meal, always goes into the kitchen of restaurants to visit the chef. He says, "I was at Uncle Tai's and went back to the kitchen for 20 minutes. He couldn't speak any English, but he'd point and show me how he did everything, talking in Chinese the whole time." The columnist notes that Dallasites can get "wild boar on the Crescent Club buffet, rabbit at Routh Street, roses as dessert, and fried yucca coming soon . . . where will it end?" One of her informants tells her, if not where it will end, where it will go next: "Cock's combs—those red things on roosters' heads. I ate them in Paris."

The *Dallas Times Herald* column is as much about food as symbol as it is about vulgar excess. Food has always been used as symbol. The fatted calf killed for the return of the prodigal; the sacrifices of Cain and Abel; the first Thanksgiving; the church's full calendar of feast and fast days. All show the symbolic nature of food for life; it reflects man's race-long preoccupation with starvation. And starvation *has been* a race-long reality. That it is not the prevalent condition in our culture does not keep the fear of starvation from being at the heart of our interior life.

When food is scarce, the impoverished dream of it, invent stories of full larders, make up rhymes about its scarcity:

> There was an old woman who lived in a shoe
> Who had so many children she didn't know what to do
> She gave them some broth without any bread
> She whipped them all soundly and put them to bed.

A part of the dream for plenty can be seen when the suitor promises the girl he wants to marry that she will not only be free from drudgery—"nor yet feed the swine"—but will enjoy a life filled with dainties. For the rest of her life, Goldilocks will "sit on a cushion and sew a fine seam/And feed upon straw-berries, sugar, and cream." Not nutritional fare, but it is as close as the lover can come to imagining the food consumed in some vague Xanadu. It is like promising the fare of an afterworld. Heaven promises "milk and honey," and the gods on Olympus dined on ambrosia and washed it down with nectar. I can sympathize because my childhood dream was to have—just once—all the chocolate-covered cherries I could eat.

The fact that history is full of famous feasts tells us that power eating is not an invention of yuppies. From Nebuchadnezzar to Trimalchio to a fifteenth century Archbishop of York, we have seen food used as a tool to intimidate and impress. The feast that took place at Carwood Castle in 1465 has been called one of the "most sensational" in England if we exclude some of the royal feasts held in Westminster Hall. The feast lasted for several days, as Mark Giroux tells in *Life in the English Country House* (25):

> Although the ostensible purpose was to celebrate the enthronement of George Neville as Archbishop of York, it must have also been planned as a demonstration of the power, wealth, and solidarity of the great Neville Clan. Seven bishops, 10 abbots, 28 peers, an as-sortment of great ladies, 59 knights, and innumerable judges, law-yers, clergy, aldermen and esquires travelled from all over the coun-try to attend it. Since they all came with an appropriate number of attendants, the total number of people involved (including those

serving and waiting) was somewhere in the neighborhood of 2500 people; the food eaten included 113 oxen, 6 wild bulls, 1000 sheep, 2000 each of geese, pigs, and chickens, 12 porpoises and 4000 cold venison pasties.

This is power eating on a scale that stuns modern imaginations. Even the late Walter Jetton never catered a feed like that for Lyndon Johnson at the LBJ Ranch.

Power eating is often reflected in the fatness of the eaters—at least when fatness is a sign of beauty or prosperity. Remember the nursery rhyme:

> Bobby Shaftoe's fat and fair,
> Combing down his yellow hair.
> He's my love for evermore
> Pretty Bobby Shaftoe.

Remember William Howard Taft: "Three hundred pounds of pure Republican." Stefan Zweig in his autobiography *The World of Yesterday* tells of Vienna in the late nineteenth century—during what he calls the Age of Security—when young men tried to look plump, prosperous, and forty in order to make their way in a world of bankers and merchants.

Nowadays power eaters can eat and stay thin. Slimness is a sign of beauty and prosperity. If the poor are all fat—as Texas Senator Phil Gramm once claimed—they may be so because they are too poor to afford shellfish, broccoli, sorbets from France, and caviar at twelve hundred dollars a pound. Irish potatoes and sawmill gravy over bread aren't slimming fare.

Eats may provide as much information about the way we live and see the world as the people we elect to office or the houses we build or the books we approve or the movies we film. Ruskin once said that the buildings we build reflect our souls—he was looking at a particularly nasty piece of town hall architecture in Bradford, Yorkshire, at the time. But it may be that the foods we eat, the way we eat them, and the imagination we bestow upon their preparation will tell historians, folklorists, and anthropologists of Buck Rogers's twenty-fifth century more about the way most of us lived than the paintings found in the ruins of the Museum of Modern Art or the books in the destroyed Library of Congress. Will we be seen as eaters of ice cream with fake Dutch and Danish names, of fish blackened beyond recognition, meat barely warmed on the outside, fish eggs found only in the Caspian Sea, snails, fungi rooted up by French hogs, or will we go down in history as a civilization devoted to red-eye gravy, collards, fried steak and chicken, black-eyed peas, baked coon, and souse meat? It will make a difference.

Eats. I am a monument to them. We all are. And they are monuments to us.

James Ward Lee

PART ONE

Eats from the Red River to the Sabine to the Nueces to the Rio Grande to the High Plains and Back

Tell Me What You Eat and I'll Tell You Where You Live

ONCE UPON A TIME, Texas could be divided into five eats areas.

Northeast Texas, where the Upper South pioneering types—Tennesseans, Kentuckians, Missourians, and Arkansawyers—came in the 1820s, ever searching for a place that would afford them the good life: chopping and plowing by day, strumming and fiddling by night, with time off for hunting and fishing.

Deep East Texas, the Piney Woods area where the ancient mound builders' village, Nacogdoches, a clearing at the end of El Camino Real, became the meeting place in the early 1800s for adventurers and drifters from Louisiana Territory, whose food supply was as near as the nearest bayou, and the Lower South settlers, whose food was whatever could be gathered, trapped, or shot.

Central Texas, that area roughly encircling Austin and including Waco to the north, Waller and Austin counties to the east—where Stephen F. Austin located his Three Hundred in 1824–25 — the Hill Country to the west, and extending toward San Antonio to the south.

South Texas, where in sparse settlements and centuries-old San Antonio, there could be heard the slap, slap, slap of women on their knees before an open fire, shaping by hand a mix of water and finely ground corn from their metates into tortillas, the flat cakes that, when baked on a rock, could be wrapped around some pieces of cabrito or beans, or spread with the sweetened pulp of some fruit.

And West Texas, everything west of Fort Worth, stretching from the Rio Grande to the Oklahoma Panhandle, where eats would become cowboy cuisine.

During the years of the Republic, waves of Upper South people rolled into North and Northeast Texas; most particularly, they came out of Tennessee, the granddaddy of Texas, it is said. They packed their few belongings into the wagon, lashed a crate of chickens to one side, a water keg to the other side, dangled a washpot from the rear, threw in some sacks of seeds, scrawled "Gone to Texas" across the weather-beaten boards of their emptied cabins, and took to the westward trail, driving their sow and leading the cow behind the wagon to provide milk for the freckle-faced urchins peering out from beneath the raised wagon sheet. They went into Arkansas, crossed over Red River, and stopped for a time. The climate was mild. Water was plentiful. A one-room log cabin could be thrown up for sleeping, cooking, eating, and whatever else went on indoors; their numerous progeny needed little clothing; the woman could make garden and gather fruits, nuts, and berries to feed the family; and the man could hunt.

Life presented few problems. They didn't even have to build outhouses. Plum thickets grew everywhere. The Indians had long before discovered and eaten the tart little fruits, throwing the seeds to the ground, where more and more little trees sprang up and grew into dense thickets, with branches that spread out close to the ground. And though it took some trouble to avoid the thorns, the thickets were good cover.

Corn was easy to grow. A hog could snuff out acorns and hickory nuts and needed no care except for a "whoo-oo-oo-ri" to call it in. Even left to find its own food, it will just "pig out," increasing its weight 150 percent in its first eight or nine months. When early Texans said "meat," they meant pork.

This way of life suited the Upper South people. They were fiercely independent; they lived in isolated places in a kind of loose kinship network, scorning town life where they would have to give up some of that independence to live socially. They belittled "larnin'" although they were known to say, when they reached Red River and saw a sign reading "This Way to Texas," that those who could read crossed over into Texas and those who couldn't stayed in Arkansas.

They held fast their dream that the good life lay westward, and they continued to live at almost a subsistence level, not putting down roots, just expecting poverty to go away, and sojourning in one place only until that day when they would hear there was better land lying somewhere beyond. It was said of one of these Texans that every spring his chickens would come running to him, cross their legs, and wait to be tied up for the next move. So the Tennesseans and their ilk spread themselves around North Texas and Central Texas, leaving in their wake a tradition of down-home cooking, called in the turbulent 1960s soul food, and, lately, white trash cooking. As the Indian threat lessened, numbers of pioneers turned westward again. On the High Plains they met the harsh, hostile climate and soil conditions head-on with stubborn endurance, the price they had to pay for the space they most wanted to protect their independence. It was no great step for them to shift from pork to beef in

A family moving west. *Courtesy the Erwin E. Smith Collection of the Library of Congress, on deposit at the Amon Carter Museum.*

their kitchens, adopt some of the Mexican ways with eats, and create a West Texas tradition of ranch and chuck wagon cooking.

The foodways of the early Texans were marked by the old familiar traditions of the land they left. But new environments necessarily brought about some changes, and pioneers were possibly influenced further by contact with other people moving west from places strange to them, some of whom may have known Randolph Marcy's *The Prairie Traveler: A Handbook for Overland Expeditions*, published in 1859. Marcy advised immigrants to put in flour, pork, coffee, sugar, yeast powder, salt, and pepper. Marcy didn't seem to have in mind the "pore" whites down South, the ones who were moving west in such great numbers. Wheat flour, when it could be had, cost up to sixty-five dollars or more per barrel, and saleratus—soda—served them when they needed leavening.

But some of his comments are of interest. Marcy advised that pork should be packed in strong, heavy sacks if the travellers planned to go to a hot climate. For more protection, it could be packed in bran and then placed in the bottom of the wagon where it would be cooler. It was possible to take butter along by boiling it, lifting off the scum, and repeating this process until the butter was clear and thin as oil. "In Texas," he wrote, "butter can be kept for a long time like this, its flavor but little impaired" (31).

Sugar was a problem because it had to be kept out of the damp in water-proofed bags. Vegetables should be dried; "airtight" (canned) vegetables were not as portable. He also encouraged the immigrants to watch for wild onions, wild greens, and grapes to supplement their supplies, and he told them they could expect to find an abundance of game—rabbits, squirrels, deer, bear, fish, and fowl.

Marcy highly recommended a "cold flour" used by the Mexicans. It was made from parched corn, pounded on a mortar until it was a coarse meal. Then a little sugar and cinnamon could be added. He wrote that a half-bushel of this corn flour mixed with a little water would keep a man going for thirty days.

There is a tale told in Fort Worth about a pioneer taken captive by the Comanches. They rode and rode, at length stopping to camp alongside a stream in the vicinity of the present-day Botanical Gardens. The captive picked up a stick, wet it in the stream, stuck it in his pack of flour, and then held the stick over the fire. He gave the browned bread to the Indians, who liked it so much they let him go free on the promise that he would bring them some of the flour. Surely that man had some Mexican "cold flour."

When the great-great-grandfather of Fort Worth lawyer Billy Couts Hutcheson prepared to leave Arkansas, where the family had settled after leaving Tennessee, he packed his wagon with the necessaries, not forgetting a hand of dried tobacco for smoking and for keeping bugs away. Nor did he forget to take sacks of seed for corn, apple trees, and whatever else. As he started to pull out of the yard, his father stuck a bag under the wagon seat, saying, "Here's a sack of peach seeds for you." The great-great-grandfather settled in the Palo Pinto area, but he didn't get around to planting the peach seeds for a season. When he did take down the sack and spilled out the contents, gold pieces—not peach seeds—fell to the ground. Needless to say, most pioneers were not so fortunate.

Folk wisdom: Anyone can count the number of seeds in an apple, but only God can count the number of apples in the seed.

Early reports of travellers to Texas add to what we know about the foodways of the pioneers. Thirty years before Marcy was preparing immigrants *for* the road, Noah Smithwick was *on* the road, leaving Tennessee in 1827 for Texas and adventure. He travelled to New Orleans and then by coastal schooner to Lavaca. Being an all-around good fellow, he was welcomed by the settlers whose cabins he happened upon, partaking of their salt pork, corn pone, and molasses with good grace.

Smithwick felt sympathy for the women, their lives marked by hardship and privation. The men pleasured themselves by hunting and fishing; sometimes they might work at, say, cutting down a bee tree. Not so the women. Their lot was to bear the children, clothe them, and gather edibles or raise a garden to feed them. Sugar, salt, pepper, and coffee were the only supplies a woman was likely to have to purchase.

Smithwick had a story about a woman who came by some flour, and, using what stores she had on hand for make-do, she cooked up some biscuits. They were hard as rocks, but she put them on the table. One of the "frying-size," "half-pint" boys picked up a biscuit, looked at it, and then ran out of the cabin. Soon he was back, asking for a second biscuit. The father couldn't think how the boy could eat the hard biscuit so fast, so he followed him outside where he found the child playing with a little Mexican cart. He had punched holes through the center of the two biscuits, attached them to a stick for an axle, and fashioned himself a toy with wheels that would roll. Smithwick added, "I assure you, from my recollection of those pioneer biscuits, they were capable of sustaining a pretty heavy load" (8).

When he reached the Colorado River, near LaGrange, he found the settlers doing well at farming and was pleased to report that some of them had milk cows. He happened along right at the time corn was in "roasting ear" and the people were feasting. They boiled the corn; they fried it; they roasted it, either by standing the shucked ears on end in front of the fire and turning them until they were browned all around, or by burying them, husk and all, in hot ashes—"the sweetest way green corn was ever cooked," he said (14).

But a revolution came about in the mid-1850s, when the early dependence on corn for bread ended. Folks began to raise wheat, and a mill was built west of Georgetown. They came from far and near to have their wheat milled, some of them having to camp several days while they waited their turn.

Most of the people Smithwick observed around the mill were Germans. He admired them, knowing they had had a hard time of it the first several years: their crops failed, and not being handy with firearms, they could not depend on game for food. He found them thrifty folk, good for their word, industrious, and important to the development of the state.

The local miller told Smithwick a story about a German who came into the mill, so poor his clothes were little more than patches. The German looked around, noticed flour all over the floor where it had been spilled, trampled on, and spit on. He asked if he might have it. The miller said yes. The German took a broom and swept up the flour, saw a little bran, swept it up, put it all in a sack, bought some shorts to make a bushel, and threw the bag over his shoulder. "Huh, bread fourteen days!" he said. The miller, feeling sorry for the man, followed him out the door, thinking to give him a good bushel of wheat. There must be starving children at his cabin. But, in the store, his pity gave way to indignation when he saw the German lay down a twenty-dollar gold piece for some goods, including tobacco (227–28).

Unlike Smithwick, Frederick Law Olmsted, who was sent to Texas in 1857 by the *New York Times* to record his impressions, registered everything he saw and tasted with Knickerbocker attitudinizing that Texans, reading his *Journey Through Texas* today, find downright amusing. Olmsted took the Louisiana route to Alexandria, on to Nachitoches, then overland to Nacogdoches. From there he travelled El Camino Real to Austin, spent some time among the Germans in the Hill Country, then turned south to San Antonio. On the return trip he followed the coast to Houston and Liberty. He seems to have travelled on his stomach, so fulsome are his comments on the food given him.

It was a bleak picture he gave of the people along the road in Deep East Texas. He reported that they lived in filthy, one-room cabins, holding stead-fast the notion that they were above work, their sole ambition to own some slaves and live like Southern aristocracy. When he and his companions were hungry, they would drop in at some poor cabin, apparently unconcerned should the woman be pregnant and overburdened. In one such instance, the woman set before him cold, fat salt pork, along with stale, dry "micaceous" corn bread, molasses, and milk—food he scorned to eat, except for the milk (49). This was the fare he would report along the way to Austin wherever the pore whites of the South had put up their cabins. The same food appeared for breakfast, dinner, and supper, in that order. Occasionally, there would be a boiled or roasted sweet potato. The coffee, when there was any, he found "revolting," as was the corn pone (61).

At a hotel in Austin, the food was worse. He was brought "burnt flesh of bulls and swine, decaying vegetables sour and mouldy like farinaceous glue, drowned in rancid butter" (112). In disgust, he and his friends scoured the town for supplies to prepare their own food as they camped along the way to the German settlements. Olmsted would probably have added a sonorous "Amen" to the old proverb, "God sends meat and the devil sends cooks."

In New Braunfels, the widely travelled Olmsted thought he had been transported to Germany. He was fed an excellent soup, two courses of meat (neither of them pork), two vegetables, a salad, peaches, coffee with milk, and buttered wheat bread. He was surprised to have butter. At a cabin in East Texas he had eaten with a settler who had a herd of a hundred cattle, but no butter. When he asked why, the farmer declared, "Too much trouble." And later he was told it was impossible to make butter in Texas, a statement he had accepted, firmly declaring that the butter would not come because of the

Some cabins had two rooms with a dogtrot between. *Log Cabin Village, Fort Worth, Texas*

filth in the households he had visited. But he approved of everything he saw among the Germans and was especially pleased that he paid them less for their good food than he had paid the East Texans for their mouldy bread and bacon (144). Moving into South Texas, Olmsted was delighted by the sight of the Mexican women making tortillas, which he called corn slap jacks. They satisfied the curiosity of the traveller in an exotic land. One woman made a hash of kid with some onions, leeks, and red peppers and wrapped it with corn shucks—a kind of tamale. He also had brown beans, boiled for twelve hours, he reported, then dried in a pan with a sauce of butter and chile colorado. Altogether, he found his meal "wholesome, nourishing, and extremely cheap," taking additional pleasure in watching the Mexicans twist a tortilla around some food and eat it from hand, without benefit of forks or spoons (349–51).

Returning by way of Houston and the low prairies, Olmsted found food much to his liking: venison and beef in ragout, hominy, sweet milk, wheat bread, modified by a soupçon of Frenchiness (365). Despite the good food he was treated to in the later stages of his journey, his exasperated—and exasperating—reports about the food of the pore whites in Deep East Texas and Central Texas made the more indelible impression on outsiders when his *Journey Through Texas* was published.

Fifteen years later—the disasters of Reconstruction fading—Edward King was sent by Scribner's in New York to traverse the ex-slave states and bring back the truth about Texas. His book *Texas: 1874* reported that Texans have "a hearty scorn for anything good to eat." It was curious to him that the sons were so "stout" and the daughters so "pretty," to look at the food they consumed (148).

Near Red River City, King heard tell of a railroad president who, on an inspection tour, stopped by a little cabin for a meal. The old woman of the house, wanting to treat her company with respect, asked him, after setting before him the usual dinner of greasy pork, molasses, bread, and bitter coffee, "Won't ye have a little bacon fat to wallop yore corn dodgers in now, won't ye?" (148).

His worst experience occurred in a hotel in a North Texas "metropolis." It was an unfinished structure without ceiling or lathing, "through whose roof one could see the stars." (Was this the Dallas hotel Alexander Cockrell was building on John Neeley Bryan's land before he was shot down in the street?) King reported: "In the long, creaking supper-room . . . a dirty cloth was laid on a dirtier table, and pork, fried to a cinder and swimming in grease hot enough to scorch the palate, was placed before the guests. To this was presently added by the hands of a tall, angular, red-haired woman, a yellow mass of dough supposed to be biscuit, a cup of bitter bean-juice named coffee, and as a crowning torture, a mustard-pot, with very watery mustard in it" (150).

"Help yourself to the mustard" is a common retort to the child who refuses to eat the food set on the table. It derives from a traveling anecdote. A hungry traveler from the East stops by a cabin for food. Looking at the salt pork on his plate, he says, "I can't eat this meat." "Help yourself to the mustard," he's told. Or he stops by a chuck wagon on the trail. He looks at the Son-of-a-Gun stew. "I can't eat this," he says. "Help yourself to the mustard," the boss of the chuck wagon answers.

•

J. Frank Dobie told this version:

"Breakfast!" the driver shouted an hour before daylight to his tired, frowsy, half-dead passengers at a stage stop on the Pecos River.

Nobody was hungry, but it was forty miles on to Fort Stockton and nothing but grass and greasewood along the way. The passengers got out and went into the station house. One was a valetudinarian.

"Boiled beans," he moaned. "They would give an ostrich indigestion at this time in the morning."

"Try some bacon," suggested the cook, indicating a platter half full of grease.

"Nothing but grease, grease," groaned the valetudinarian, too lifeless to really fulminate.

"There's corn bread." The cook slammed it down in a tin plate. "I'm not an Indian or a mule," the delicate man mumbled.

"Then, damn it," the driver paused from his gorging to advise, "help yourself to the mustard." (*The Flavor of Texas*, 108)

King, unlike Olmsted, didn't take to Mexican cooking. The Mexican, he said,

> learned to turn American curiosity about his cooking to account. Entering one of these hovels, you will find a long, rough table with wooden benches about it; a single candlestick dimly sending its light into the dark recesses . . .; a hard earth floor, in which the fowls are busily bestowing themselves for sleep; a few dishes arranged on the table, and glasses and coffee-cups beside them. The fat, tawny Mexican materfamilias will place before you various savory compounds, swimming in fiery pepper, which biteth like a serpent; and the tortilla, a smoking hot cake, thin as a shaving, and about as eatable, is the substitute for bread. (109)

> Knock, knock! Who's there?
> Red.
> Red who?
> Red pepper—ain't that a hot one?

King's *Texas: 1874* was one part of an eight-hundred-page book about the South. It was considered a truthful picture and attracted international readership. But the accounts of a couple of travellers don't make truth; however, they were so widely read as to give outsiders the impression that in Texas one could not expect a decent meal.

When Edna Ferber wrote *Giant* in 1952, another generation of outsiders took it for an accurate picture of Texas. The genteel bride from Virginia, taking her first meal on the ranch, sits down at a long table bearing catsup bottles and jars of other condiments. Two Mexican girls ply the family with food: "There was steak . . . enormous fried slabs, flat, grey, served with a thick flour gravy. Mashed potatoes. Canned peas. Pickles. Huge soft rolls. Jelly. Canned peaches. Chocolate cake. It was fundamental American food cooked and served at its worst, without taste or imagination" (136–37).

Many visitors to Texas, however, would not consider their visit complete without a *good* chicken fried steak:

CHICKEN FRIED STEAK

Take one round steak about one-half inch thick. Cut it into four pieces. Pound it with a meat pounder, beat it, stretch it, then pound

---

it some more, until it is as thin as a thin pancake. In a shallow dish, beat two large eggs and two tablespoons of milk. In another plate, mix one-fourth cup of flour with salt and pepper. Dip each steak first into the egg mixture, then into the flour mix. Melt two tablespoons of margarine in a skillet and brown the steaks, two pieces at a time.

For the cream gravy, melt two tablespoons of margarine, stir in two tablespoons of flour. Cook and stir until blended. Add one cup of milk slowly, sprinkle with salt and pepper. Cook slowly and stir constantly until the gravy is smooth and is a not-too-thin and not-too-thick consistency.

This will make one cup of gravy. Double the recipe if you want more. With more gravy you can stretch the meat and add a guest at the table.

Although Texas foods reflected regional differences for almost a century, a few nineteenth-century developments did affect Texas cooking. Some of the changes were cultural. Around the turn of the century, the younger generation picked up a little learning and were able to help the older folk who had missed out. Furthermore, some of the men were persuaded to leave the log cabins and build frame houses in town.

In 1883 the ladies of the First Presbyterian Church in Houston published the *First Texas Cookbook*. Since everyone knew that meats were to be fried or boiled, there were only ten pages given to entrees. And everyone knew to boil vegetables until they were tender, so they got short shrift: just a few suggestions to cook cabbage sixty to ninety minutes, spinach an hour, green beans three to four hours. The ladies were striving for sophistication, and there are some elaborate recipes. Almost half are for sweets. Cakes especially. They recommended using baking powder, which had been suspect ever since it was first advertised. But the Presbyterian ladies wrote: "It is in every way satisfactory—wholesome as well as efficacious" (116).

Another revolution took place in the kitchen when cookstoves became available. Mrs. Malissa C. Everett, whose farm was near Garden City, Texas, wrote this account in 1923:

> now I will tell Somthing funny its my experiance with my first Cook Stove Their was a lot of people moved away from around Gainsville & couldent take their Stoves with them, they left on accout of the Indians & a man by the name Scott that lived on dry Elem Creek, near Gainsville that bought Several Stoves those people that was moving away. one of my friends went up there & bought one She had never had a Cook Stove & was highly pleased with it, So She put at me to go & get me one, we wove lots of cloth. Cloth was the currency of the Country. So I got my husband in notion to go I gave the man 13 yards of Cloth for a cook Stove, the Second I ever Saw

dident know one thing about one. he would laugh at me & Say he
had no Idea it would Cook a lick So I Couled hardly Sleep good for
fear it wouldent Cook, old Mother Garner had Saw a good many
before She Came west, She Said She thought Sure it would cook,
we aimed to put it in the fire place & let the pipe run up the chimney
it was to cool to quit fire in the fire place So we Set it in the hall
waiting for wormer weather So one day they was all gone from
home. I thought now was my time to try it. the wind was in the
South I drug it to north Side of the hall So the Smoke would go out
of the house & built afire in it, put on Some corn bread the hardest
thing to cook of anything. I Kept putting in fuel & it wouldent Cook
at all. the bread looked like it had been Seting in the Sun, So I took
it & gave it to the hogs Cleaned out all the ashes & drug it back to
its place, So when the folks came home, I got a chance & told old
Mother garner for She was like a mother to me, I told her that Stove
wouldent cook a lick, Said how do you Know I Said because I have
tried it, She walked out in the hall & asked me where the pipe was
I Said I dident have any She Said Child it wont cook without a
pipe, She asked me if I turned up the damper I hadent evan found
it, I said what part does that play She Said it reggulated the heat. I
said why dident they call it a regulater She Said She dident think I
need to be uneasy She was Sure it would cook all right. it dident
entirely Satisfy me. but I felt Some easier So the time Came to Set
up the Stove I new if it dident cook I never would hear the last of
it, So asked the ole Lady what to get to make the hottest fire, She
told me & I made the fire all was Standing around looking on to See
the out come, I went to work to get Supper, it got red hot right now
it looked all most like it would Set the house on fire it burnt up
everything I put about it. My husband Said he would give it up he
was Satisfide it would Cook & I was mitily relieved, now that is my
experiance with my first Stove.

Audrey Parker Brooks of Moran has written that, though she did not learn
to cook on her mother's enormous wood-burning stove with its big warming
oven and hot-water reservoir on the side, she did learn how to build a fire in
it—no little achievement. Cooking in a wood-burning stove is an art; the fire
has to be just right, she says. One time she attempted to make biscuits in it,
but they "were rock-hard disasters. My brothers made such insulting remarks
about the chunks of baked flour that I threatened to throw the things at
them." Facing such dangerous weapons, the boys must have desisted.

When Audrey married, she had a more up-to-date kerosene stove, and
though it smelled and smoked, at times filling her kitchen with black soot,
this was the stove on which she really learned to cook (April 16, 1987).

But cultural changes, cookbooks, and revolutionary gadgets did not radi-

A family living in a tent with stove in the open. *Courtesy the Erwin E. Smith Collection of the*

Library of Congress, on deposit at the Amon Carter Museum.

cally alter regional cooking styles. Into the twentieth century, eats in Texas were still reflective of the five cultural areas: Northeast Texas, Deep East Texas, Central Texas, South Texas, and West Texas.

A TEXAS MENU
by Gordon A. Hyatt

Many of our pioneer forefathers took their food and drink seriously, and may have named their communities after their favorite food, or were influenced by the availability of a particular food in their county. [The town name is followed by its county and by date or dates referring to the years the post office was open]:

BREAKFAST
Melon (*Frio*) 1909
Oatmeal (*Burnet*) 1853
Cream (*Parker*) 1879–1880
Pancake (*Coryell*) 1884–1908
Bacon (*Panola*) 1903–1905
Ham (*Henderson*) 1901–1912
Blackberry Plain (*Fannin*) 1871–1873
Plum (*Fayette*) 1880–current
Coffeeville (*Upshur*) 1852–1915

LUNCH
Fruit (*Smith*) 1894–1900
Crawfish (*Floyd*) 1892–1893
Salmon (*Anderson*) 1902
Antelope (*Jack*) 1852–current
Okra (*Eastland*) 1899
Tomato (*Callahan*) 1893–1898
Bean Creek (*Hunt*) 1853–1855
Noodle (*Jones*) 1900–1924
Olive (*Hardin*) 1884–1920
Onion (*Jones*) 1905
Gourdneck (*Rusk*) 1880–1881

DINNER
Sherry (*Red River*) 1902–1923
Catfish (*Henderson*) 1888–1910
Whitefish (*Donley*) 1896–1905
Frijole (*Culberson*) 1916
Lamb (*Kimble*) 1892–1893
Alligator (*Brazos*) 1888
Quail (*Collingsworth*) 1902–current
Rice (*Navarro*) 1872–current

Turkey (*Hall*) 1893–current
Cherry (*Red River*) 1901–1907
Peach (*Wood*) 1902–1929
Raisin (*Victoria*) 1892–1914
Cheeseland (*Angelina*) 1857–1886
Rich Coffey (*Coleman*) 1879–1882
Cogniac [*Cognac*] (Jasper) 1903–1904

BREAD
White (*Scurry*) 1890–1907
Rye (*Brazos*) 1904–1906
Alfalfa (*Ochiltree*) 1900–1924
Pepper (*Rusk*) 1902–1905
Salty (*Milam*) 1894–1909
Scrap (*Red River*) 1903–1924

T. J. Parrish farming in Rains County. *Courtesy the Southwest Collection, Texas Tech University.*

Corn ready for harvesting.

Eats in Northeast Texas

Living Off the Land

One for the blackbird,
Two for the crow,
Three for the cutworm,
And four to grow.

CORN PLANTING CHANT

ROM the Indians, the frontier folk who spilled over into the Red River country and across the Sabine from the Upper and Lower South had learned that corn was to be had for the planting—and some tending. It would not grow wild, as most grains will.

Among the Cherokees, there was a belief that a naked squaw walking up and down the corn rows under a bright moon, while dragging her clothes behind her, would bring a good harvest.

Corn was the staff of life to the Indians. Their first name for it was *zea mays*, meaning "our life." Early settlers called it simply Indian corn, the word "corn" an old-world name for grains in general. The Indians had found many ways to prepare corn: they popped it; they developed a sweet corn for roasting ears; they cooked grits; they leached the corn with lime and hulled it to make hominy; they made corn puddings; they ground it into meal and used the meal for mush, pone, and cakes. The pioneers had little to add to Indian ways of preparing corn for eating.

After the corn was gathered, it was cut off the cob and put in the sun to dry. Then it was sacked. A few roots of sassafras kept the bugs out of dried foods. When the corn was needed, it could be ground into meal for bread, or it could be soaked and boiled with pork for soup.

> Why can't you tell a secret in a corn patch?
> (*Answer: Too many ears.*)
>
> What has ears but can't hear?
> (*Answer: Corn.*)

The pioneers could have taken another lesson from the Indians and ground mesquite beans into meal. The beans are so hard one would not think them useful for anything, but the Indian women did grind them on their metates into a fine flour. William H. Leckie has written in *The Buffalo Soldiers* that the men of the Tenth Cavalry in West Texas found sacks and sacks of mesquite beans in Kiowa and Comanche encampments (146).

Acorns, too, were ground to make meal and used to make bread. When the bitter—and toxic—tannin was removed, the acorns were sweet. The Indians used wood ashes and water (to make a lye solution) to remove the tannin. It could also be removed by boiling the acorns two or three hours, changing the water every time it became discolored from the tannin. Then the acorns were dried and ground.

Or they could have made cattail flour, as the Indians did, by peeling the fiber from the roots of the cattail and then pulverizing it. Of course, this would have been woman's work. Texas was hell on women and horses, fine for men and dogs.

Pioneers brought with them knowledge of edible plants, fruits, and nuts already learned from Indians back in the Upper South. Lamb's-quarters, wild lettuce, curly dock, nettle leaves, dandelion greens, sorrel, and poke were picked when the leaves were young and tender and then boiled with salt pork. Even the early spring shoots of tumbleweed and thistles could be boiled until they were edible.

A vendor at the Weatherford Trade Day one spring in the 1960s was overheard to say as he sold his last mess of poke that when word got around he had some, he sold out in thirty minutes, so eager were folk for it. It was hard to find, he went on; in fact, he had to put on his waders to go into the swamps to get it. He warned his customers that it had to be "parebiled"—that is, boiled and drained and boiled again—or "it's sure pizen. The Safeway stores," he added, "didn't know it was pizen. They had so many calls for poke that they got some and canned it. Those people who bought it all got sick, and Safeway is still in court trying to settle all the cases brought against them just because they didn't know enough to parebile their poke."

Jim Byrd of Commerce says, "Folks just don't know about poke. Some think it grows around outhouses and 'hawgpens', but it will grow anywhere the soil is rich—along roadsides, even—and it is not hard to find." He says the poison stories are exaggerated. The Cherokees advise that the leaves be picked when they are no more than three or four inches long, and, when they are prepared properly, they are sweet and delicious—not poison. Besides, they are a good tonic and restore youthful vigor. They make you feel "frisky as a snake that had shed its skin," one informant told him.

Poke is most often spoken of as "sallet." The settlers no doubt poured hot bacon grease over greens and called the dish sallet—not to be spelled s-a-l-a-d. Byrd says folk speech in Tennessee and East Texas uses sallet to refer to almost any kind of greens (61–62).

Mrs. J. B. Yates, of Wolfe City, gave him the recipe which follows:

POKE FOR THE MOST DISCRIMINATING TASTE

Simply pick the tops of tender buds. Wash them. "Pareboil" them about about half an hour and drain. The boiling and draining will get rid of a strong taste as well as a supposed poison. Put in half a cup of bacon drippings. Cook until all water has been evaporated. For every two cups of cooked poke, stir in five beaten eggs and scramble. Add salt and pepper. Serve with corn bread.

Wild fruits were abundant: mustang grapes, wild plums, blackberries, muscadines, mulberries, may apples, may pops, and mayhaws. When flour and leavening were available, persimmon pulp was used for cookies and cakes.

> What is white as snow, but snow it's not;
> Green as grass, but grass it's not;
> Red as fire, but fire it's not;
> Black as ink, but ink it's not?
> (Answer: Blackberries.)

Among the Cherokees mustang grapes were used for a dumpling dish that became traditional for weddings. (The groom's family had to provide venison.) The recipe assumes the cook knows proportions:

CHEROKEE MUSTANG GRAPE DUMPLINGS

Bring mustang grapes to a boil and add sugar to sweeten to taste. Make dumplings of flour, lard, a little sugar, and some leavening. Dampen the flour mixture with a little grape juice. Drop the dumplings by spoonfuls into the boiling juice and cook covered for 10 or 15 minutes.

In Elithe Hamilton Kirkland's *Love Is a Wild Assault*, the historical Harriet Page, abandoned in the Brazos swamps, keeps her children alive by feeding them haws. Marcia Thomas of Jefferson has written a one-woman play about the indomitable Harriet and her tumultuous romance with the deceptive Robert Potter of Texas Republic fame. Marcia concludes her performances with a tasting party of mayhaw jelly, which she has served to such noteworthies as James Michener, Suzanne Morris, Elithe Kirkland, Mary Costa, and Ladybird Johnson. Mrs. Johnson knows about the haws and what good jelly they make, as her childhood home was a plantation alongside Caddo Lake near Jefferson. All speak of the jelly in eloquent terms and associate it with old-fashioned homemade biscuits, fresh-churned butter, and the reputation the old Red River port had for fine food.

This is what Marcia writes about the haws:

> Since I grew up here in Jefferson, I was always aware of mayhaws, and earliest recollections bring memories of blacks coming along the highways to the back door to sell them by the gallon. They had always been in abundance until recent years, though they were always a bit hard to get to since they grew in swampy areas of our bottomlands. Today it is very difficult to find them—I believe the ecology is changing—and even more difficult to find someone to harvest them. Fortunately, there have always been some folks around who can get enough for jelly-making, and I have been able to keep an adequate supply for the last several years.

When Marcia began dramatizing Harriet's story, her interest in mayhaws became more than casual. Her research turned up seventy-eight species in the United States alone, and the one she knew she identified as *crataegus opaca*, a kind of brushy hedge-like plant that grows in wet soil around shallow ponds. The low country around Jefferson was ideal for its propagation. "May" refers to the time it ripens and "haw" to the kind of flowering plant. The white blossoms are very much like those of the pear tree, but the haw is thorny, its little branches having very sharp points. She continues:

> Because it is a favorite food of songbirds, game birds, and squirrels, but also of foxes, raccoons, and deer, only a diligent picker will return home with a full pail (and with scratched arms!). Most people are now reluctant to venture into the snake-infested thickets for them. But I suspect it was a great spring adventure for the family to go out into the wilderness to gather mayhaws before fences kept them out. Even as little as thirty years ago the berries could be gathered from the river or bayou when they dropped into the early-spring-flooded channels and floated alongside your boat.
>
> My grandmother used to make the jelly yearly and, while I was too young to be involved, I do remember it was an all-day affair

which put her in a somewhat grouchy mood the whole day. Now I know why. The following is a recipe from Cissie McCampbell and "Sister" Wagner. Cissie was the long-time manager/chef of the Excelsior Hotel until her death a few years ago. "Sister" is still living and makes the jelly every few years. First, a large container is required to "juice-out" the berries, preferably porcelain or granite. It is prudent to start with only a couple of gallons so as not to overwhelm your ambitions. Rinse berries thoroughly, discarding all debris and bad fruit, but do not remove green berries as they contain the pectin that makes the jelly "roll." You can, of course, use "sto-baught" pectin if you want. Cover the berries with just enough water to cover completely and bring to a boil. Cook until the juice turns bright pink (about 15 minutes). Pour juice and berries into a cheese-cloth bag or old flour sack, hang it on a nail or other holder and place a large container underneath to catch the liquid that drips through. After first skimming off the foam (be sure to squeeze the bag thoroughly to get every bit of juice), boil the juice again to a high rolling boil (about 220 degrees), add two cups sugar to every three cups juice, and boil for exactly one more minute. Take from heat and pour quickly into sterilized containers. When cool, seal with paraffin or if you want, you can store the juice for an indefinite period in the freezer—though I have noted that the juice tends to fade in color over the months and color is part of the beauty of the product.

The haw deserves its place in the history of our state for it is obvious that humans and animals alike survived on the little marble-sized fruit during hard times in those early days. Like Texas' pioneers, it was born a fighter, struggling for available space with a fierce determination to survive the elements.

Other uses of wild fruits and berries come from Jack H. Hittson's account:

> Pioneer cooks [who had drifted from East Texas into the Palo Pinto hills] used wild plums, wild grapes, and sometimes chaparral (or agarita) berries in preparing their tasty fruit dishes.
>
> A hunk of roasted bear meat smiling on the platter really tasted good when served up with a sliver of tangy wild plum jelly. Wild turkey dinners were always improved with the inclusion of green grape cobblers for dessert.
>
> All of these early-day culinary artists have passed away, and no doubt many of their prized recipes have gone along with them, but their wild fruits and berries still remain in places as reminders of those happy days of long ago.
>
> J. H. (Ham) Baker came to Palo Pinto County in the late 1850's.

He used homemade cane syrup instead of sugar in preserving wild plums.

His son, Ed Baker, lived many years in Mineral Wells. I remember spending the night in his home on several occasions. On one of these visits, Ed came out with a large bottle of wild mustang grape juice. This was by far the most delicious grape drink I had ever tasted. It had no alcoholic content. Ed's father was the first and foremost prohibitionist amongst the pioneer settlers and [I] am sure Ed was influenced with the moral teachings of this good man. Instead of wine, he served pure grape juice.

Two species of grape are native to this area. The mustang and the tiny sweet grape known locally as a winter, or fox, grape. The mustang is noted for its long, high-reaching vines. Records claim that these vines reach upward 100 feet. It makes a heavy potent wine when generous amounts of sugar are added to its fermenting juices. When gathered and canned green, as during the period when the seeds are soft, it truly makes a cobbler fit for a king and likewise the peasant.

The little fox grape (or winter) is equally as good for all the uses of other grapes, but its smallness makes it tedious to gather and process.

Two native varieties of plums are found in this section of the country. The Mexican tree-plum grows in creek and river bottoms [and] has leaves, large and woolly below white fragrant flowers, in early spring. Plums are purplish-red and very tart. Chaparral berry, or agarita (wild current), is our only edible native berry used here for cooking and canning.

Blackberries and its several species came along with the first settlers and are found growing wild in places. I know of several peach trees growing wild back in the hills.

Our native stretchberries are used by children to make their chewing gum bubble. Some of the older generation, thus having no store-bought gum, looked for gum elastic found in the sap of the native Chittum tree.

A combination of Chittum gum and the pulp from a few stretchberries served the purpose for making a first-rate bubble gum—a lot of bubble with a noisy pop.

School teachers frowned on this form of misbehavior in the classroom. They made threats of punishment only. Down under, I think they welcomed these noisy pranks, as it probably awakened all the pupils for the first time in weeks. (155–156)

There were also nuts: hickory nuts, chinquapins (called chinkypins by the Tennesseans), and pecans. The Kiowas have a legend about the origin of the pecan: Many, many years ago, the Great White Father lived among them on the Great Plains. They were a happy people, for the Great White Father had led them in many triumphant battles against their enemies. He had also brought them good fortune on their hunts. But the time came when he told them he had to leave them to go to the spirit world. The Indians took the body and buried it in a stream bed, covering it carefully with rocks. All the Kiowas looked on the grave as a sacred place. One time, some of the men, when paying a visit to the grave, noticed a small green plant coming out of the site. They nurtured the plant knowing it was sacred. After many years, nuts began to fall from the tree, and from these nuts, other trees grew until there were many, many trees bearing the delicious nuts. This was the pecan, an Indian word meaning "nut," which the Kiowas regarded as their special gift from the Great White Father (G. T. Bludworth, 79–80).

October was the time to pick up hickory nuts. A box or pail of them would be placed beside the hearth with a good-sized hammer alongside. The fellow who sat down before the fire was expected to crack a few nuts and dig the goodies out. It was a task not to be anticipated because mashed thumbs just naturally go along with cracking the hard nuts. But if there was going to be a hickory nut cake for Christmas, everyone had to take turns with the hammer.

In Dobie's *The Flavor of Texas*, there is a story about another way to crack hickory nuts. A crony of Bigfoot Wallace, Dan Smith of San Antonio, told how Bigfoot stuffed his clothes with hickory nuts to protect himself from Indians. They spent their arrows on the giant and then fled in terror when he did not fall. What they never knew was that they had split open two bushels of hickory nuts (61).

Archaeologist David Jurney says that early sojourners depended mostly on deer, rabbit, and turtle for meat. Hunters who ranged beyond the pine forests into the Texas savannah would find buffalo. Possum and bear were rendered for fat (the Indians' and pioneers' substitute for butter or mayonnaise, something to help that dry corn pone slide down, Jurney says), as was the wild hog—DeSoto had brought a herd of swine into Texas, and they had wandered off and adapted to the wilderness. The meats were salted, dried, or smoked for preservation—jerky and pemmican, for example:

JERKY

Cut meat into strips about two inches wide. Cut with the grain of the meat. You will need a green wood pole hung four or five feet high—out of the reach of the dogs—and in a sunny place. Leave the meat until all the juices are dried up.

For extra flavor, build a fire underneath the meat, but sprinkle water on it from time to time so that it is only smoldering. The smoke will season the meat, especially if the wood is hickory or mesquite, and it will keep insects away. The strips should be turned from time to time.

After about a day's smoking, the meat should be stiff and dry. It will take longer if the sun doesn't shine.

PEMMICAN

To make pemmican, pound up a quantity of jerky. Then take some animal fat and cut it into walnut-shaped hunks. Fry these out over a slow fire, never letting the grease boil.

Pour the hot fat over the pounded jerky, mixing the two together until it has the consistency of sausage. At this point, you may add dried berries or fruit.

Pack the mixture in commercial casings or waterproof bags. Indians were known to put the pemmican in gourds for storage.

> The nearer the bone, the sweeter the meat.

For fowl, the settlers had quail, wild turkey, prairie chicken, ducks, and geese. They also fished, gigged frogs (the legs won't jump out of the skillet when they are fried, but they will jerk unless the tendon is cut), and they hooked turtles for soup.

> One day two fathers and two sons went fishing. Each fisherman caught a fish, yet only three fish were caught. How is this possible?
> (*Answer: A boy, his father, and his grandfather went fishing.*)

There was also wildlife that some folks get squeamish about eating, but other folks would eat: rattlesnake, armadillo, coon, possum, alligator, and prairie dog. Daisy Atkins told a tale about eating prairie dog. Actually if the dogs had been called prairie squirrels, they would have been an acceptable edible. Daisy wrote about frontier life in West Texas, and her story does show something about food preferences:

> [They] resemble ground squirrels, very cunning, shy but graceful little animals. . . . They should have been good to eat for they ate only best of grass—but because of the name and their bark were seldom eaten, however the young were very palatable. My brother killed and dressed some; Mother fried them as rabbits. The supposing rabbits were served to Mo [Missouri?] girls who was visiting in

our home. Alas!, a youngster who knew what they were, asked for more dog when eating. Dad said, "What's that kid asking for?" The secret was let out. None of us had to give up our dinner; the girls who were game to any prank said they were sure good. (38)

On a smuggling expedition out of Mexico with contraband tobacco, torrential rains forced Noah Smithwick and his companions to strike camp. The men killed a mustang and fried some steaks. Noah held out. He would not eat it. But, on the third day without food, the smell of the meat being fried over the campfire was so tempting that he reached over for some cracklins one of the men had lifted from the skillet. It was mighty tasty eating, so he helped himself to a steak and liked it—not well enough, however, that he would look forward to eating it again, he wrote (29).

Honey was easy to come by but required some labor on the part of the men to get it to the table. Noah Smithwick told this story about bee-keeping:

My nearest neighbor on Brushy was Jimmie Standefer. . . . He was very devout, but didn't allow that to interfere with business. . . . Jimmie had domesticated a number of hives of bees, the increase of which he was anxious to save. . . . [But the bees] were allowed to take their own way and time for moving. This they did by swarming in the spring. Having noticed an unusual activity among his bees, Jimmie left some of his children to watch them while he went to breakfast. Before the rather long grace was finished, his ear caught a suspicious buzzing which caused him to hurry up the ceremony, but it had to be finished according to custom, though his impatience caused the introduction of a sentence not down in the ritual. Casting an anxious glance through the door as the concluding sentence fell from his lips, he called to the children: "Children, ain't them bees a-swarmin'? Amen." (218)

Besides honey, sorghum and molasses provided sweeteners. In August the settlers would go into the fields, strip the sorghum cane stalks of leaves, cut the stalks, and haul them to the mill. Charles Linck recalls that on his father's farm, the stalks were fed by handfuls into three upright rotating iron cylinders geared to a long pole that a team of mules pulled round and round to keep the cylinders rotating. As the juice ran out, it was funneled into a big bucket beneath the cylinders. The juice was then put into one end of a long rectangular pan made for this purpose. It had dividers, each with a gate. The pan was placed on a slant above a long brick fireplace. Slowly the juice was released from gate to gate until it was thick. As it was moved down and back and forth from section to section of the pan, it would get thicker and thicker. Sorghum is the ultimate product, long in the making. If the sorghum is cooked even longer, it becomes molasses. "On fresh baked bread, it's great," he says. "It has a tangy taste one never forgets."

From The Open Hearth

"AND IT'S ALL THEY CALL FOR IS 'DOUGH, BOYS, DOUGH'"

Come all you Mis-sou - ri girls and lis-ten to my noise, And don't you
mar-ry them Tex - as boys; Take you out on a sand flat hill And that will
be a- gainst your will, And that will be a- gainst your will.

 . . . When they go a-courting they take a chair,
And first thing they say is "Daddy killed a deer,"
And next thing they say when they set down,
"Lord God, johnny cake's cooking rather brown,
Lord God, johnny cake's cooking rather brown."

If they have a cow they milk her in a gourd,
Set it in a corner and cover it with a board;
Some gets a little and some gets none,
And that's the way with a Tex-i-un,
And that's the way with a Tex-i-un.

If they get hungry before they go to bed
They build up a fire at the husband's head,
Rake away the ashes and roll in the dough,
And it's all they call for is "Dough, boys, dough,"
And it's all they call for is "Dough, boys, dough."
 —William A. Owens, *Tell Me a Story, Sing Me a Song,* 80.

  The Southern girls who came to know Tex-i-un ways had to cook on the open hearth. They had few utensils: "kittles" of different sizes for boiling, at least one large enough for corn dumpling stew with whatever small game the hunter brought home. A "skillit" for frying. Later, town folk would say "frying pan"; "spider" for skillet was heard in Texas only from an occasional Carolinian. There would be, if the woman was of Scots ancestry, a "girdle," her name for a griddle. Wooden bowls for mixing and spoons for stirring were hollowed out and carved by hand; these were passed down from generation to generation.
  A crane was attached to the inside of the fireplace, like a long arm, from

Elly Hutcheson at Fort Worth's Log Cabin Village, 1987.

Utensils for cooking on the open hearth.

which the woman could hang her kittles and a tin bucket for boiling whatever ground-up beans she used for coffee. She also could have some andirons to hold a spit for roasting meat.

Her most important pot was the three-legged Dutch oven, which she could stand above the coals. Or she might have a stand with stubby legs to set a flat-bottomed heavy iron pot on. The pot must have a flanged lid, that is, a lid with a collar to hold coals for faster cooking and browning. The bread was sometimes cooked in the Dutch oven, and the woman had to be very skillful to heap the coals around the bottom and on the top and keep moving them for even cooking and browning.

> An eggshell thrown into the coffeepot after it has boiled will settle the grounds.
>
> If coffee was not to be had, tea could be brewed from a variety of herbs: horsetail, peppermint, catnip, and mint.

Lyman Brightman Russell wrote in his memoirs about cooking over the open hearth. The father had moved his family from a log cabin into a clapboard house, fourteen by twenty-eight feet, called "California style." The house was never ceiled, but, about the time of The War, the father was able to buy cheesecloth to cover cracks in the walls and after that they felt "mighty tony." Before closing up the cracks, though, he recalled that during old-time blue northers the children would stand around the fireplace "like spare-ribs hung in front of the fire to roast in hog-killing time."

There was an old shanty behind the house that we used for a kitchen. This had a chimney of which the lower part exposed to the fire was of limestone, and the flue of sticks and mud. An iron bar ran across the throat of this chimney, upon which were hung several iron hooks, which were used to hang pots on for cooking vegetables and meats. There was also a "trivet" or three-sided iron triangle with legs about six inches high, which was for baking bread in a skillet, giving ample room for a bed of hot coals beneath it. We also used this trivet for baking chicken-pie. My! My mouth waters to this day, when I think of those old-time chicken-pies made in a castiron oven with ears to it for lifting with the double pothooks which worked like a pair of tongs. For company, an oven was used that would hold about a half bushel. Three or four frying chickens, or a couple of hens, were cut in pieces and stewed an hour or so in a separate pot. Meantime, a batch of flour dough was made up and rolled out into flat disks large enough to cover the bottom of the oven, and laid closely, with the sides extending up around the edges. A few pieces of chicken were distributed around on the bottom and these interspersed with strips of dough. Then another layer of dough large enough to cover the whole; then some more pieces of stewed chicken, with strips of dumpling, and another layer of dough, and this was built up to about four or five stories on the inside of the oven, and the whole then topped off with another layer of dough, carefully joined to the side walls of dough. The oven was then placed on the trivet, the cover put on and a slow fire kept above and beneath it all for about an hour, care being taken to see that the fire never got hot enough to scorch the crust. When it was done, the top crust was of a rich brown, and the side crusts and bottom also. Chicken-pie is not as good now as it was in "them good old days." (5–6)

Many foods were cooked in hot coals raked to the front of the fireplace: sweet potatoes covered with mud, corn, onions, nuts, even corn pone. It was claimed that the ashes improved the taste of the pone, so they gave it a name—ash pone. Pone is the settlers' way of saying Cherokee *sup-pawn*.

With frontier ingenuity, the women devised better ways of baking bread. Sometimes they put the pone on a hoe or shovel and held it over the fire. Or they took the handle off the hoe and propped the metal piece among the coals. This was called hoecake. Johnny cake is an early Virginia and Maryland name for pone. The name, they said, came from "journey cake," because they gave travelers or hunters or Indian fighters the leftover pones for their forays. But "johnny" and "journey" are really only attempts to imitate the Algonquin *shawnee*, meaning "bread." Settlers were also likely to call pone "scratch cakes" because the tops of the cakes were so rough.

Corn dodgers were pone cakes that had been browned in a hot skillet, so hard that if they were thrown, the intended victim knew that he had better dodge fast. Denise Anderson in Austin recalls a neighbor who, still cooking over a wood-burning stove in the twenties, gave pone to her family every day, but, being somewhat citified, she called it hot-water corn bread. The woman would take equal amounts of cornmeal and boiling water, add a little salt, a couple of tablespoons of butter and an equal number of spoons of chopped onions, and mix it all to make a thick batter. She would wet her hands, shape the batter into round patties, and brown them in a sizzling greased skillet.

This same recipe is used for hush puppies, so named, the story goes, when a cook, trying to get bread to Massa's table on time, was bothered by yelping pups. Ever so often she would throw a bit of bread to the pups and shout, "Hush, puppies." The batter is shaped into little balls and fried in deep fat.

Denise remembers a black cook in her mother's kitchen who insisted pure Southern corn bread had neither sugar nor wheat flour in it. Both of those additions, she said, were Yankee ways. The Texans were too poor to buy sugar and flour.

A pestle for pounding corn.

REAL SOUTHERN CORN BREAD

1 cup sour milk
1/4 teaspoonful soda dissolved in 1 teaspoonful water
1 egg yolk
1/2 teaspoon salt
1 1/2 cups cornmeal
1 egg white, beaten stiff

Mix ingredients in order given. Heat 2 tablespoons of butter or bacon grease in a heavy iron skillet. When sizzling hot, pour half the grease into the bread mixture. Mix gently. Pour the batter into the hot skillet and bake in a moderate oven for 20 minutes. To save time, use the whole egg at one time, instead of separating it, but the texture will not be quite as good.

NORTHERN CORN BREAD

1 cup cornmeal
1 cup white flour
2 cups sour milk
2 tablespoons fat, melted
2 tablespoons sugar
1 1/2 teaspoons salt
2 well beaten eggs
1 teaspoonful soda

Mix dry ingredients: meal, flour, sugar, salt, and soda. Add the milk, eggs, and fat gradually. Bake in a shallow iron pan for 30 minutes in a moderate oven.

Back to the pioneers. The early travelers, had they looked around, would have seen native fruits drying on the mantel or in some sunny place like the window sills—if there were windows in the cabin. There would also be strings of dried wild onions, sacks of pecans, parched corn hanging near the fireplace, and a hand of tobacco. Cucumber peelings (when the settlers began to garden) thrown into the pantry kept weevils out of the meal. And horse apples from the bois d'arc tree—native to the Northeast Texas area—lying here and there, kept other insects away.

The old saying that necessity is the mother of invention held true. The settlers made graters for the corn out of old tin coffeepots. The pot was ripped open, spread on a board, and punched full of holes. The tin was then bent into an oval shape and the straight edges were nailed to the wall or a board.

Or the woman would take the corn outside where, Indian style, she ground it into fine meal in the hollowed-out stump of a tree. A tree was cut three or four feet above the ground—depending on the height of the woman who did the work—and scraped and burned out until it would hold a good amount of corn. A pestle was shaped out of a heavy piece of wood, and the woman could then pound the corn into meal. If the man of the family was industrious, he would attach the pestle to the end of a long pole which was then swung into the fork of a nearby tree. This was a labor-saving device for the woman, for, by pulling the pole up and down, she could grind the corn much easier, or even put one of the children to the task.

When wheat flour became cheap enough to be had, corn bread gave way to biscuits. They could be made with soda, which the women had. And then came baking powder, a decade or so before the turn of the century. It made baking easier, and whatever was easier was bound to make the woman in the kitchen appear lazy. Also, it was new-fangled. Some folks actually feared to use it. The opening chapter of Hart Stilwell's *Uncovered Wagon* is one account of the trouble baking powder could create for one family. The Old Man would go into a rage if the biscuits were made with baking powder and sweet milk instead of soda and sour milk. "God-damn baking powder biscuits," he said.

"If you want to poison me, why don't you put strychnine in my food?" Then he would yell, run out of the house in a frenzy, and return with his sharpened ax, threatening to kill the whole family (5).

It was commonly known that whichever woman in the household failed at quilting became the bread-maker. "My stitches were too big," Anna Hartman of Fort Worth said sadly. "Mother would not let me quilt. I had to do all the cooking for the family." Is it any wonder that Texas households had so many quilts?

These were the foodways common to the Upper and Lower South people. But it was the Upper South pore whites, the pioneering types from Tennessee, Kentucky, Arkansas, and Missouri, moving restlessly from here to there, who spread throughout the state a tradition of down-home cooking. Texas eats begin and end with the Davy Crockett types who pushed their way into Northeast Texas in the wake of the retreating Caddos, content to live at a subsistence level so long as there was a frontier holding out the promise of a better way of life.

Frontier Folk Food Recipes
As Told by Early Settlers

WILD GREENS

1/2 pound salt pork
2 quarts water
1 peck wild greens—wild lettuce, polk [poke] shoots, or wild onions
   Cook salt pork in water for 45 minutes. Add greens and cook one hour, or until the greens sink to the bottom of the pan. Salt and pepper to taste. Serve with corn bread.

GREENS AND POT-LIKKER

   Place in pot 1/2 pound piece of salt pork and boil in 3/4 cup cold water for 45 minutes. Wash young turnip greens. Place them in pot with salt pork and boil slowly another hour. Drain and save the water [the likker] from the pork and greens, chop the greens finely, and season with salt and pepper. Place greens on a hot dish and decorate with slices of salt pork. Pour over the meat and greens about 1 1/2 cups of the likker in which the greens were cooked. Corn meal doggers are served with this to sop up the likker [or crumble corn bread into the likker left in the bottom of the dish and spoon it up].

WILTED LETTUCE

Fry 4 or 5 slices of bacon. Remove bacon when crisp. Add to the hot grease 1/4 cup vinegar, 3 tablespoons water, 1 tablespoon sugar, 3 young green onions (chopped fine), salt and pepper. Add 2 quarts shredded leaf lettuce. Cook 'til wilted. Add crumbled bacon on top before serving.

JOHNNY CAKE

Two cups Indian corn, one cup wheat,
  One cup [4] good eggs that you can eat,
One-half cup molasses too.
  One big spoon sugar added thereto,
Salt and soda, each a small spoon.
  Mix up quickly and bake it soon.

PIE DOUGH

Use pork lard for the best consistency and taste of pie dough.

EGG BUTTER

An old Kentucky recipe, used to make do when the cows went dry and butter was scarce. Kids still liked their bread and butter after school.

Bring to hot 1 pint sorghum. Add two eggs, well beaten. Sprinkle with about 1/2 teaspoon nutmeg. Beat well. Then bring to boil and remove from fire before it burns. Beat again and pour into jar and keep cool.

WOODMAN'S JAM OR PRESERVES

This is old, old, old. Used when in need of a spread and no other source is available. Will not be thick until cold. 1 1/2 cups sorghum molasses and 2 eggs beaten together. Cook in double boiler until eggs are cooked. Stir constantly while cooking. Cool. When cool it is the consistency of most jams.

Old settlers had barrels of homemade sorghum. And of course gingerbread and ginger cookies were favorites with them too when they were too far from a town or could get there but did not have the money to buy sugar.

PARADISE PUFF PILLOWS

2 cups flour
1 1/2 teaspoons baking powder
1 teaspoon salt
2 teaspoons shortening

Mix the above ingredients, adding enough lukewarm water to reduce sticking to hand. Knead the mixture until smooth. Divide into two loaves, and roll each out to 1/8″ thick. To cook, drop small pieces into extremely hot oil. Turn almost immediately.

HOMINY

Tie live oak ashes in a thin white cloth sack and place it in the washpot with the shelled corn. Boil it for two hours. The lye from the ashes seeps out of the sack and gives the hominy its good flavor, the husks fall off the corn kernels, and the eyes slip out. After the first cooking, the corn must be washed thoroughly and then put back into the pot in clean water and boiled for five more hours. Stir it frequently to keep it from burning and add more water if it gets too dry. When cooked, put it in glass jars and seal.

VINEGAR

No vinegar was bought. Daisy Atkins wrote in *'Way Back Yonder*, "we made it all—of fruit juices, left over sugar—any sweets—like rinsing of preserves kettle—all this strained through a cloth into a keg placed near the stove—then a piece of brown paper was put into this mixture, paper forms what is known as a mother to help sour the vinegar. Remember this old riddle: What is vinegar without a mother? Answer: An orphan very poor" (27).

VINEGAR PIE

1/3 cup flour
3 tablespoons [cider] vinegar
1 tablespoon butter
1 cup sugar
1 teaspoon nutmeg
1 1/2 cups water

Crumble butter and flour together. Add sugar and nutmeg. Add vinegar and water. Stir. Pour into unbaked pie shell. Bake at 400 degrees for 15 minutes. Reduce heat to 350 degrees and bake until bubbles form on top.

VINEGAR PIE WITH RAISINS

1 cup seedless raisins, chopped or cut
1/4 cup butter
2 cups sugar
1/2 teaspoon allspice

1/2 teaspoon cinnamon
1/4 teaspoon cloves
4 eggs, beat until light and foamy
2 1/2 to 3 tablespoons of 5% cider vinegar
Dash of salt

Combine ingredients in the order listed. This is a two-crust pie. Pour mixture into unbaked pie shell. Cover with second crust. Bake in a moderately hot oven (425 degrees) for 15 minutes, then reduce heat to 300 degrees and bake 20 minutes longer, or until the top is nicely browned and center of filling is jelly-like.

LORA GARRISON'S TEXIAN VINEGAR PIE

In a 13 × 9 inch pan, put:
2 cups water
1/3 cup apple cider vinegar
1 1/2 cups sugar (can use raw sugar)
1 tablespoon butter

Crust:
2 cups flour
2/3 cups shortening (butter, margarine or Crisco)
1/4 teaspoon salt
1/4 teaspoon baking powder

Add enough water to make a stiff dough. Roll dough to a big 1/4-inch thick square. Dot generously with butter, cover with 2/3 cup sugar. Sprinkle with cinnamon. Roll up as a cinnamon roll and slice in 1-inch pieces; place in pan with sauce of vinegar and water. Spoon sauce over the rolls. Bake in 350 degree oven until slightly brown. This was an old settlers' recipe, my father's favorite.

STACK CAKE

For the filling:
Cook 1 pound sun-dried apples 1 1/3 hours. Cool and mash. Add 1 cup brown sugar, 1/2 cup white sugar, 1 teaspoon cinnamon, 1/2 teaspoon allspice, and 1/2 teaspoon cloves.

For the cake:
1 cup sugar, 1/2 cup butter, 2 eggs, 1 cup buttermilk, 1 teaspoon baking powder, 1/2 teaspoon soda, 1 teaspoon salt, 2 teaspoons vanilla, and enough flour to make a cake dough (2 to 3 cups). Bake at 425 degrees in round cake pans. Use seven pans total, filling with about 1/4" of dough in each pan.

When browned lightly, take out and cool. Alternate the baked layers with the above filling.

OLD-FASHIONED POUND CAKE

1 pound butter (2 cups)
1 pound flour (3 cups)
1 pound sugar (2 cups)
1 pound eggs (9 average)

Cream butter and sugar. Add a little flour and 1 egg at a time. Beat well each time until all is added. Bake in loaf or tube pan in slow oven for two hours.

POUND CAKE

Beating is the secret of pound cake.

3 cups sugar
6 eggs at room temperature
1 teaspoon almond flavoring
4 cups flour
1 pound butter, softened
3/4 cup milk
1 teaspoon vanilla

Combine sugar and butter. Cream until light and fluffy. Add eggs one at a time; beat one minute after each addition. Add flour to cream mixture, alternately with milk, starting and finishing with dry ingredients. Beat 7 minutes. Stir in flavoring. Pour batter in well-greased and sugared 10-inch tube pan. Bake at 300 degrees for one hour and 40 minutes or until cake tests done. Try some fresh fruit over this.

To test a cake, take a clean broomstraw. Stick it into the center of the cake. If it comes out clean of crumbs, the cake is done.

At socials, Noah Smithwick always enjoyed "yellow bread"—pound cakes—which, he said, "warranted full weight, that deluding inflationist, baking powder, not having as yet found its way into that neck of the woods" (234).

The tale of the yaller bread has traveled all over Texas. This is a retelling of J. Frank Dobie's version:

A daughter of a settler was being married. The dinner was prepared and on the table, ready for the wedding guests. Down the trail came Old Heavypaw, a neighbor, on his way to the mill with a sack of corn. His hair "looked as if the bear grease had not been washed out of it in years" and his clothes looked "cured, so much dirt and blood and taller from butchering had been rubbed into them." He was not one of the guests, but no one was ever sent away without being fed. He settled down to eat, helped himself to chicken, venison, greens, and potatoes, and, reaching across the table, took a big slice of pound cake. He sopped it in his gravy and devoured it in one gulp. The uneasy hostess pushed corn bread in front of him, but he shoved it aside and reached for the cake. She was really alarmed when Old Heavypaw got up, took off his belt, sat down again and resumed eating. She ran to the cooking cabin and brought back a plate of hot biscuits. "Oh, Mr. Heavypaw," she said, "do have some biscuits. We don't have them often and I know you'll like these." "No thank ye, ma'am," was his answer. "You jes' save them there biscuits for the company here. This yaller bread is good enough for me." And with that he helped himself to another big piece of the yaller bread and washed it down with a saucer of black coffee (*The Flavor of Texas*, 44–45).

BY-GUESS-BY-GOSH-GINGERBREAD

I always take some flour, just enough for the cake I want to make. I mix it up with some buttermilk if I happen to have any of it, just enough for the flour. Then I take some ginger, some like more, some like less. I put in a little salt and pearl ash [potassium carbonate, or potash, for leavening], and then I tell one of my children to pour in molasses till I tell him to stop. Then the children bring in wood to build up a good fire, and we have gingerbread. (Anonymous)

SCHNITZ UND KNEPP*
Apples, Ham, and Dumplings

Pick over and wash one quart dried apples. Cover with water, let soak overnight or several hours. Next cover a three-pound piece of ham with cold water and let cook four to five hours. Add apples and apple water to drained ham and boil until all are well done. Add two tablespoons brown sugar, remove ham from pot and set aside. Make buttons and add to schnitz [apple and ham broth] and cook covered for 15 to 17 minutes.

For buttons:

Use 2 cups flour, 4 teaspoons baking powder, 1 egg beaten, 3 tablespoons melted shortening, and 1 teaspoon salt. Add milk to make dough the consistency of biscuits. Drop by spoonfuls into hot liquid.

*Schnitz: slices, bits and pieces; knepp: buttons

LEATHER BREECHES BEANS

String tender green beans. Fill a long needle with a long, strong thread. Push the needle through the center of the bean, pushing the beans together at the end of the thread, filling from the knot end to the needle. Hang up the string by one end in the warm air, but not in direct sunlight. This gives the beans a better flavor. Let them remain hanging until the beans become dry. Store in a bag until ready to use.

To cook, remove thread from beans and drop them in a pot of scalding water. Then add a good hunk of salt pork and cook all morning.

It is an old saw that a quart of dried beans "biled two hours," said Josh Billings, "comes out a gallon and a half." And he said, "There ain't but phew things that can beat a bean climbing a pole."

RABBIT

On the range, rabbit was stewed with dumplings, or it was skewered and roasted over an open fire. Fried rabbit is a favorite:

1 rabbit
1 cup flour
1 to 2 teaspoons salt
1 teaspoon pepper
1 to 2 teaspoons paprika or chili powder

After the rabbit is dressed and cut into pieces, wash it well in cold water and dry it. Mix the flour and seasonings. Dip the pieces of rabbit in the flour mixture. Have the fat hot but not smoking. Brown the rabbit lightly, turning it so that all sides are browned. Add a small amount of water. Cover the skillet with a tight-fitting lid and cook over low heat for about an hour. Uncover and continue to cook until the pieces are brown and crispy.

When you are out hunting, if you see a rabbit running uphill, you will have good luck finding game.

•

Hunt rabbits only in months that have R in them.

•

Before a boxing match, never eat rabbit meat, because you will be timid like a rabbit.

Eats in Deep East Texas

THE LOWER SOUTH FOLK—Alabamians, Georgians, Mississippians, and Louisianians—who moved into Deep East Texas brought some different cooking traditions with them. Many of them were pore whites; they lived as the Upper South hill people did—at a subsistence level. They had a corn patch, hogs, perhaps a cow or two, and gathered wild berries, fruits, and edible weeds. They differed, however, from the restless, pioneering folk in Northeast Texas. For they came to settle, their dream to be plantation gentry, grow cotton, and, when they were not hunting or fishing, to sit on a cool veranda sipping mint juleps or Planter's Punch and count their slaves, the measure of their wealth.

Their hunting expeditions may not have been unlike this more recent account by Francis E. Abernethy of Nacogdoches:

> Three of us splash-banged down an old logging road in Alfred's '39 Chevy, dodging stumps and praying through mudholes and finally got to the camp. A half-a-dozen men—as compared to us early-20s boys—were sitting around a fire. Two were cleaning squirrels; two were telling them how; two were refereeing the operation. Alfred, who was younger than Hubert and I but acted older, introduced us around and gave us a couple of beers out of an iced washtub to show that he was one of the official hosts. We stood around awhile until we got Alfred settled down by the campfire; then we got off to the woods.
>
> We had a good hunt. There was a lot of mast that year, and the leaves had fallen enough that you could see to get a shot. We hunted along the road—Hubert on one side, I on the other—so we wouldn't wander off in the wrong direction and then whistled each

other in about dark. It was good and dark by the time we got back, and the camp was settled down in another dimension, ringed by trees, in firelight and long shadows with voices bouncing out into the darkness. They had set the washpot on the fire and had it cradled in rocks so it wouldn't tip over. An old pickup and a jeep had arrived with more Jernigans, and everybody was laughing and talking and doing things to the pot.

We skinned our squirrels and quartered them and tossed them in the pot. The stock was already boiling and squirrel parts were cooking tender. Somebody had tossed in some young cat squirrels, heads and tails, and they periodically rolled to the surface to see what was coming next. A young coon and a rabbit were added to the pot, and some uncle threatened the stew with armadillo that was snuffling around in the brush just outside the firelight.

When the meat started coming off the bones, the cooks— everybody there—added carrots, potatoes, onions, and God knows what else, canned or cut. One old man kept seasoning the broth with cigar ashes. Other creative souls contributed splashes of beer, whiskey, and coffee "to add character," they said, to the mixture. I heard somebody say, "Dammit, Casey, quit spittin' in that pot." I'm sure he was just joking with those of us who were new to the tradition.

I was starving to the point of eating my hat and gloves when the head cook forked into a piece of meat and finally announced that the stew was ready. We all lined up with a variety of bowls, cups, and coffee cans while the cook ladled it out. It didn't look like the stew you have around the house, probably because there was so much of it, but it smelled about the same, maybe a little stronger. Hubert and I looked over at each other when we sat down to eat, wondering how much of a new experience our stomachs would stand. Alfred was already slurping away as if he had washpot sunovagun at every meal. We might have hesitated but the moment was short, and we ate with hunger-whetted appetites. My God, but that was good stew! I don't know how to describe how good that stew was except to say that that stew took place about 40 years ago and I can still savor it on tongue and palate. Everybody was eating and carryin' on about how good it was and the whole scene was like a communion, with people sitting on the edge of the firelight, with stars sparkling on the blue-black sky and owls 6 feet tall hoo-haing across the river at each other.

The Lower South ladies brought the plantation tradition of fine foods and Southern hospitality to the Texas savannahs along the rivers coursing toward the Gulf of Mexico or the Mississippi. Their recipes were learned in the

A turn-of-the-century hunting camp. *Courtesy the John Black Collection, East Texas State University.*

kitchen alongside their mothers who cooked with a pinch of this, a dab of that, and a handful of the other. Sometimes, tucked away among family papers, in a letter, a diary, or on a slip of paper, there would be a "receet." But usually the receet was carried in their heads, like the 1-2-3-4 cake:

- 1 cup butter
- 2 cups molasses
- 3 cups flour
- 4 eggs
- 1 teaspoon soda in 1/2 cup buttermilk

The cake was good just as was, or the cook could throw in a handful of hickory nuts or pecans, some ginger, or some spices, should she have some. She was limited only by her imagination.

The ladies served their guests much fish and game—venison, duck, and quail. And they followed the meal with an assortment of cakes, pies, and puddings.

Senator Ralph Yarborough tells this story about Sam Houston at a plantation dinner. The tale was a favorite of J. Frank Dobie:

> Sam Houston sent word to the Thomas plantation on the Colorado River that he was coming. The Thomases invited all the bellwethers in the country, put the big pot in the little one, fried the skillet and threw away the handle. Dinner, of course, was in the middle of the day. It was election time and Houston was full of talk. His enemies may have been men with the bark on, but he peeled it off. He had a lusty appetite. His eating did not interfere with his talking and his talking did not interfere with his eating.
>
> After an enormous bait of pork and turnip greens, roast beef and fried venison, baked sweet potatoes and Irish potato salad, roasting ears that were roasted and red beans boiled with fat bacon, both cornbread and biscuits, along with trimmings and buttermilk, the dessert came. It was hot rice pudding—than which nothing can be hotter. It was served in ample bowls with ample spoons.
>
> In the midst of an accusation of a certain character whom Houston often denounced as "nothing but a damned vegetarian," he clapped a heaping spoon of the hot rice pudding into his mouth. Immediately, if not sooner, he ejected it back into the bowl and on to the surrounding territory. Then pausing, spoon suspended in mid-air, he calmly interposed: "Many a damn fool would have swallered that."

The folk with Lower South plantation heritage thought tomatoes and wild greens, except for salad lettuce grown in their own gardens, unfit to eat. Sam Sewell of Richardson recalls an elderly Georgia uncle who would not allow greens on the table except for wilted lettuce cooked over high heat in bacon grease. String beans were weeds, he said, and he demanded his patient-Griselda wife wait until the beans had matured to cook up "shelled beans" especially for him.

Originally there was a great deal of skepticism about the foods found in the New World. The Indians had given the early settlers *batatas*, sweet potatoes; *papas*, white potatoes; and *tomates*. The *batata* is a swollen root, quite different from the *papa* that grows from a tuber. And since both the *tomate* and the *papa* belong to the nightshade family, they were thought to be poisonous. When the Spanish took the tomato back to Europe, it was given the name "love apple" because it looked so much like a red apple, to which romantic notions had long been attached, but it was not considered fit to eat until about the 1850s.

The plantation ladies were able to purchase spices, but they alone held the keys to the spice cabinets and zealously guarded their hoards. The spices, along with herbs from their gardens, encouraged the cooks to create dishes served with delicately flavored sauces.

The truth is that it was mainly the imagination of the brightly turbaned black Mammys in the separate kitchen house behind the main building who created what we call plantation cuisine. At their own cabins they kept small plots for gardens where they planted sweet potatoes, cabbage, and corn. And at butchering time they were given the parts of the animal Ol' Massa didn't want. So they found ways of preparing hogs' innards (also called the lights), hogs' heads, hogs' feet, chicken necks, fish heads, and so on. In time these foods would become regular fare for Texans.

Heléne Curry of Denton recalls opening the pot of flavorsome chicken gumbo that Bea, the Mississippi cook, had simmering on the stove. And there, close to the top, were the chicken feet. Good gumbo, though!

Food in the big house was altogether different. Working at the large hearth in the kitchen, Mammy could, with great flair, cook up quail and serve it with a delicately flavored wine sauce, with hot, flaky biscuits on the side; roast turkey with corn bread dressing, often with oysters added; many kinds of preserves and relishes; potatoes, whipped with eggs, butter, and cream, until they were light and fluffy—potatoes to the early Texans were sweet potatoes or yams, the two words not synonymous then. And there would be cakes and pies. Her meats were juicy, turned on a spit in the fireplace until golden brown by one of the smaller boys from her cabin. Corn bread was served with every meal, Southern Spoon Bread being a favorite, soft in the middle like a pudding. This recipe dates from the days of the Confederacy and is handed down by descendants of Stephen F. Austin, the Dr. John Caldwell family in Freeport:

SOUTHERN SPOON BREAD

1 cup white cornmeal
2 cups sweet milk
2 tablespoons butter
1 teaspoon sugar
Dash of salt
3 eggs, separated

Cook the cornmeal in the milk for 3 to 4 minutes [stirring constantly]. Add butter, sugar, and salt. Allow to cook. Fold in the well beaten egg yolks, then fold in the stiffly beaten egg whites. Turn into a well greased baking dish that has been heated. Bake in a moderate oven for 45 minutes, until the center is set.

As the houseboys hurried along the walkway between the kitchen and the main house, they had to whistle so that they could not sample the foods bound for the big table. This walk came to be called "Whistler's Walk."

Recipes from Deep East Texas Kitchens

VENISON ROAST

Cut long strips of sliced salt bacon and put into the venison ham with a skewer. Add 4 to 5 cloves of garlic cut into slivers and inserted into the meat. Spread with mustard, black and red pepper, salt, and Worcestershire sauce. Add just a few drops of Tabasco sauce. Slice 1 large or 2 medium onions very fine and about a cupful of tomatoes. Add a little thyme (about 1 teaspoonful), one apple and one orange, cut up. Put all of this in the roasting pan.

Before starting to bake, the venison should be seared to prevent loss of the fat pork larding. Then put a small amount of flour on the roast and brown. Now add roast to all the vegetables in the roast pan. Cover with lid. Bake first in a hot oven (about 450 degrees) for at least one hour. Remove the cover, cut down the heat to 350 degrees and baste with beer. Continue basting and cooking 2 more hours.

As you baste with the beer, dip up juices from the pan and baste with the drippings from this mixture. Continue cooking until roast is brown and tender.

Serve with pan gravy and garnish with mint. A good sauce may be currant jelly, currant mint sauce, muscadine or wild grape jelly. Currant mint sauce is made by stirring 1 tablespoon chopped mint leaves and the grated rind of half an orange into a glass of currant jelly.

FRANK DOBIE'S VENISON STEAK

Frank Dobie thought venison should be eaten in the camp and his advice was: "Cut off a steak, salt and pepper it, chunk it in the flour and throw it in the grease. That's the best way to cook venison."

QUAIL IN SHERRY

Allow a quail for each serving.
2 tablespoons of butter
1 teaspoon chopped parsley

1 tablespoon chopped onion
2 tablespoons flour
1 cup canned mushrooms, including liquor
1 cup sherry wine
1 teaspoon salt
Pepper and Tabasco to taste

Put butter, parsley, onions in deep pot and fry until onions are light brown. Add flour, brown slightly, add mushrooms and liquor, wine, salt, pepper, and Tabasco. [To avoid lumps of flour, stir flour with a little cold water first and strain into cooking pot.] When the ingredients are thoroughly cooked, place the quail breast side down in the pot. Add water to half-cover the quail and cook 30 minutes, or until the juice from the quail, when forked, is clear. This amount of sauce is for 6 quail.

Some cooks prefer to split the quail, season them, coat with flour, and brown them on both sides in hot oil. Remove from the skillet. With two tablespoons of the drippings in the skillet, proceed as above, adding an equal amount of flour, stirring until smooth. Then add the parsley, onion, and mushrooms. Add the sherry last. Stir this mixture until it is thickened. Return the quail to the skillet, cover, and simmer until the quail is fork tender.

There is a saying that it is impossible to eat a quail a day for thirty days. Pat Flynn, newspaperman for the Amarillo *Advance*, said he reached his twenty-first day after being challenged by his publisher, Gene Howe.

Pat found the first fifteen days easy going. After that it became more difficult to find ways to prepare the quail so that it would be easy to swallow. Finally he admitted defeat. "When I stopped," he said, "I not only was making sounds like a bobwhite but was beginning to think like a quail—easily flushed by anything." (Hittson, 113)

STUFFED RED SNAPPER

Scale and clean a 3-to-4-pound red snapper. Cut on inside along the backbone to make room for the stuffing. Do not cut through.

6 tablespoons butter
1/4 cup fish stock, or hot water
2 cups bread, cubed
1 medium onion, chopped
1 clove garlic, finely chopped

2 tablespoons parsley
1 peeled tomato, chopped
1/2 cup celery, chopped
1 tablespoon ham, chopped
Salt to taste
Pepper, both black and red, to taste

Melt butter in liquid and pour over all the ingredients. Add whatever fish bits you have: oysters, baby clams, shrimp (optional). You may add 1 well-beaten egg yolk to bind the ingredients, but do not plan to refrigerate leftover dressing with egg in it. It spoils easily.

Place the stuffed fish in a baking pan greased amply with bacon drippings. Add white wine and fish stock to cover 1/4 of the fish. Baste frequently.

Bake 10 minutes per pound at 400 degrees or until the fish is flaky. Serves 6. Garnish with plenty of lemon wedges and parsley.

Serve with a white sauce:

1 cup Sauterne
1/4 cup parsley, chopped
1/2 tablespoon chives
1/2 tablespoon tarragon
1/2 pound butter
2 egg yolks
1 teaspoon pepper, white preferred
1/2 teaspoon salt

Bring wine to boil. Simmer herbs in the wine for a minute. Bring to boil and turn heat off.

Beat egg yolks well. Spoon half a cup of boiling wine slowly into egg yolks and stir briskly to avoid lumps; then add to wine along with the salt, pepper, and half the butter. Beat well with an eggbeater. Add remaining butter and blend some more. Serve immediately.

RICE WITH HERBS

Sauté 3 tablespoons minced onions, 1 teaspoon minced garlic, in 4 tablespoons butter. Add 2 cups raw rice, 2 bay leaves, 1 teaspoon thyme, 1/2 teaspoon basil, 1 teaspoon marjoram. Cook over low heat until rice is no longer opaque. Add 4 cups hot chicken broth to the rice. Add salt and pepper to taste. Cover and simmer for 30 minutes or until rice is soft. Remove the bay leaves before serving.

FRITTER FRIED OKRA

1 cup all-purpose flour
1 tablespoon baking powder
1/2 teaspoon salt
2 eggs, well-beaten
1/3 cup milk
5 cups thinly sliced okra
Hot vegetable oil

Mix flour, baking powder, and salt in a medium-sized bowl. Add eggs and milk, beating until smooth. Add okra, stirring until coated. Spoon the okra into the hot oil in a large skillet, a little at a time as you do not want to crowd the okra. Fry the pieces until they are golden brown. Lift from the skillet and drain.

FRESH CUT CORN

Take two dozen ears of fresh corn, shuck them, and taking one ear at a time, cut away the corn, taking care not to cut deeply. You want to barely cut the tops of the kernels. Then scrape the cob with the blunt edge of the knife to catch the milk. This will not work with store-bought corn.

Heat 1/2 cup butter in a heavy iron skillet or Dutch oven. Add a cup of cream. Stir in the corn and milk from the cobs. Add salt and pepper to taste. Cook over medium or low heat, stirring occasionally to avoid sticking until the corn is done, 20 to 30 minutes. If the mixture begins to dry out, add some milk and butter.

You may want to add an onion and a bell pepper. If so, sauté the finely chopped onion and pepper in the butter before adding the cream and the corn.

CORN BREAD WITH SAUSAGE

1 cup white cornmeal
1 cup flour
1 1/2 teaspoons salt
4 teaspoons baking powder
1 tablespoon sugar
2 eggs
1 1/2 cups buttermilk

Mix the dry ingredients together, combine the eggs and buttermilk and add to the dry mixture. The batter should be thick.

Corn bread is best when cooked in a heavy cast iron skillet. Heat short of smoking 2 tablespoons of oil, bacon drippings, or cooking oil left over from frying chicken. Swish the hot oil around the sides of the skillet, then pour half of it into the batter.

Now crumble into another skillet about a pound of sausage, preferably a hot, spicy sausage. Add a chopped onion. Brown the sausage and drain off the grease.

Now take a can of cream-style corn and pour it into the middle of the corn bread batter. Sprinkle the sausage over the top of the corn. Cover the sausage with a cup of grated rat trap cheese.

Pour the remaining batter over the corn-sausage-cheese mixture. Bake in a hot oven (400 degrees) for about 30 minutes, or until golden brown.

ORANGE BLOSSOM MUFFINS
from the Excelsior House, Jefferson

1 slightly beaten egg
1/4 cup sugar
1/2 cup orange juice
2 tablespoons salad oil or melted shortening
2 cups biscuit mix
1/2 cup orange marmalade
1/2 cup chopped pecans

Combine first four ingredients; add biscuit mix and beat vigorously for 30 seconds. Stir in marmalade and pecans. Grease muffin pans or line with paper baking cups; fill 2/3 full.

Topping:

1/4 cup sugar
1 1/2 tablespoons flour
1/2 teaspoon cinnamon
1/4 teaspoon nutmeg
1 tablespoon butter

Combine sugar, flour, nutmeg, and cinnamon; cut in butter till mixture is crumbly. Sprinkle over batter in each muffin cup. Bake at 400 degrees for 20 to 25 minutes. Makes 1 dozen.

PRALINES

Take a heavy iron pan and bring to a boil 2 cups of sugar, 1 cup of half-and-half cream, and 1 tablespoon butter. In a separate heavy pan, melt 1/2 cup sugar until it is caramel colored. Add the first mixture to the caramel sugar. Add pecans and cook to the soft ball stage (235 degrees on the candy thermometer). Remove from heat and beat until it thickens. Drop onto wax paper to harden. Yields 2 dozen pralines.

Some cooks insist that good pralines must be made in heavy iron pans and dropped on marble to harden quickly.

MINT JULEP

Use a silver julep cup or a large clear glass and crush a few sprigs of mint all around the inside of the glass, then throw the mint away. Fill the glass with finely cracked ice. Slowly pour in a measure of bourbon whiskey, then add about 2 tablespoons of water in which a lump of sugar has been dissolved. Do not stir. Place a sprig of mint in the top of the glass.

Adding to the distinctiveness of Deep East Texas food lore is Cajun cooking. Texas Cajuns are descendants of the peasants from Acadia who, removed from French Canada, migrated to Louisiana and made the marshlands and swamps their home. Some of them had moved westward and crossed the Sabine in the days of the Republic. Then in the oil-booming early decades of the new century, they came in large numbers, looking for jobs along coastal Texas.

Their food was that of French peasants, but they were quick to adjust to their new environment, where they hunted, fished, and farmed. At the same time, they adapted what they liked of Afro-American eats—okra, for example, which had been brought from Africa by the slaves. And they took what they wanted of the Spanish ways with food, making theirs hot and spicy, not with expensive imported spices like black pepper from India, but with their own cayenne—red peppers which they could grow.

One can't really talk about a Cajun tradition. Cajun cooks change and adapt constantly, for they are very creative. Food is not eaten for sustenance alone but for pleasure too. The food is a long time in the making (that is the reason blackened redfish is not considered true Cajun) and a long time in the eating. They like to linger over their coffee, and they may end a meal with singing and dancing.

A daughter may learn to cook Cajun in her mother's kitchen, but her recipes will be different. She will bring her own imaginative skills to her kitchen, and her inspiration rests in her aim to make whatever she cooked yesterday be better today.

Still, there are certain basics. Nearly all recipes begin with a roux—light brown, medium, or dark. And there must be a good stock made by boiling for hours whatever is not to be eaten: fish heads, shrimp peelings, the necks of poultry, chicken backs, and crab claws; add some onion and carrot and let it simmer. Pepper is also basic. Finally, there will be rice, a food introduced by the Spaniards and quickly adopted by the Louisianians.

Meats are frequently smoked. On the open hearth, smothering was a common practice. Whatever meat was to be cooked could be braised, that is, cooked in hot fat briefly and then covered with stock (or water) and a little flour and left to cook slowly for hours. Because Cajuns cook their food a long time, none of their peas or beans rattle on the plate.

Sam Sewell, who counts some Cajun families among his best friends, emphasizes the creativity of the cooks: "They take whatever is at hand, possum, crawfish (you don't say crawdads and you don't say crayfish), alligator, chicken, or pork, and cook it in a sauce with mushrooms, onions, some vegetables, and lots of pepper. I sat down at the table once and they brought out blackbirds. Sure, they were good, covered up with that Cajun sauce. And alligator in a gumbo is no surprise."

Crawfish are a delicacy. The Cajuns gather them from the rice fields. They boil them, Sam says, in stock and bring them to the table in tubs where they are dumped onto newspapers for the eaters. Then "You squeezes de tail and sucks de haid." You squeeze and break off the tail, he explains, and pull out the string-like intestine to get to the strip of sweet white meat. His friends told him to suck the head to get the brains. Brains or whatever, what you suck out is hot and spicy like the stock the crawfish has been boiled in, he says.

Étoufée is served on the side. It is basically a roux but must have some crawfish fat. To get at the fat, the cook has to take the live crawfish, avoid its pincers while she twists off the tail, rips open the body, and scoops out the yellow globules of fat. It is possible to buy crawfish fat if you know whose store to go to.

It is a mistake, Sam says, to think of Cajun food as chiefly seafood. Sure, they like oysters, though only in the months that have an "r" in the spelling; they say the oysters are milky during the other months and don't taste right. But Cajuns have always been trappers and farmers, not just fishermen. Like their Lower South neighbors in Deep East Texas, they have chickens, hogs, some cattle, cane, corn, rice, vegetables, pecans, and sweet potatoes.

Sam says, "Ask a Cajun what a seven-course meal is and he will answer, 'A six-pack and boudin'." Boudin is a delicacy to be ranked with crawfish and étoufée. It is a soft sausage made of cooked pork scraps left after butchering, onions, seasonings, and some rice. Then bring out the fiddles and the party is on. The Cajuns enjoy life—and good food.

Cochon, Cajun for pig, roasted on a spit over charcoal, is a favorite for big celebrations. Sally Gates Cobb, formerly of Pasadena and now Assistant Director and Food Coordinator for the New Orleans Jazz and Heritage Festival, frequently prepared cochon for wedding celebrations when she operated Sally's Country Inn outside New Orleans. The roasting was done over a pit, lined with sheets of corrugated tin on three sides for directing the heat toward the pig. The pig was scalded and the hide scraped clean of hair and dirt. Then it was gutted, cleaned thoroughly, folded up in a piece of metal fencing, and suspended in front of and above the coals. The pig must be turned from time to time—Sally's husband fashioned a rig that kept the pig turning the entire cooking time. The pig may be seasoned with salt, pepper, and garlic before beginning the roasting, or the seasoning may be left until the cooking is done.

Sally points out that Cajun cooking is different from Creole. It is the difference between country and city cooking. The Cajuns use the gravy-like roux that is hot, peppery, and heavily spiced; the Creoles can purchase herbs and exotic spices for delicately flavored sauces. One thing they will agree on is how to prepare red beans and rice. Here is Sally's recipe, with others from her kitchen:

RED BEANS AND RICE

2 pounds red kidney beans, washed and soaked overnight
2 cups chopped onion
1/2 cup green onion tops
1/2 cup chopped bell pepper
2 tablespoons minced garlic
2 tablespoons minced fresh parsley
1 pound baked ham, cut into cubes
1 or 2 ham hocks or ham bones
1 tablespoon salt
1/2 teaspoon black pepper
Dash cayenne pepper
Pinch crushed red pepper pods
2 whole bay leaves, broken in half
1/2 teaspoon dried thyme
1/2 teaspoon dried basil
3 to 4 quarts of water

Put all ingredients into a 10-quart pot. Bring to a boil, then lower the heat to simmer 3 to 4 hours, or till beans are tender and a thick natural gravy has formed. May need to add more water if beans appear too dry. Stir the beans frequently during cooking to prevent scorching. When the beans are cooked, turn off the heat. Ladle about 1 1/2 cups of beans, meat, and gravy over about 2/3 cup of boiled rice. We serve a 3- to 4-inch length of boiled smoked sausage on the side.

Serve with corn bread or French bread and a garden salad. If beans do not thicken by themselves, take a cup of the beans and mash them with a fork. Return mashed beans to large pot and let simmer 15 to 20 minutes. Delicious.

SALLY'S PRIZE-WINNING GUMBO

There are as many different recipes for gumbo as there are cooks to make it. It may be made with okra or filé to thicken. Filé is powdered sassafras root and was made long ago by the Choctaw Indians. Always add filé *after* the gumbo is cooked and removed from the heat. Boiling gumbo after filé is added tends to make the gumbo stringy.

I love okra and always use okra to thicken. Filé may be set on the table for personal use. Many people simply like the flavor that filé imparts.

Gumbo is a great way to use up bits and pieces of leftovers. (Jambalaya is a good way also.)

I always save the bones from chicken, turkey, or ham, boil them down, and use that rich stock for the gumbo. If you are lucky enough to get fresh shrimp, use the heads and shells to make a stock. Gumbo can be simple or fairly complicated. Gumbo is what meat you have combined with a roux, vegetables, and seasonings, cooked long and slow. It is almost always better the second day. When using seafood, especially oysters, the roux should be thicker to make up for the water exuded by the oysters:

CHICKEN (OR TURKEY)-SAUSAGE GUMBO
(*Serves 8–12*)

1/2 cup oil
1/2 cup flour

First you make a roux. In a large Dutch oven or black skillet heat the oil over medium-low heat. Add the flour and cook over medium heat until very dark—at least the color of hazelnuts. Stir constantly while browning. If the roux burns, throw it out and start over. I always use a wooden spoon to stir.

Now add:

1 pound fresh or frozen okra
2 cups chopped onions
1/4 cup bell pepper
3 pods garlic (or more), chopped fine
3 to 4 large Creole tomatoes

Cook till okra loses its stringiness and the vegetables are translucent. Add 1 to 2 quarts of water or stock.

Now add:

1/2 to 1 pound smoked sausage (kielbasa), cut into 1/2-inch thick rounds
1 3-pound fryer that has been cut up and browned, or the meat from leftover turkey
1/4 pound baked ham, cut into cubes (optional)
1/4 cup finely chopped parsley
1/2 cup green onion tops, thinly sliced
1 jalapeno pepper (or 1 to 2 teaspoons crushed red pepper)
1/2 teaspoon basil

1 teaspoon salt

1/2 teaspoon freshly ground black pepper

Cook till done. All vegetables should be mushy. Chicken should be falling apart.

For seafood gumbo use shrimp, oysters, and crabmeat instead of sausage, chicken, and ham. Add lemon juice (1 tablespoon) and use seafood stock for liquids. Add seafood to the okra mixture and cook about five minutes over medium-high heat, until the shrimp turns pink.

Serve over boiled rice. I prefer brown. Enjoy!

JAMBALAYA

2 tablespoons vegetable oil

1 fryer (3 to 4 pounds), cut up, rinsed, and dried

4 cups chopped onion

3/4 cup chopped green pepper

3/4 cup thinly sliced green onion tops

1 tablespoon finely minced garlic

3 tablespoons finely minced fresh parsley

1/2 cup chopped lean baked ham

1 pound lean pork, cut in 1/2-inch cubes (optional)

24 inches smoked sausage (kielbasa), sliced 1/2 inch thick

3 teaspoons salt

1/2 teaspoon fresh ground black pepper

1/4 teaspoon cayenne

1/2 teaspoon chili powder

2 bay leaves, crushed

1/2 teaspoon dried thyme

1/8 teaspoon cloves

1/4 teaspoon basil

1 1/2 cups long-grain rice

3 cups water or stock

In a heavy 7–8 quart pot, heat oil over high heat. Brown the chicken, turning parts frequently to insure even browning. Remove parts to platter. After chicken is browned and removed, add the vegetables, parsley, ham, and pork to the pot. Reduce the heat to medium and cook for 15 minutes until all is browned.

Add the sausage and seasonings and cook and stir for 5 more minutes. Add chicken, rice, and water. Mix gently. Raise the heat to high and bring to a boil. Cover pot and turn the heat to low. Cook for 45 minutes; uncover occasionally to stir. Uncover pot last 10 minutes of cooking and raise the heat to medium. Stir gently as rice dries out. Eat! *Serves 4.*

CRAWFISH ÉTOUFÉE

1 pound butter
2 cups flour
8 cups onion
2/3 cup chopped bell pepper
2/3 cup chopped celery
2/3 cup chopped green onions (the white part)
1/2 cup finely minced garlic
6 pounds crawfish tails and fat
2 tablespoons salt
2 1/2 teaspoons fresh ground black pepper
2 teaspoons cayenne
1/2 teaspoon crushed red pepper
1/2 teaspoon cumin
2 tablespoons fresh lemon juice
1/2 cup fresh finely minced parsley
1 cup thinly sliced green onion tops
10 cups cold water

In heavy pot, melt butter over low heat. Gradually add the flour, stirring constantly. Cook over low heat until a medium brown roux is formed (15 to 20 minutes). Quickly add the onions, green pepper, celery, and garlic and continue to cook till vegetables are glazed and tender.

Add crawfish tails, crawfish fat, salt, black pepper, cayenne, lemon juice, onion tops, and parsley, and mix well. Add 3 to 4 scant cups cold water and bring to a boil, then lower heat and simmer for 12 minutes or till crawfish tails are just tender, stirring frequently. Add the rest of the gravy. Let steep 1 hour.

You may make étoufée with shrimp or chicken.

MAKING A ROUX

Use equal amounts of flour and shortening. Add flour to hot shortening, lower heat slightly and brown flour while constantly stirring and smoothing. The secret is to push the browning to the darkest degree possible without scorching the flour. It should become the color of chocolate. Turn heat very low before adding water. Add water slowly and blend thoroughly each time until mixture has the consistency of a thin paste, then water may be added more rapidly in larger quantities. In the early stages of blending, it may be necessary to lift the pan from the heat or even remove it temporarily to keep roux creamy.

PECAN PIE

Boil for two minutes:

1 cup brown sugar

1 1/2 cups white Karo syrup

Beat 4 eggs till lemon-colored. Slowly pour hot syrup into egg mixture. Beat constantly so that the egg does not cook. Add 2 tablespoons melted butter and 1 1/2 teaspoons vanilla. Add 1 1/2 cups pecans or pieces.

Pour into unbaked pie shell and bake for 45 minutes at 350 degrees.

Irrigation. *Courtesy Amon Carter Museum, Fort Worth, Texas.*

Early farming. *Courtesy the Erwin E. Smith Collection of the Library of Congress, on deposit at the Amon Carter Museum.*

58

Eats in Central Texas

T HE THREE HUNDRED brought by
Stephen F. Austin to make their homes in his colony were, as said earlier, the
pioneering frontier folk from the Upper South. Like their relatives and friends
of East Texas, they lived at a subsistence level, and their foodways differed
very little even into the first decades of the twentieth century.

To see them at their best is to observe them when the preacher comes to
dinner. Itinerant preachers "ate around" and no doubt ate better than the
folks they prayed for.

Alma McGee of Commerce tells this story about a friend who had invited
the preacher to dinner. It was always an occasion. Everyone scrubbed up, wore
clean clothes, and was reminded of manners. A fresh white tablecoth was laid
out, along with the best dishes, the best tableware, and store-bought glassware
instead of jelly glasses. This woman was an Episcopalian, a devout church-
goer, and everything must be just right for her priest.

There would be two meats—fried ham and chicken—black-eyed peas,
string beans, creamed corn (there had to be at least two vegetables), hot biscuits and butter, slang jang for the peas, pickles and relishes, jams and jellies,
a cake and a pie or cobbler, and plenty of iced tea with some of the mint that
grew beside the back door. It would seem that this preacher was in for a good
feed.

It was cotton picking time and everyone liked to be in the fields to lay by
some extra money. All the maids, houseboys, and yard boys would leave. The
missus' maid asked to go pick too, so another black woman was brought in as
a temporary replacement. Now this woman had a good reputation for cooking,
washing and ironing, cleaning house, all those things expected of a maid, and,
above all, she was known to be reliable.

Alma's friend's husband had the store in town and she was accustomed to

Children in chicken yard, Clifton, c. 1900. *Courtesy Amon Carter Museum, Fort Worth, Texas.*

helping him on busy days. A shipment had come in on this Monday morning and she had to leave the house early to work with him.

Monday is washday. Everyone knows that. Nothing interrupts washday—except having the preacher come to dinner. So the missus wrote a note, telling the new maid *not* to wash but to prepare the dinner after she had cleaned house. And she wrote out a list of what the maid should cook.

About 11:00 she became somewhat apprehensive about things at home, since dinner was served at 12:00 sharp, so she called. "How are you getting along?" she asked when the maid answered.

"Fine," was the answer.

"What are you doing now?"

"I'se washin'," was the response.

With some consternation in her voice, the lady of the house asked, "Washing? Why?"

"It's Monday," the maid said.

"I know it's Monday. But what are we having for dinner?"

"Corn bread. Beans."

The missus was frantic. "Corn bread! Beans! Didn't you see my note?"

"Yas'm," was the answer. There was a long pause. Then, "What do it say?"

SMOTHERED CHICKEN

Before the advent of the cookstove, chicken was stewed in a kettle on the open hearth. The chicken was cut up, put into the Dutch oven, and covered with water. When it was tender from stewing, salt and pepper were added, and a blend of equal amounts of melted butter—or fat, whatever was on hand—and flour was added for thickening.

BILL OWENS'S FRIED CHICKEN

This is Southern Fried Chicken, Virginia style, Texas style or whatever. First of all, mix some flour with salt and pepper and put it into a paper sack. Cut the pieces of chicken into normal size for frying. Chill the pieces in iced water before cooking. Drain well and dry. Apply a light coating of mustard to the pieces, then drop them into the sack and shake up and down until all are well coated. Don't put too many pieces in the sack at once. Next, carefully put the pieces in a heated skillet with pretty hot fat, about 1/4 inch, just enough to keep the chicken from burning. Fry 30 minutes on one side; turn the pieces and fry 30 minutes on the other side. This chicken is well done.

And then make Southern white gravy. Drain off the fat. Put a little brandy in the skillet to scrape loose what is sticking. Mix a couple of tablespoons of flour from the sack with the scrapings in the skillet. Add about a cup of milk, or enough to allow the gravy to cook to the desired consistency.

Corn patch. *Courtesy Southwest Collection, Texas Tech University.*

SLANG JANG

1 tomato, fresh from the garden, chopped
1 sweet green pepper, chopped
1 medium onion, chopped
2 stalks of celery, sliced
About 1/2 pod of hot red pepper
A pinch of salt and sugar
3/4 cup vinegar
1/4 cup water
  Combine all ingredients. Add hot pepper and seasonings to taste.

PEACH COBBLER I

  Heat about a quart of sliced fresh peaches and sugar to taste in a saucepan. Mix well 1 cup sugar, 1 cup flour, 1 teaspoon salt, 3 teaspoons baking powder in a bowl. Add 1 cup milk to the dry ingredients, a little at a time. Melt three tablespoons butter in a baking pan. Pour the batter into the pan. Spoon the fruit over the top of the batter. Bake for 30 or 40 minutes in a hot oven (400 degrees) until golden brown. Serve with cream.

BUTTERMILK BISCUITS

The oven must be very hot, preheated to 450 degrees.

Sift together 2 cups flour, 1/2 teaspoon salt, 1/4 teaspoon soda, and 1 tablespoon baking powder. With the tips of your fingers, or with a pastry blender, cut in 5 tablespoons shortening. Make a well in the middle of the mixture and pour in 1 cup of buttermilk. With a fork, toss lightly only until the flour is moistened. Turn out on a floured board and knead two or three times. Just push the dough with the palm of your hand. Pat the dough out to about 1/2-inch thickness. Cut with a biscuit cutter and place in a buttered pie tin. Bake for 12 to 15 minutes until nicely browned. Brush tops with melted butter.

Stick your finger into the middle of a biscuit to make a hole; fill it with honey or corn syrup.

An old story tells about a preacher who began his career during early times in Texas as a Baptist circuit rider. It might be a hard ride over rough terrain in dark or rain, but unfailingly at the end of the ride there would be a meal worth the ride at some ranch house or country place. He remembered one such meal when the subject of fried chicken came up. Not allowing even a flicker of humor to play across his face as he put both hands behind his head and locked them, he said something like this:

I went to this one house one time and they had fried chicken. There was a lot of other good food too—mashed potatoes, all white under light brown cream gravy, fresh vegetables and plenty of 'em because it was summer, big ole loaves of bread, and fruit pies, the kind with top crusts and not that meringue stuff. There was a bunch of us at the table, some were older children, some adults, and one young boy about eight years old. There was a good white cloth spread on the table and plates that were pretty well matched up. It would be a chore to keep from dropping food on that white cloth, but we were all expected to try. The little boy sat next to me. After the food was passed around, I noticed that he didn't take any chicken. I asked him if he didn't want some chicken and picked up the plate to pass it back to him. He said he didn't want any and ducked his head and wouldn't look up any more. Well, the meal went on and everything, all of it, was passed again. Still the boy wouldn't take any chicken or anything else. I insisted again, telling him that it would all be gone and there wouldn't be any left later. When he didn't say anything at all, I tried to persuade him one more time. On my last try, the child raised his head, looked me straight in the face, and said, "No, I don't want none of that chicken. That's the one that fell in the slop jar and drowned last night and mama cooked him for dinner." He ran off from the table and some others left too.

"Buffalo Wings," chicken wings fried crisp—first served in a bar in Buffalo, New York—will have little appeal to the Texan who had to eat what the adults left on the platter of fried chicken—usually the wings. The men always got the choice pieces. And children usually had to wait until second table for their eats.

One Texan said she did not know there was both white and dark meat on a chicken until she was cook in her own kitchen. Nor had she ever heard that a chicken had a breast!

But these preacher stories are only intended to show that when the Texans put on the dog, their tables groaned with down-home cooking.

Daily fare for the early Texas folk was soup or stew. A pot was kept simmering at the hearth or at the back of the stove. It is said that French settlers never let a pot go empty and that some families were known to keep their soup going for generations. These folk had to be thrifty. Nothing was thrown out, and leftovers went into the pot for soup. Elly Hutcheson, popular speaker in Fort Worth on folkways and foodways of early Texans, says squirrel stew with dumplings was the all-time favorite.

SQUIRREL STEW WITH DUMPLINGS

Soak the squirrels overnight in salt water or a solution of half vinegar and half water. Leave the squirrels whole or cut into parts. Cover with water and boil slowly until tender. Add salt, pepper, and a little bacon grease or butter for seasoning. Remove the squirrel. Drop dumpling dough—either corn or wheat flour will do—in the boiling liquid. Cover and cook for 10 minutes or so.

Dumplings: Melt 8 tablespoons butter in 2 cups of boiling water. Add 2 cups flour to which 1 teaspoon salt has been added. Stir and cook for a short time, until the mixture begins to leave the side of the pan. Cook a little and then add 4 eggs, one at a time, stirring well after each addition. On a floured board, and with floured hands, pat out the dumpling mixture to the desired thickness. Cut into narrow strips, about 1 inch by 2 inches.

Meantime, mix 1/4 to 1/2 cup of flour with 1/2 cup of water. Strain out any lumps. Add to the hot broth, stirring constantly until it begins to thicken. Drop the strips into the boiling broth. Let them cook for 10 minutes in the covered kettle.

But not all residents of Central Texas came from Upper South families. This area of the state has distinctive communities of German, Czech, and Polish immigrants as well. Living as they did in close societal clusters, they kept alive their ethnic traditions, including foods.

Clinton Machann and James Mendl write in *Krásna Amérika* about the food traditions of the Czechs, whose culture respects good cooks and recognizes that foods are one important way of continuing their traditions. "Bread was the most venerated food, and special customs were associated with it. In some families, a loaf of bread was blessed before and after baking, and the sign of the cross made upon it was supposed to cause it to last longer. Another superstition prohibited cutting a loaf of bread from both ends. The early Czech settlers preferred rye bread, but in Texas they learned to accept corn bread as an occasional substitute" (141).

They had beef in great quantities. Lamb, too, was a good source for meat, but "pork was the favorite . . . especially *vepřová pečeně* (roast pork) with the usual trimmings of *knedlíky* (dumplings) or *zemáky s máčkú* (potatoes with gravy) and *zelí* (sauerkraut), usually flavored with caraway seed, in addition to cooked garden vegetables. Fresh pork was consumed only during the winter months. Almost every farmstead had its own smokehouse" (140).

Goose and duck were favored kinds of poultry, though chicken is now popular. Roasting and boiling were preferred ways for preparing the meats, although the custom of frying foods has been accepted.

> Soup (*polevka*) was an important part of the noon meal (*oběd*). Rolled-out, paper-thin egg noodle dough spread on a table or draped over chairs was a common sight in a Czech home. After drying, the sheet of dough was rolled and cut into thin strips, to be used in various kinds of noodle soup. Another favorite was liver dumpling soup. Fresh beef liver was crushed and mixed with flour and seasoning. Little balls were fashioned with the fingers and dropped into boiling broth. Various kinds of *guláš* (stew) were also common. (140)

Most enduring of Czech culinary traditions are the pastries. "Today the only Czech word that many Texans know is *koláč*—the term for the famous circular tart made of a special double-risen dough whose center is topped or filled with a sweet sauce made of *mák* (poppy seed), cottage cheese, prunes, peaches, or another fruit. Less well known are the *buchta* and *houska* variations with fruit or fillings baked into a loaf of square-pan form of *koláč*-type dough" (140).

The German traditions also added to the distinctiveness of Central Texas foods. In *A Yankee in German-America Texas Hill Country*, Vera Flach gave her account of butchering and making sausage:

> Sausage making is dependent upon certain conditions. It must be cold weather. No dinky little half-hearted norther will do. [It also

Getting ready to butcher. *Courtesy Amon Carter Museum, Fort Worth, Texas.*

must be while the moon is getting full so the meat won't shrink during cooking.] Venison will be used, so a buck must be hanging somewhere and the pig (the bacon type) should have a weight of about three hundred pounds.

First of all that pig must be killed. I stayed as far away as possible from the pig whose hour had come. Most farm women were in at the kill and caught the blood which would later go into the famous German Blood Sausage, Blut Wurst. The hog was hung up, cleaned and scraped and left overnight to cool, and a piece was sent to be tested for trichina.

In the morning a great heavy wooden table came from one of the barns to the back yard. A fire was built and the immense copper kettle, black as sin on the outside and shining like the sun inside, was hung from an iron tripod and filled with water. At our house there were always five or six people around on sausage-making day. It took three men to get that pig into a wheelbarrow and onto the table. My mother-in-law being in charge, my job was to carry things that were not too heavy, wash pans and knives as necessary, and cook dinner for the gang. I stood by that table as little as possible.

First the long, ugly, shining knives cut off the two hams and a slab of bacon. A big grinder was attached to the end of the table with a flat pan beneath it. One person cut the meat from the bones, another one or two sliced it into strips and dropped them into the grinder, which was turned by one of the men. It was a back-breaking chore and the man at the grinder gladly changed jobs with a meat cutter every now and then. As the pan became full it was dumped into a washtub and the mountain of meat grew higher and higher. At first there was much talk and laughter around that greasy table, but as the day wore on there was more and more silence. After the pork was ground, the venison went through the same process. Some people used beef, but our family preferred venison.

Then came the business of mixing, adding spices, and grinding that mountain a second time. There would be three kinds of sausage—meat, liver and blood. The first was smoked, the other two cooked in that great copper kettle. During this process the water would boil down and to this juice cornmeal would be added to make pannas. . . .

But wait, don't go away. We are only half done, or a third. There is the fat meat to be cut into cubes, dumped into that indispensable kettle and sizzled into lard. (Lard was usually made the next day.) A few of the cracklings went into the pannas—and did we feed the rest to the chickens? No, siree. We saved them for *soap*!

It was like my one hundred pounds of flour. Everywhere I looked there was meat. Mixed and reground, it was in dishpans, crocks, roasting pans—and, sure, washtubs. As they were emptied, they arrived in my sink to be washed. There were thousands of them, it seemed. . . .

Lard, too, was everywhere—gallon ice cream cartons, two-pound coffee cans, big crocks, little crocks. There was so much of it that every year some of it spoiled in warm weather. . . .

But let's get on with it. While the meat was being mixed, someone (good grief, not me!) was sent to the river with a washtub of entrails. There they were washed, thoroughly I'm sure, turned inside out, washed again, and brought back to be sausage jackets.

In place of the grinder, a sausage stuffer with a funny-looking long snout was now attached to the table. The entrails were cut into pieces ten to twenty inches long and tied at one end with sausage twine. They had to be tied very tight, for who wants sausage squirting all over the smokehouse? That tying took wrists and fingers of iron and even those would get callouses. The open end of the jacket was held over the stuffer snout and the meat pushed in by means of a flat metal disc with a long handle that controlled it. Then, of course, the other end must be tied tightly. The twine was cut long enough so a second knot could be tied, thus forming a loop. These two loops were slipped over long metal rods, and on them a dozen or so sausages traveled to the smokehouse. Wires held them above the fire which would later be built, using sawdust from Spanish oak or cherry wood.

For anyone interested in recipes, our family used two-thirds pork, one-third venison; forty-four pounds of meat to one pound of salt, and coarse ground pepper to taste. One-half teaspoon of saltpeter was added. This recipe is for meat sausage. To be really good, sausage should be smoked six weeks, adding coals to the sawdust each morning, skipping a day if it turns warm.

So now—as someone trotted back and forth to the smokehouse, another someone cleaned up that slippery table, and hooray, we started the cooked sausage. Liver sausage contained, besides the liver, the jowls, some of the lightest-colored hog meat, and less venison than the meat sausage. The more venison used, the less greasy the sausage will be. When they were stuffed and tied, into the good old kettle they went to cook for half an hour. Then off to the smokehouse with them.

The blood sausage was made last. The big flat pan of blood which had been stirred several times during the day to prevent coagulation was combined with the darker pork, milt [the spleen], kidneys, lungs, and tongue (which was diced, not ground). Sometimes venison ribs were boiled and this meat added.

I forgot to say that all the meat for these last sausages had to be cooked first. It makes me weary even to write about it.

So—with all these goodies added to the blood, these were stuffed, tied, cooked in the kettle again until a needle stuck in a sausage no longer drew red blood. It was then pressed between two boards with bricks on top to remove any excess moisture and then off it, too, went for smoking.

Now, then—all that was left was to make the pannas, pour the lard into containers, cover the tops with brown paper, tie them with string and carry them to the basement. To stir that cornmeal into the meat juice took a good-sized wooden paddle and *two* hands. It could not be done with one hand.

And then—we cleaned up! The horrible table was scrubbed and scrubbed again, the grinder and stuffer taken apart, washed and stored away, the copper kettle scoured with salt and vinegar, the kitchen floor mopped. Hands that were nearly frozen from working outdoors in the cold were rubbed or held near the range to thaw out. . . .

Guests in our house were very fond of the sausage and usually took one home. As for me, in all the years I have never eaten a bite of sausage after I saw it made. (16–20)

Using the Whole Hog
From *Texas Living: Past and Present,* 16–19

PIG'S FEET

Put pig's feet in cold water. Scrape and clean well. Place in a pot and cover with salted water. Boil until tender or until meat slips from bone. Eat as is or roll foot (with meat on) in corn meal and fry.

CHITTLINS

Thoroughly clean intestines using the larger ones for sausage casings . . . cut the smaller ones in pieces and boil until tender. Roll in cornmeal and fry.

PIG SKIN

Cut up hog's hide with the fat on it and render the fat by frying to a crisp. Save the rendered fat in large lard cans or stands for use in cooking. Press the fat from the crisp skin in lard press or two boards made into a press by connecting with a leather strap nailed to one end of each. The skins were the cracklins. It could be eaten as such or made into cracklin corn bread.

CRACKLIN CORN BREAD

1 1/2 cups cornmeal
1/2 cup flour
1 teaspoon baking powder
1/2 teaspoon salt
1 egg, beaten
1 1/2 cups milk
1/2 cup cracklins

Sift together cornmeal, flour, baking powder, and salt. Combine egg, milk, and cracklins with dry ingredients. Beat well and pour into a greased pan or iron skillet. Bake in a moderate oven until done. Should be brown.

CRACKLIN CORN CAKES

1 cup white cornmeal
1 cup yellow cornmeal
1 teaspoon salt
1 1/2 cups cracklins, put through food chopper
2 cups boiling water
2 tablespoons shortening

Put cornmeal and salt in mixing bowl. Stir in cracklins. Add boiling water and mix thoroughly. Melt shortening in 9-inch pie pan. Shape mixture into pones, put in pan and flatten. Be sure the prints of your fingers show. Bake at 400 degrees until golden brown.

HOG'S HEAD CHEESE OR SOUSE

Headcheese is easy to make. Cook heads, tongues, skins, hearts, and other pieces. Make deep cuts in thick pieces of meat, cover with water and simmer until the meat is well done and slips easily from the bones. If you use the skin, cook it in a net or sack; then you can remove it when so tender that you can push a finger through it. The thick ears and snout require longer cooking than other skin. Grind the skin, using the plate that has 1/8-inch holes. Bone jowls and other pieces after cooking. Grind these with the boneless pieces, such as the heart, using the plate that has 1/2-inch holes. You may prefer to cut the tongue and some of the larger pieces of fat into strips instead of grinding them.

Mix finely ground skin and coarsely ground pieces of meat with enough of the soup—the water in which the meat was cooked—to make the mass soft without being sloppy. Return this mixture to the kettle and bring to a boil. This reheating mixes the headcheese and makes it thicker. Pour it into shallow pans and chill it. Then you can slice it without difficulty.

Add seasoning at the beginning of the second cooking. Usually it is safe to season to taste. The following quantities of seasoning per 100 pounds of cooked meat, including the added soup, are a satisfactory guide:

2 to 2 1/2 pounds salt
3 to 5 ounces black pepper
1/4 to 1 ounce red pepper (if desired)
1 ounce ground cloves (if desired)
1 ounce coriander (if desired)
2 ounces sweet marjoram (if desired)

If you stuff headcheese into casings, season and stuff it before the second cooking. Return the stuffed headcheese to the remaining soup and let it simmer until it floats. This will take 10 to 30 minutes. Chill in cold water and store in a clean, cool place.

Usually headcheese is eaten cold, sometimes with vinegar.

SCRAPPLE I

3 pounds pork bones (meat to make 1 1/2 cups)
4 cups water
1/4 teaspoon sage (if desired)
Salt and pepper to taste
1 cup cornmeal

Cover bones with water and simmer until meat falls from bones. Strain stock and remove fat. Pick bones and chop fine. Set aside. Add sage, salt, and pepper to broth and bring to boil. Slowly add cornmeal, stirring constantly. Cook until a thick mush. Add meat and cook a few minutes. Pour in a loaf pan and let set overnight. Slice, dust with flour and fry until crisp.

SCRAPPLE II

Cornmeal mush, boiled for hours until it is very thick, can be sliced cold. It is served with molasses poured over it or spread with apple butter. This was a good after school treat.

BRAINS AND EGGS

1/2 pound brains
1 teaspoon salt
5 tablespoons butter

6 eggs, slightly beaten
1 teaspoon salt
1/4 teaspoon Tabasco sauce
2 tablespoons minced scallions

Wash the brains, then soak them overnight in enough water to cover and a teaspoon of salt. In the morning, drain and rinse under cold running water and remove the outer membrane with a sharp knife. Cut the brains into 1/2-inch cubes. Melt butter in a heavy skillet over medium heat until it foams. Pour in the brains and sauté until most of the moisture is gone. Add lightly beaten eggs, 1 teaspoon salt, and cook over low heat until partially set, but still very moist. Don't overcook. Serves four. Hot sauce and scallions can be sprinkled on top.

"Meals in German-America," Vera Flach wrote, "were never hastily thrown together." She commented on some of the German dishes that she had not known in the North:

Cabbage Loaf: Shred the cabbage and cook till soft in boiling salted water. (Don't overcook it.) Drain. Add an egg or two, bacon cubes, onions, celery, salt, pepper, and bread crumbs. Wrap in the outside leaves of cabbage, tie in a bag and boil about an hour.

Wine Soup: Make a thin tapioca and water mixture. Cook till clear, add sugar, cinnamon, and wine. Good for sick people—or anybody else.

Kochkaese (cooked cheese): takes forever. First, put your clabber in a bag (pointed like a jelly bag) and let the whey drip out. Let the remaining cream cheese dry—*very* dry. Then grate it, add salt and caraway seeds. Put in a pan with a little butter and cook a very short time. Look out or you'll ruin it. . . .

Zwieback: Make a yeast dough with milk, flour, and eggs. Let it rise. Add sugar, butter, salt, and more flour. Make nice round rolls and let 'em rise again. Bake the things. Then all you have to do is cut 'em in half and bake 'em again—slowly. My children ate buckets of these things.

There were special Christmas cookies—pfeffernusse, molasses and honey cookies, makronen. They made so many of these to be sure there would be enough for all Christmas visitors that these cookies often turned up at a Geburtstag [birthday celebration] in April.

Coffee there always was, and in summer, iced tea—never, never hot tea.

Turkey dressing was made with raisins and was faintly sweet.

Lots of lemons were used, little vinegar.

German brown bread was, and still is, a specialty of the house. . . .

Three loaves take 3 cups of water, 1/4 cup oil, 1/4 cup salt, and 3/4 cup brown sugar (or honey or molasses), 1 yeast cake, 2 quarts white flour and one of whole wheat. After stirring for three minutes in the mixer, allow it to double in bulk. Make into loaves, let rise once more, and bake at 350 degrees for about 50 minutes. The dough should be quite stiff.

Those women could turn out a meal for two or twenty in no time flat. Their ease and competence in the kitchen never failed to astonish me. Their fancy tea cakes made French pastry take a back seat. They never moaned about doing the dishes. They just did them— and *visited*. (65–67)

One of the mysteries that confronted Vera was a crock about two feet tall, almost eight inches in diameter, with a lid that had a hole in the top, and a wooden plunger with a disk full of holes in the end. She found out in time that it was a churn.

Making butter sounded easy. She poured her cream into the churn, put the lid down over the plunger, got a book to read, and sat down to mindlessly work the plunger up and down.

Did she get butter? No. She was told to get some ice: the cream must be too warm. Still no butter. She was then told that the cream was too cold: it should stand awhile to warm. Still no butter. The pigs got that bucket of cream.

Then there were times when, with a few stirs of a wooden spoon, she would get "beautiful butter." From her account, the making of butter remains something of a mystery (*Yankee*, 21).

SAUER KRAUT

With heavy heart he kneeled him down
And humbly breathed this prayer:
    "O Lord, Thou knowest why it is
I've lost most all my hair:

    "Whene'er the hash-house door swings wide
To greet the hungry horde,
    The stench of sauer kraut bars my way
Like Eden's flaming sword.

· · ·

    "Dost note that buzzard sailing high,
Eye on this earthly dwelling?
    He thinks there's something dead down here—
That's sauer kraut he's smelling.

"Methinks my bones will be his fare
If this keeps up much longer.
  As day by day I weaker grow
That sauer kraut grows stronger.

"More maddening than the 'third degree,'
More painful than the knout,
  The agony that twisteth me
When I eat sauer kraut.

"The hosts of Hell assemble
When I take my couch at night,
  And prick and pinch and grin and dance
And yell and fuss and fight.

"O Lord, behold my withered form;
Thou knowest all I've been through;
  Have mercy on thy servant, Lord—
For God's sake change the menu."

—Carlos Ashley

Daisy Atkins recalled making sauerkraut in *'Way Back Yonder:*

Another food which meant much work was making sour kraut—cabbage had to be thoroughly cleaned—then sliced with a kraut cutter—the containers were usually five or ten gallon kegs. First a layer of cabbage was placed in the keg and salted—this was mashed with a mall, to form a water or juice; continued on in this way until the keg was full, then placed in a warm spot—near the stove was best—until it began to sour, the odor was not so sweet. Sure was "scrumptious." (28)

Eats in South Texas

A Conversation with Mrs. Alonzo (Sylvia) Sosa, Native of Harlingen

> *Señor, bendice estos alimentos que vamos a tomar, y bendice a los que los han preparado. Da pan a los que no lo tienen, en el nombre de Nuestro Señor Jesus Cristo, te lo pedimos. Amen.*
>
> (Lord, bless these foods that we are about to partake, and bless those that prepared them. Give bread to those in need, in the name of our Lord Jesus Christ, we ask you. Amen.)
>
> THE PRAYER BEFORE MEALS
> —Sra. Francisca H. Sosa, Harlingen

SYLVIA, when I was in New Mexico, I had *bizcochitos*. Do you make them? My friends said they were a blessing the good Lord had chosen to give the people of their lovely land of *poco tiempo.*

I know they are little breads that must be made with lard. Shortening won't do. I really don't know how to make them. My mother says she used them only for *bautismos.*

You know *las posadas?* When the children come to the door at Christmas time, re-enacting Mary and Joseph as they tried to find an inn in Bethlehem? And you were supposed to have a sweet to give them? *Bizcochitos* are made at Christmas time for that purpose, too.

There should be different things to give the children. Like *empanaditas.* They are little fried pies *con carne o frutas.* Or they can be baked in the oven.

Buñuelos are good. They are little fried puffs sprinkled with sugar. Some people call them *sopapillas*. Another sweet she gave us was like *una trenza*, a braid. It was called *chongo*.

I read that the Mexican women had to work so hard just making tortillas to feed their families day by day that, when holidays came around, they took great pride in making fancy breads and cakes and cookies and candies. This is the reason the Mexican women have such a good reputation for their cooking. Would you agree?

I don't know about that. My mother never waited for celebrations to give us good foods. Let me tell you about a food used throughout our area, even in my own home now.

Cut some corn tortillas into small bite-sized pieces. Pour some oil into a pan and let it get good and hot. Put the pieces of corn tortilla in the hot oil all at once and stir them. Sprinkle with chili pepper. If you want to, throw some *chorizo mexicano*, sausage, in there. And add seasoning. A little onion, chopped tomatoes, and green pepper. This is called *migas con carne*.

Or you can cook up eggs with the tortillas and your seasonings and have *migas con huevos*.

It sounds like a nice change from plain scrambled eggs.

Yes, my children prefer *migas con carne*. Then they put catsup on it.

Where I lived, the franchise places, like Taco Bell and Jack-in-the-Box, sell *migas*. And they are found in hospitals and are sold by the vendors around the federal buildings, everywhere. But these traditional dishes stay down there. They are totally new to people away from the border. But they are so good.

Do you make flan?

That's new to me. It's a custard but I don't make it. I did grow up with *champurrado*. It's delicious.

What you do is take cornmeal and brown it in a skillet. On the side you have milk and brown sugar brought to the boiling point with some cinnamon in it, always the cinnamon. Then you stir the browned meal into the milk mixture. You can drink it.

I have heard the Cherokees talk about this drink. They say it is grainy and you have to acquire a taste for it, but they really like it.

What kind of bread did you have in your home? Tortillas, of course.

Yes, and I grew up with *pan de maíz*. My mother took corn just at the time it was losing its tenderness, almost to the parching stage. The corn has to be at the stage when there is just a little juice left in it. Then she would scrape the corn off the cob until she had about 2 cupfuls. She would add a handful of cornmeal, a cup and a little more of milk, several spoons of oil, about a teaspoon of salt, that much baking powder, perhaps a couple of tablespoons of sugar. At the last, she would put in a couple of well-beaten eggs, mix it all up, and bake it in a hot oven.

Some people think it is better if you add a handful of wheat flour to the cornmeal. And some like to put a little grated onion in it.

Did you have potatoes?

Certainly. Sweet potatoes are native to Mexico. I like baked sweet potatoes. Once when Alonzo's mother came to visit, I had some on hand to bake. But she took them and made *empanaditas* with a sweet potato filling. *Empanaditas* are little fried pies. She always makes different things.

What about green vegetables?

When I was growing up, my mother made sure we had lots of vegetables. *Calabacitas* (squash), *ejotes* (string beans), *tomatillos*, *tomates*, *elotes* (corn on the cob), okra, tomatoes, and greens. I can't remember complaining about having to eat them the way my children do. They want *carne*. My mother had eight children, and she kept us healthy.

I want my children to know the traditional foods of Mexico. Like *nopalitos*. But it's not easy to get my children to eat them.

After I married Alonzo, I learned to make fish stew. Cut the fish into fillets. Boil some water. I don't know about measurements. I started cooking at twelve. I had to cook cereal for the whole family before school. So I've just always calculated what I thought I needed.

Put the fillets aside. Take the head and all the bones and boil them for 5, 6, or 7 minutes. Strain and put this aside.

Now take a skillet and put a little oil in it, sauté some celery, bell pepper, onions, and tomatoes. Cook them just soft enough. Add a little flour to make a roux with the vegetables. If you have some shrimp, throw it in at the last minute.

Dissolve some bouillon cubes in the broth which you are going to use for the roux. Add seasonings. Now I'm ready to take my fillets and cut them, not too large, not too small. Then I go back to the head and the bones and flake the meat off. You have to work fast at this stage.

Put the fillets in the roux and cook, but do not overcook. Take the pieces out of the pan when you begin to pour everything together so that they do not break up. Use all of the broth but do not let the sediment spill into your pan.

Now everything is cooked. Combine the roux, the broth, and the cooked fillets. Cook for 5 or 6 minutes. Do not overcook the fish. You want the pieces whole. It is delicious! Delicious!

Don't leave out the cilantro.

I can make a big pot of this, and my family will eat it all. I don't serve anything with it.

Did you have some special foods for Christmas?

Yes, tamales. When I was growing up, my mother would say sometime before Christmas that we were going to the market. We were looking for a hog's head. The grocer had so many orders that you had to sign up to get one, and sometimes there would be a sign on the hog's head that this head belongs to so-and-so.

After we had got the head, my mother would invite her neighbors and relatives and friends to come in to make tamales. On the day they arrived she would cook the head. She put it in a big pot and boiled it with spices, garlic, whole peppers, and cilantro. She kept this broth to mix with the *masa*.

The corn husks had to be gathered, separated, and cleaned. They are called *hojas*. My mother would wash and scrape them, and, having separated the husks, she would cut them into uniform rectangular shapes. I learned later that they could be bleached and prepared more easily by putting them in boiling water.

Homemade tamales. *Courtesy John O. West, El Paso.*

My mother bought her *masa* at the store. She would ask for the processed cornmeal. Then she would cook it for a few minutes in a little water with salt and maybe some chili powder. She put this in a big tub. Then she would take lard and work, and work, and work the lard into that cooked cornmeal until it was worked up fine and smooth. All the time she was working it, she was adding seasoning to her liking. Preparing the *masa* just right took a long time.

Now the meat from the hog's head had to be ground. It took big pots to hold all the meat. After it was ground, it had to be cooked again with spices. At this stage everyone wanted to taste it. When it was approved by all the ladies, the meat was said to be ready to be laid on the *masa*, which had been spread very thinly on the shucks.

The shucks had to be rolled up just right, folded just so, and tied. Then the tamales were stood in big pots, but they must not touch the bottom. My mother would lay her tablespoons on the bottom of the pot to support something—maybe a tin pie plate—on which to stand the tamales and lift them out. Then boiling water was poured over them. A clean cloth was laid across the top of the pot for a cover, and they were steamed for 30 to 45 minutes.

Then one of the ladies would take one out and taste it. This was a time for talking, laughing, exchanging *dichos*. They stopped their work and had coffee. When all was done, everybody would take some tamales home.

My mother liked to have tamales on hand to give as gifts to the peddlers who came regularly to our house, the postman, and all those service people. The tamales and a bottle of her tomato juice made a nice gift.

In the summer, my mother would gather up big brown beer bottles and she would make tomato juice, bottle it, and cap it. Then she had tomatoes on hand all winter.

When I was a child, we had breakfast, dinner, and supper. Now we have breakast, lunch, and dinner. What does a typical South Texas family consider the main meal?

It was our tradition to have five meals a day. My mother had to cook a lot. There was early breakfast—*desayuno*, just to get started. This was light: tortillas or *pan dulce*, a sweet roll, with milk or coffee. In midmorning, *almuerzo*, a large breakfast, was served. We would have fruit, eggs, beans, tortillas, salsa, and coffee.

The *comida*—dinner—was served in midafternoon. There would always be a soup, *caldo*, followed by a dry soup, *sopa*. *Sopa* is something like pasta or rice with vegetables or seafood. The main course would be some kind of meat or fish. And there would be cakes or sweets and coffee to finish the meal.

The *merienda* is a late afternoon meal, just refreshments really, like a sweet bread or chocolate. This would be a drink made by our mother, nothing you could buy in a carton.

Then about nine o'clock in the evening there would be *cena*, something like your supper.

I've heard that fajitas are not a Mexican dish, just something made up by Texas chefs. Is this right?

We had friends who asked us to come over and have fajitas with them, and I thought, this is a new dish. Fajita only means skirt, the loose pieces or trimmings left after butchering, not really choice. So we had these strips of meat that had been browned, or sautéed, in a skillet, and served with salsa.

Well, I've made that dish for years. We take the tougher, cheaper cuts of meat, cut them into very thin strips, and I boil the strips for one or two hours until they are real tender. I use very little fat at my house, so I just drain them well and salt them. That's the way my children like them. I serve a salad of lettuce, tomato, celery, and onion with them.

I never heard of burritos until one time when I came north with my mother to Corsicana, visiting. And our friends talked about going out to buy burritos.

Well, that means little donkeys. I don't know where these names come from. I didn't grow up calling these foods what they are now called.

Another thing is crispies. They are sold at Del Taco. They are little breads sprinkled with sugar and cinnamon. The real name is *buñuelos*.

You take flour, no baking powder, a little pinch of salt, an egg, some butter, water, and cinnamon. I can't give you measurements. Then you roll the dough out until it is almost transparent—paper thin. We cut them into squares. Drop them in hot oil, a few at a time. You must use oil. They will puff up, if done right. Then you drain them and sprinkle them with cinnamon and sugar.

I've heard that you should not drink milk with Mexican food. Is that right?

Well, beans and tortillas are very nourishing. With milk, where's the problem? I suppose it would be a case of how much chile you used.

My grandmother told me that if I ate avocado, I must not drink milk. I wanted them both. I wish I had asked her what would happen. I had to find out. Some chemical reaction takes place.

I've read that the beans Mexicans like are red.

There are frijoles of many colors. In southern Mexico, they eat black beans. I've had those about four times in my life. They taste different. Our beans are called red by some, but they are little brown pintos. Where we lived, we could get them fresh. They are so good! But they are not your red kidney beans.

Let me tell you about some other native foods. *Nopalitos* are eaten during Holy Week when you are not eating meat. They are the leaves from the nopal plant, which is the prickly pear. We would go out into the fields and cut them and bring them home. My mother would remove the needles.

She would use a very sharp knife or a razor blade—like a straight-edge razor. She would hold the leaf with a clothespin and shave off the needles.

There are many ways to prepare them. She would dice them and boil them, and they are just like okra. So I have tried many different ways of cooking them. I have steamed them, you know, with the water underneath. Then they are not slimy. This is what you do. After they are steamed, you mix them with some sausage, *chorizo*. Toss them together and then fry them with the sausage.

It's good to break eggs into the mixture. These are *nopalitos con huevos*. Or just eaten alone, they are a good source of protein. We use them in the spring when the leaves are very tender. But now the Mexicans are losing their cactus. We have to buy them in the store for $2.00 or $2.50 a pound.

The Indians and the Mexicans grew up with food like this. They knew what was nutritious. I want my children to learn to eat them. So this is what I do.

I take *nopalitos* and cut them like French-style green beans. Then I mix them with green beans, cook, and use lots of seasoning. My children can't tell the difference, and they have learned to eat them this way.

Another food we like is the flowers from the yucca plant. You know all those white flowers?

I've heard them called God's Candlestick.

That's right. Don't try to use the stem, as it is very bitter. Just the petals. You can make a good soup with them. Gather about a quart of them; wash them in cold water. Take several spoons of butter, melt it in a skillet, add some chopped onion, and sauté the flowers with the onions. Don't let them get brown; just cook until the onion is transparent. Add a quart of cream, or half-and-half if you do not want it too rich. Blend two tablespoons of flour with a little of the cream until it is smooth. Add it to the soup. Cook and stir all the time until the soup is as thick as you want it. Season it with salt and pepper. The flowers can also be fried.

This is another traditional dish used during Holy Week. People have gotten away from these foods.

The fruit of the prickly pear is good, too. Eat them fresh. Peel them first. Some are yellow, red, purple; they are lots of colors. They make good candy and jelly also.

You haven't said anything about chicken. I thought chicken was a favorite with Mexicans.

It is. The favorite way is to serve it with *molé* sauce. It has been about twenty-five years since I have seen someone make good *molé*. It must have pumpkin seed in it.

Chicken with *molé* is traditional for elaborate weddings, communion, or baptismals. Our weddings sometimes take three or four days. There is lots of food prepared for a wedding.

Another food I had while I was growing up was *menudo*. Not very many people like it. It was eaten after an animal had been freshly killed. It was the stomach of the animal cleaned and spiced. It was cut up into small pieces and boiled. It gave off a pungent odor—like boiling an animal. It was cooked with garlic, boiled for 1 1/2 to 2 hours, or however long it took to make it tender. It was cooked very slowly. It was a different kind of dish. My mother always seasoned it with lots of red chile.

When I say chile, I mean peppers. Chile to us is the seasoning. This is the number one food in Mexico, the essential ingredient. It is very special. It has all the vitamins we need. It does irritate some people, and I have heard there is medical research going on to determine why.

A good salsa is served with every meal. You can make it with a can of tomatoes, mashed up. Add a chopped onion, a cup of green chiles, more or less, as you like it, and some salt to taste.

I attended a banquet one time where bread pudding was served for dessert. We were told it was a Mexican tradition. Is this right?

Yes, you are talking about *capirotada*. It is served at Easter time. I suppose because bread is a symbolic food.

A Mexican plate, hot from the kitchen, Casa   A cook at Casa Jurado, El Paso, makes a taco.
Jurado, El Paso. *Courtesy John O. West, El Paso.*   *Courtesy John O. West, El Paso.*

I know *taco* means bite or snack, and it was a word used ever so long ago
for a tortilla folded over some meat. But what about enchilada? How did it
come into use? Someone said the word looks like *entre* and *lado,* meaning
between the sides. With chili in the middle? Is this a Tex-Mex dish? Or
something a traditional family like yours would prepare?

I try to have a Mexican dish at least once a week, and enchiladas are a
favorite. I'm not sure where they originated.

Mexican tamales were such favorites, writes Elizabeth Hurley in "Come
Buy, Come Buy," that nearly every town had a street vendor, sometimes ring-
ing a bell to get customers, sometimes singing a little ditty, or chanting something like "Ta-mal! Ta-mal!" In East Texas it was usually a black who sold
them. A Denton vendor was known to cry: "Hot tamales, two in a shuck." In
Lufkin the tamale man had a sense of humor: "Hot tamales. Three in a shuck.
Two of 'em slipped and one of 'em stuck" (118–19).

PEPPER WISDOM

Eating plenty of chili peppers is good for ague.

Swallowing whole small chilis will cure a cold.

Boiled pods mixed with buffalo tallow are good for burns.

All peppers have strong aphrodisiac properties.

For a bad cold or sore throat, eat jalapeño peppers or chili peppers that are very hot.

If you feel some kind of harm is going to happen to you, sprinkle your shoe with red pepper to ward off all evil.

A pepper plant in the yard brings good luck.

Plant pepper plants while you are angry and the peppers will be very hot.

Mean people have the best luck with pepper plants.

Mexican Recipes

TACOS

Taco means roll and came to have the added meaning of snack or bite. It is a soft tortilla, not the fried, crispy kind, which is rolled around, or wrapped around, or folded around some filling—meat, beans, cheese, eggs, or whatever is on the table. It is the bread at the meal and is eaten out of hand.

ENCHILADAS

The enchilada is like the taco except that the tortilla is first dipped in hot fat to soften it, then dipped in a sauce. Stack as many dipped tortillas as you plan to serve, then pour off the extra sauce. Put a filling of chicken, beef, pork, cabrito, or cheese in the center of each one and roll it up tightly. Place the rolled up enchiladas in a pan, pour more sauce over them, top with cheese, and heat in a moderate oven.

ENCHILADA SAUCE

1 medium onion

1 chopped green chiles

1 teaspoon ground cominos (cumin)

1 teaspoon ground oregano

1/4 teaspoon garlic powder

1 teaspoon salt

3 cups tomato juice

Sauté the onion with the spices and green chiles. Add the tomato juice and simmer for 15 minutes or so. Blend the sauce until it is smooth.

CHICKEN ENCHILADA CASSEROLE

1 chicken, stewed, boned, and cut in pieces
1 can cream of chicken soup
1 can cream of mushroom soup
1 can green chiles, chopped
1 small to medium onion
1 1/2 cups grated cheese
1 package frozen tortillas

Heat together soups, chiles, and half the chicken pieces. Dilute with water if too thick. Separate frozen tortillas under running water. Heat each a few seconds in a hot skillet, lightly oiled. Roll each tortilla with chicken, cheese, onions, and place in baking dish; layer it if necessary. Cover with soup and remaining chicken pieces. Top with grated cheese. Bake at 375 degrees until bubbly. Serve with green salad and bread.

CARNE ASADA

Carne Asada is nothing more or less than a tenderloin flattened thin by pounding, seasoned with garlic salt, salt, and pepper, and broiled at 500 degrees or fried in a hot, thick iron pan.

For a typical Mexican platter, serve this with guacamole, tacos, refried beans, and rice.

CHICKEN MOLÉ

One 2 1/2 to 3-pound ready-to-cook broiler-fryer chicken, cut up
1/4 cup butter or margarine
1/4 cup blanched almonds
1/4 cup chopped onions
1/4 cup finely chopped green pepper
1 small clove garlic, minced
One 7 1/2-ounce can tomatoes, cut up
1/2 cup chicken broth
2 teaspoons sugar
1/2 teaspoon chile powder
1/8 teaspoon ground cinnamon
1/8 teaspoon ground nutmeg
Dash ground cloves
1 tablespoon sesame seeds
Dash bottled hot pepper sauce

1/4 of a 1-ounce square unsweetened chocolate
2 tablespoons cold water
1 tablespoon cornstarch

In a large skillet, brown chicken slowly in butter. Season lightly with salt and pepper. Set chicken aside; cover.

Place almonds, green pepper, minced garlic, tomatoes, onion, chicken broth, sugar, chile powder, ground cinnamon, nutmeg, cloves, sesame seeds, and hot pepper sauce in a blender or food processor. Blend at a high speed until a smooth purée. Pour the molé into a separate skillet and simmer it, stirring constantly, for about 5 minutes. Add the chocolate and cook until it is melted.

Add the chicken to the molé sauce. Cover and reduce heat; cook until the meat is tender, about 45 minutes. Remove chicken to a serving platter to keep it warm. Slowly blend cold water into cornstarch; stir into sauce. Cook and stir till thickened and bubbly. Pour sauce over chicken. Sprinkle sesame seeds on top. Serves 4.

GUACAMOLE

4 to 6 avocados, depending on size
1 1/2 teaspoons salt
2 teaspoons vinegar
2 tablespoons mayonnaise
1 teaspoon salad oil
4 to 6 drops Tabasco sauce
1/2 cup peeled tomato, finely chopped
1/4 cup onion, finely chopped
Crisp lettuce

Place skinned and seeded avocados in bowl, mash with a fork, and add remaining ingredients. Several avocado seeds in the bowl will help prevent discoloration. Serve immediately on crisp lettuce. Makes 4 servings.

CAPIROTADA

Take 3 cups of sugar and let it turn to a golden brown in a skillet over low heat, stirring constantly. Or use brown sugar, firmly packed. Add 6 cups of water (twice the amount of sugar you use, or enough water to fill your skillet). Add a short stick of cinnamon and a whole clove. Bring the mixture to a boil and cook to a light syrup, about 10 minutes. Remove the spices and set the syrup aside.

Butter a pan. Toast 6 to 8 pieces of bread lightly and cube them. Usually the Mexican cook will use the whole slice without cutting it. Place layers of the toasted bread in the pan, add a layer of apple slices, raisins, nuts, and cheese (a cheddar or Monterey Jack). Repeat layering until all the ingredients are used. Dot the top with a tablespoon of butter. Sprinkle powdered cinnamon over the top. Now pour the syrup over all. Bake in a preheated oven (350 degrees) for about 30 minutes.

You will need 3 to 4 apples, peeled, cored, and sliced. Some cooks prefer using prunes. Also, a cup of raisins, a cup of almonds or pecans, and 1/2 to 3/4 pound of cheese, depending upon how much bread you use. This recipe invites the cook to use her imagination.

To keep the pudding from drying out, add anise tea as needed. Or use wine when the capirotada has been removed from the oven.

SPECIAL MEXICAN HOT SAUCE

4 cloves bud garlic, chopped fine
1 medium bell pepper, chopped fine
Tabasco hot sauce to make as hot as wanted
2 #2 cans tomatoes, mashed very fine
2 #2 cans tomato juice
1 teaspoon black pepper
Salt to taste

Place this hot sauce in glass jar or container with lid and keep under refrigeration. Sauce is more flavorful the next day after it's made. Serve hot or cold.

To test salsa, drop some on the tablecloth. If it fails to burn a hole in the cloth, it is not a good sauce.

FRIJOLES

Wash and clean 1 pound of pinto beans. Place in cooker with about 1 1/2 inches water (enough to cover). Boil 30 minutes. Pour off this water. Add more hot water and return to the fire. Add 2 cloves chopped garlic, 1 teaspoon comino, 4 tablespoons chile powder, 1 cup salt pork or 12 slices bacon, salt, and pepper. Let cook until good and done—about 2 hours.

When done, beans should have 1/2 inch of broth above them so that when they cool they can absorb this broth. This makes the beans softer and easier to mash. Let cool thoroughly before refrigeration.

To refry, place 4 spoons bacon grease or shortening in the skillet and add 4 cups cooked beans. Mash with potato masher. Fry slowly adding salt and pepper to taste and water to get the right consistency.

Variations:

1. Garnish with raw onion rings and grated cheese.

2. Garnish with shredded lettuce and triangles of fried tortilla.

3. Add cubed cheese (any mild creamy cheese will do) to the beans, allowing them to remain in the the frying pan until the cheese has melted.

4. Add 1 tin of sardines and 1 tablespoon of finely grated onions to the beans. Fry until thoroughly heated. Roll into thumb-sized rolls, sprinkle with grated Parmesan, garnish with strips of avocado dipped in lemon juice.

CHRISTMAS BUÑUELOS

1 teaspoon cinnamon (ground)
1 teaspoon baking powder
4 cups flour
1/4 cup butter or oil or fat for frying
1 teaspoon salt
2 teaspoons sugar
1 cup water
Sugar and cinnamon mixture

Sift all dry ingredients together. Slowly add water and a little oil. Turn onto a lightly floured board and knead until dough is smooth and elastic. Divide into about 40 small balls; roll out into approximately 4-to 6-inch circles. Fry in very hot oil (hot and deep) until delicately browned on both sides. Drain on paper towels and sprinkle with cinnamon and sugar mixture.

FLAN (CARAMEL CUSTARD)

1 3/4 cups sugar
3 egg whites
8 egg yolks
2 tall cans evaporated milk
2 teaspoons vanilla
6 tablespoons brandy or rum

Put 1 cup sugar into a 9 by 9 by 2-inch square loaf pan in which custard is to be baked, and place over heat. Stir constantly until sugar melts and turns golden. Remove from heat and tip pan back and forth until it is entirely coated with caramel. Let cool while mixing custard. Beat egg whites and egg yolks together well and add milk, remaining sugar, and vanilla. Beat until sugar dissolves, then strain custard into caramel-coated pan. Cover custard, place pan in a larger pan containing 1 inch of hot water, and bake in moderate oven (350 degrees) for 1 hour. While still hot, turn out on serving platter. When ready to serve, pour brandy or rum over pudding, and send to the table burning. Serves 8.

LECHE QUEMADA (BURNED MILK CANDY)

1 quart pasteurized milk
2 cups granulated sugar
1/8 teaspoon cream of tartar
1/2 cup chopped pecans or pecan halves

Place milk, sugar, and cream of tartar in a saucepan. Stir to dissolve. Cook over low flame about 1 hour or until mixture begins to thicken. Stir occasionally and later constantly. When mixture thickens, check by caramel method (dropping a drop of the mixture into a cup of cold water until a soft ball forms) or use candy thermometer and let it be 232 degrees. Remove from heat, add chopped pecans. Pour into wax-paper-lined square cake pan and let it cool; cut into squares. Top with pecan halves for decoration. Other suggestions: Omit chopped pecans. Pour mixture by the spoonful onto wax paper, top with pecan halves on each candy. Makes 2 dozen small squares.

SPICED PECANS

1 cup sugar
1/2 cup water
1 teaspoon cinnamon
1/4 teaspoon salt
1 teaspoon vanilla
2 1/2 cups pecan halves

Combine sugar, water, cinnamon, and salt in saucepan and cook over medium gas flame to 232 degrees or thread stage. Remove from flame. Add vanilla and pecans. Stir until nuts are well coated and mixture becomes creamy. Pour onto greased platter or baking sheet. With spoons or forks, separate nuts as they cool.

MEXICAN WEDDING CAKES

1 cup butter or margarine
3/4 cup confectioners' sugar
1 teaspoon vanilla
2 cups flour
1 cup finely chopped walnuts
Extra confectioners' sugar

Cream butter, 3/4 cup confectioners' sugar, and vanilla. With a spoon gradually blend in flour. Mix in walnuts. Shape into 3/4-inch balls, rolling in palms. Place about 1/2 inch apart on ungreased cookie sheet. Bake in 325 degree oven for 30 minutes; cookies should be creamy color. Remove to wire rack until just warm, roll in a little of the extra confectioners' sugar. Cool entirely. Roll again in a little of the confectioners' sugar. Store in a tightly covered container. Cookies will be a rounded shape with flat bottoms. Makes 3 1/2 dozen.

BIZCOCHITOS

1 cup sugar
2 cups lard
1 teaspoon anise seed
2 eggs
6 cups sifted flour
3 teaspoons baking powder
1 teaspoon salt
3/4 cup water

Cream lard thoroughly with hand, add sugar and anise seed. Beat eggs and add to lard mixture. Blend until light and fluffy. Sift flour with baking powder and salt and add to first mixture. Add water and knead until well mixed. Roll 1/2 inch thick and cut into fancy shapes. Roll top of each cookie in a mixture of 1 teaspoon cinnamon to each 1/2 cup sugar. Bake in a moderate oven until slightly brown.

Senator Ralph Yarborough recalls what a practical joker J. Frank Dobie was. In 1929 National Geographic sent a team to do a feature article on the Big Bend. Ex-ranger John Townsend, living in Alpine, was host to the writers and photographers who had been sent to do the job.

While Townsend and his party went down into the canyon, Dobie and his Mexican buddy stayed in camp, offering to have a hot meal for the men when they returned.

It happened that Dobie and his friend saw a mountain lion, followed it, and killed it. They butchered and barbecued it.

That night, the party returned. Dobie said, "My Mexican friend here has cooked his favorite meat for you. Cabrito. It's real, genuwine barbecued goat."

Captain Townsend knew Dobie was pulling some kind of joke and he wouldn't touch a bite. But the outsiders ate heartily, all agreeing it was the best cabrito they ever expected to eat.

DICHOS (FOLK SAYINGS)

Ten cuidado que no te den gato por liebre. (Beware that they don't give you cat meat instead of rabbit.) This seems to be the equivalent of "Buyer, beware."

Comiste gallo? (Did you eat a fighting cock?) The Anglo would say, "You must have gotten up on the wrong side of the bed."

. . . como agua para chocolate (like water for chocolate). If a person is angry, his temper could be like that of one who has been given water when he ordered chocolate.

Lo pescó en las tunas. (He was caught in the *tunas*, the fruit of the nopal.) Since the *tunas* cause a man's hands to become red when he picks them, the *dicho* is like the saying, "He was caught red-handed."

No creas que la luna es queso porque la ves redonda. (Don't think the moon is cheese because it looks round.) The *dicho* comes from a coyote story: The coon talks the coyote into plunging into the lake to get the cheese, which is really the reflection of the moon. The folk truth is that appearances deceive.

Panza llena, corazón contento. (Belly full, heart easy.)

No puede beber el caldo y quiere tragar la carne. (He can't drink the soup, yet he wants to swallow the meat.) This is the Mexican way of saying, "He has bitten off more than he can chew."

No descubres el pastel. (Don't uncover the pie.) Don't spill the soup.

No menear el arroz aunque se pegue. (Don't stir the rice even though it sticks.) Practice moderation. Don't stir up a hornet's nest.

El que nace para tamal del cielo le caen las hojas. (He who is to be a *tamal* will be, even though the shucks have to come from heaven.) *Tamal* has a double meaning: It can be either a tamale or a worthless person. The *dicho* says that if a person is destined for a certain position in life, he will have that position despite all.

El que nace para guaje nunca llega a ser jícara. (He who is born a gourd will never be a finished vessel.) This is the equivalent of "You can't make a silk purse from a sow's ear."

Grano a grano llena la gallina el buche. (Grain by grain the hen fills her craw.) This is like the saying, "Little by little, dripping water will wear a rock away."

Al pescado que se duerme se lo lleva la corriente. (The fish that sleeps is carried away by the current.) The *dicho* teaches one to be on guard.

Me *dió las calabazas.* (I was given the pumpkin.) This marks the end of a boy-girl affair. The pumpkin is yellow, as is its blossom, and yellow signifies rejection.

—Wesley, "Ranchero Sayings"

Eats in West Texas

 B EEF WAS what West Texas was all about—at least until the days of the oil barons and irrigation.

Beef is still prime in palaver about West Texas food. But from the Mexicans the West Texans adopted the absolute necessity—beans, better called frijoles. Beef, beans, and bread—these are the staples. It is possible to exist without beef and bread, but beans—well, beans are to a West Texan what potatoes are to an Irishman, spaghetti to an Italian, and rice to a Chinaman. These frijoles are pintos, the little speckled brown bean that gets better every time it is reheated.

Pintos, also called West Texas or Pecos strawberries, are a stimulus to the cook's creativity. A basic recipe calls for about three cups of beans to feed a dozen people. They may be soaked overnight and cooked four to six hours the next day. It is still customary in many homes in Texas to start the beans before the coffeepot is put on the stove for breakfast. Or they may be put unsoaked into the pot (preferably an earthenware pot) and left to cook all day. Give them plenty of time. It's best not to salt them until an hour or so before serving time, as salt causes them to harden.

Use only a wooden spoon to stir them. If you want a thick sauce, stir them the last couple of hours and increase the heat. They can be cooked with some bacon or salt pork. Some onion and garlic. Or chili and tomatoes. Or mash them until they are smooth, put them in a skillet, and, without stirring, let them brown around the edges. Serve as they are, or roll them up like an omelet and put grated cheese on top. The possibilities are unlimited.

Pintos are cheap, will keep forever, and are high in protein and carbohydrates; yet folks don't think eating beans is exactly living high on the hog.

A square nail *or* a cup of Coca-Cola (diet or otherwise) *or* a tablespoon of brown sugar *or* a pinch of soda and a tablespoon of mineral oil per cup of uncooked beans added an hour before they are served may help avoid the necessity to back off from friends in a social situation.

"One of the best ways to cook Mexican beans," wrote Daisy Atkins, "is to dig a pit, build a fire in it of wood that makes plenty of coals, after the ground is well heated, remove the fire, place a container with a tight lid, in which the beans have been brought to a boil—well seasoned with salt bacon or ham. Now put the container in pit, cover with dirt—build a fire on top. After a night there the beans are ready to eat. Sure have a grand flavor as no steam can escape" (11).

Paul Patterson says talk of beans brings to mind a story about young Whistler, of *Whistler's Mother* fame. As a babe, he was doing poorly—very poorly indeed. As a consequence, Whistler's mother brung him West of the Pecos and raised him (reared sounds too vulgar) on burro milk and frijole beans. Ever thereafter he was knowed as *Mother's Whistler.*

One tale calls for another. Two Texans went hunting. About nightfall they set up their camp, roasted some rabbits on sticks over their fire, and bedded down. Next morning, before leaving, they put on a pot of beans so they would have some vittles for dinner.

When the sun got high, they came back—to a mess! The fire was scattered, the pot overturned, the beans all gone. "Bear," they said.

It wasn't hard to track that bear until they got into rough country. Then the signs all played out. They were just about to give up the hunt when a little breeze wafted a strong smell in their direction, so strong it nearly knocked them down. "Beans," they said.

So, with guns cocked, they went after that bear, following him from whiff to whiff!

In a letter from Roy Bedichek to J. Frank Dobie, found in William A. Owens's *Three Friends*, there is another version of this bear story. The bear comes into the camp while the men are gone and eats a bag of beans. When the men return, they look over the havoc and take to the trail to track down the bear. Along the way they begin to see holes in the snow showing up between paw tracks. It is curious. The holes get bigger and bigger. The bear seems to be dragging something. It is his stomach. Then the men hear sounds like a motorcycle putt-putt putting. Suddenly, they come upon the bear, resting his enormously swollen belly on a rock, all the trees around him unleaved (106–07).

Besides the Mexicans, those Upper South people who kept moving, moving westward until they found the wide-open spaces, influenced West Texas cooking, too. Stella Hughes, in *Chuck Wagon Cookin'*, lists a menu of down-home eats served on a ranch for a festive occasion about 1868. This could have been the menu anywhere in Northeast Texas—Pilgrim's Rest, Kiomatia, or Noonday:

> Roast venison with brown gravy
> Fried catfish (caught from the river that morning)
> Squirrel stew
> Black-eyed peas
> Corn on the cob
> Corn bread with fresh churned butter
> Cold buttermilk
> Wild honey
> Plum jam
> Sliced cucumbers with sour cream
> Watermelon rind pickles (24)

Even cowboys sang the praises of East Texas cooking. In an early film, *Rio Grande*, John Wayne sings:

> I want some black-eyed peas,
> I want some mustard greens,
> I want some corn pone on the side,
> I want my chicken fried
> With a golden hide . . .

Chicken fried steak may have originated with these Upper South folk. Some had brought their cows along and could even boast of a churn in their kitchens. But they didn't have beef to eat, probably until after the War of Northern Aggression, when the cattle drives out of South Texas began. The beef was not tender in those days. A good pounding was necessary, and then it would be browned in the skillet and a gravy poured over it to make it more palatable.

This was only one step from ham and red-eye gravy, a dish Tennesseans credit Andrew Jackson with. It seems that Jackson and some of his cronies had been drinking and gaming most of the night. The next morning at the breakfast table, he called out, "I'll have a thick slice of ham and gravy as red as the eyes of that fellow yonder."

After the ham was fried, thickening was added to the drippings, then water, and the gravy was stirred until it was the right thickness. A little coffee gave the gravy its reddish color.

Stopping at the chuck wagon for a cup of coffee. *Courtesy Erwin E. Smith Collection of the Library of Congress, on deposit at the Amon Carter Museum.*

The culinary arts in West Texas were also shaped by blacks. After The War, many Southern blacks came West either to join up with the military or hire on as cowboys at some ranch. Often they were given the job of chuck wagon cook. They knew how to cook the small game found on the trail; they knew which native plants were edible; they knew palatable ways to cook up the dried fruits packed along. In fact, they brought home cooking to the range. Their stamp is indelible.

So put together meat right off the hoof, Mexican and Upper South foodways, the cooking tradition of the blacks, and you have West Texas eats.

> There were three flies in the kitchen; which one was the cowboy?
> *Answer: The one on the range.*

The cook inspects the son-of-a-gun stew. *Courtesy Erwin E. Smith Collection of the Library of Congress, on deposit at the Amon Carter Museum.*

THE GALLOPING GOURMET

The real artist of West Texas cooking, according to John O. West's account, is the chuck wagon cook:

> The day-to-day routine of the cook gets him up hours before breakfast to rustle grub for a bunch of unruly, and often unapprecia-tive, cowpokes. Then there is the day-long battle to keep ahead of the herd, arriving at pre-designated meal-stops with enough time to spare to put together a meal that would stick to the ribs. . . .
>
> Frank S. Hastings, veteran manager of the SMS ranch, wrote that "A Ranch in its entirety is known as an 'Outfit,' and yet in a general way the word 'Outfit' suggests the wagon outfit, which does the cow-work and lives in the open from April 15th, when the work begins, to December 1st, when it ends." Thus for three-quarters of a year

the chuck wagon was home for a dozen or so cowpunchers, and the cook was the center thereof. The cowhands stuck pretty close to camp: "They rarely leave the wagon at night," says Hastings, "and as a result of close association an interchange of wit or 'josh,' as it is called, has sprung up. There is nothing like the chuck wagon josh in any other phase of life, and it is almost impossible to describe. It is very funny, very keen and very direct."

"Jack" Thorp . . . described "A Chuck Wagon Supper" for the New Mexico Federal Writers Project of WPA days. . . .

"A chuck wagon arrives at Milagro Springs. The cook, who has been driving, hollers, 'Whoa, mule,' to the team of four which has been pulling the load. Getting off the seat he throws down the lines, and calls to the horse wrangler, who is with the *remuda* of saddle horses following the wagon, to 'gobble them up,' meaning to un-hitch the team and turn them into the *remuda*.

"The cook now digs a pit behind the chuck wagon, so when a fire is built, wind will not blow sparks over the camp and the punchers surrounding it. The chuck wagon is always stopped with the wagon tongue facing the wind; this is done so that the fire will be protected by wagon and chuck box. The horse wrangler, with rope down, drags wood for the fire. The many rolls of bedding are thrown off the wagon, and the cook brings forth his irons. Two of them are some four feet long, sharpened at one end, and with an eye in the other end. The third is a half-inch bar of iron some six feet long. Once he has driven the two sharpened irons into the ground above the pit, the long iron is slipped through the eyes of the two iron uprights; this completes the pot-rack, or stove. Cosi, as the cook is usually called—which is an abbreviation of the Spanish word *cocinero*—hangs a half dozen or so S hooks of iron some six inches long, on the suspended bar, and to these are hooked coffeepot, stew pots, and kettles for hot water.

"The rear end of the wagon contains the chuck box, which is securely fastened to the wagon box proper. The chuck box cover, or lid, swings down on hinges, making a table for Cosi to mix his bread and cut his meat upon, and make anything which may suit his fancy.

"The *cocinero*, now having his fire built, with a pot-hook in hand—an iron rod some three feet long with a hook bent in its end—lifts the heavy Dutch bake oven lid by its loop and places it on the fire, then the oven itself, and places it on top of the lid to heat. These ovens are skillets about eight inches in depth and some two feet across, generally, but they come in all sizes, being used for baking bread and cooking meat, stew, potatoes, and so forth. The coffeepot is of galvanized iron, holding from three to five gallons, and hanging on the pot-rack full of hot coffee for whoever may pass. Then Cosi, in a huge bread pan, begins to mix his dough. After filling the pan about half-full with flour, he adds sour dough, poured out of a jar or tin bucket which is always carried along, adds salt, soda, and lard or warm grease, working all together into a dough, which presently will become second-story biscuits. After the dough has been kneaded, he covers it over, and for a few minutes lets it 'raise.' A quarter of beef is taken from the wagon, where it has been wrapped in canvas to keep it cool. Slices are cut off and placed in one of the Dutch ovens, into which grease—preferably tallow—has been put. The lid is laid on, and with a shovel red hot coals are placed on top. While this is cooking, another skillet is filled with sliced potatoes, and given the same treatment as the meat. Now the bread is molded into biscuits, and put into another Dutch oven. These biscuits are softer than those made with baking powder, and as each is patted out, it is dropped into the hot grease and turned over. These biscuits are then put in the bake-oven, tight together until the bottom of the container is full. Now comes the success or failure of the operation. The secret is to keep the Dutch oven at just the right heat, adding or taking off the right amount of hot coals, from underneath the oven or on top of the lid. If everything goes right, you may be assured of the best hot biscuits in the world. Sometimes a pudding is made of dried bread, raisins, sugar, water, and a little grease, also nutmeg and spices; this is placed in a Dutch oven, and cooked until the top is brown. This is the usual cow-camp meal, but if there is no beef in the wagon, beans and chili are substituted.

"Along in the evening, as the men are through with the day's roundup or drive, tired horses are turned into the *remuda*, and Cosi hollers, 'Come and get it or I'll throw it out.' The punchers in their chaps, boots, and spurs flock to the chuck wagon, and out of the drawer get knives, forks, and spoons, and off the lid of the chuck box take plates and cups that Cosi has laid out. They then go to the different bake ovens and fill their plates, which like the cups are made of tin; the knives, spoons, and forks are of iron or composition. Lots of banter usually passes between the punchers and Cosi, though he generally gives as good as he receives. Plates filled, the boys sit around on the different rolls of bedding, the wagon tongue, or with crossed legs either squatting on the ground or with their backs against a wagon wheel. Of course, there is no tablecloth on the chuck box lid, but it is usually scrubbed clean enough for the purpose of eating—though no one uses it.

"As the boys finish their meal, plates, cups, knives, forks, and spoons are thrown into a large dishpan placed on the ground under-

Dinner at the chuck wagon. *Courtesy Erwin E. Smith Collection of the Library of Congress, on deposit at the Amon Carter Museum.*

Washing up. *Courtesy the Erwin E. Smith Collection of the Library of Congress, on deposit at the Amon Carter Museum.*

neath the chuck box lid. If some luckless puncher should place his 'eating tools' on top of the lid, he would be sure to be bawled out by Cosi. All the eating tools, when washed, are put on shelves or in drawers of the chuck box, while the heavy Dutch ovens and such are put into a box bolted underneath the wagon bed at its rear end. . . ."

The original chuck wagon, according to tradition, was created by pioneer cowman Charles Goodnight, who took a "government wagon" and had it altered, replacing the wooden axles with iron ones, and adding the chuck box at the rear. The chuck box was widely copied, says Ramon Adams: two to three feet deep and four feet high, it had shelves and drawers covered by the hinged lid. The inside thus resembled a kitchen cabinet, holding some supplies, pots, and simple medical nostrums—including horse liniment for man or beast. With sideboards added to the wagon bed, there was room for sacks of beans and flour, and canned goods.

Not to be forgotten is the "possum belly" or "cooney" (from Spanish *cuna*, cradle), where firewood was carried, or, in treeless areas, "prairie coal"—cow or buffalo chips. It was simply a cowhide stretched beneath the wagon while still green, and filled with rocks to stretch it.

Of course, there was no such thing as a school for cooking for cowboys nor soldiers nor lumberjacks—they just grew. . . .

Frequently the chuck wagon cook was a stove-up cowboy who could no longer handle regular range chores, but he soon became master of his small, vital kingdom, guarding it jealously from any encroachments. . . . A version I picked up from a contestant at a rodeo in Odessa, Texas, in 1960 tells of the outfit whose cook had been run off by the sheriff, and no replacement was at hand. So the foreman had the hands draw straws, and the short straw-drawer was elected cook, to serve 'til somebody complained. Well, nobody complained for a good while, and Cosi wasn't too happy in his job—so he started getting careless; but nobody dared complain, since whoever complained had to take the job himself. Finally he got desperate, and dumped a double handful of salt into the beans and served 'em up. One of the boys took a mouthful and nearly strangled. "By God," he hollered, "them's the saltiest beans I ever et!" About then he noticed the cook starting to take off his apron. "But that's jest the way I like 'em!" he concluded.

One old timer recalled a double killing that arose out of a cowboy's brashness:

"French and a fellow named Hinton got into it over Hinton digging into the chuck box, which was against Frenchy's rule, as it was with any good cooky. They did not want the waddies messing up the chuck box. Hinton seemed to get a kick out of seeing French get riled. . . . Frenchy never refused to give anyone a handout, but Hinton insisted upon helping himself. The evening that the fight took place, Hinton walked past Frenchy and dove into the chuck box. Frenchy went after Hinton with a carving-knife and Hinton drew his gun. The cooky kept going into Hinton slashing with his knife and Hinton kept backing away shooting all the while, trying to get away from the knife, but French never hesitated . . . ; finally he drove the knife into Hinton's breast and they both went to the ground and died a few minutes after."

The huge coffeepot was the first item to go on the cook's fire when it was built, and generally the last to come off when breaking camp. "Around chuck wagons," says Francis Fugate, "early Westerners re-newed their energies with coffee, the aromatic brew that 'quickens the spirit, and makes the heart lightsome.' Chances are that Arbuc-kles' was the brand in all those coffeepots. In fact, the use of Ar-buckle Bros. coffee was so widespread that its brand name came to be synonymous with the word 'coffee.' . . ." The cook (strongly sup-ported by the cowhands) believed in making it stout: "A recipe went the rounds from ranch to ranch, confided by cooks to greenhorn hands: 'You take two pounds of Arbuckles', put in enough water to wet it down, then you boil it for two hours. After that, you throw in a horsehoe. If the shoe sinks, the coffee ain't ready.'" One of the reasons the brand was so popular was the premiums used by John Arbuckle to stimulate sales—and thereby hangs a chuck cook trick: a stick of sugar candy included in each bag lightened the cook's load. "If a cook wanted the next day's supply of coffee ground, he would call out 'Who wants the candy?' and get a rash of volunteers to turn the crank on the coffee grinder, which was inevitably fastened to the side of the chuck wagon."

One of the proofs of the existence of a folk group is a shared language—and the chuck wagon scene had its share of useful terms:

Air tights	*canned goods*
Biscuit-shooter	*a waitress*
Chuck	*food of any kind*
Dough-gods	*biscuits*
Dough-wrangler	*cook*
Feed-trough	*to eat at a table*
Fluff-duffs	*fancy food*
Frijoles	*beans*
Gouch hooks	*irons to lift the heavy lids of cooking vessels*
Lick	*syrup (or a salt lick)*

A meal in camp. *Courtesy the Erwin E. Smith Collection of the Library of Congress, on deposit at the Amon Carter Museum.*

Salt pork went by "'sow belly,' 'hog side,' 'sow bosom,' and 'pig's vest with buttons.' Bacon was often sarcastically referred to as 'fried chicken,' 'chuck wagon chicken,' and 'Kansas City fish.' It was not used to a great extent, because it became rancid in the heat and anyway the cowman preferred fresh meat." Of course there were names for particular dishes, son-of-a-gun stew, for example, which was also called by its more natural, less polite name. Ramon Adams says it was made of practically everything the cook had at hand, excepting "horns, hoof, and hide." And perhaps the name came from the first cowboy who tasted it, and hollered, "Sonofabitch, but that's good." But Adams also notes the tendency for an outfit to call the dish by the name of some enemy—"a subtle way of calling him names which one dared not do to his face." The good chuck wagon cook learned to make do with whatever he had. A mixture of sorghum and bacon grease was a substitute for butter, for example, and it was a mighty poor cook who couldn't spice up the usual menu, which was always strong on "meat and whistle-berries [beans]." Dried apples and raisins were staples on many wagons, and they served to make pies—one item cowboys dearly loved. Cosi would roll out his dough with a beer bottle, put it in a greased pie pan and add the previously stewed fruit, then cover it with another layer of dough—with the steam escaping through the outfit's brand cut in the crust. "Spotted pup"—raisin and rice pudding—did pretty well, especially with sugar and cream (when it was available), but as a steady diet it could produce mutiny! "Some cooks were expert at making vinegar pies," reports Ramon Adams, concocted of a combination of vinegar, water, fat, and flour, all turned onto a layer of dough in a pie pan, and then covered, cobbler style, with crisscrossed strips of dough and baked. And then there was "pooch"—tomatoes, stewed with left-over biscuits and a little sugar—that the cowboys enjoyed as much as dessert. Rather than pack a lunch, a hand would carry a can or two of tomatoes to tide him over if he was going to be gone over the meal hour; they served as both food and drink.

Another side of the grouchy cook—the very one who died defending his turf in the story above—is presented by John Baker:

"The belly-cheater on the Holt outfit was a fellow called Frenchy, a top cooky. He was one of them fellows that took enjoyment out of satisfying the waddies' tapeworm. Frenchy was always pulling some tricks on us waddies and we enjoyed his tricks, because he always made up for the tricks by extra efforts in cooking some dish we hankered after. He could make some of the best puddings I ever shoved into my mouth. One day at supper we were all about done eating and French said: 'If you dam skunks wait a second I'll give you some pudding. It is a little late getting done.' Of course we all waited and he pulled a beauty out of the oven. We all dived into it and took big gobs into our mouths. We then started to make funny faces. What he had done was to use salt instead of sugar when he made it and that pudding tasted like hell. We all began to sputter and spit to clean our mouths. He then pulled a good pudding on us and that sure was a peach. We had forgot that the day was April 1. He would use red pepper on us in some dishes we hankered after, also cotton in biscuits, but we knew something extra was coming up to follow."

The cowboys often cussed the chuck and the cook, and called him names like Vinegar Jim, and Bilious Bill, and Dirty Dave—not to mention some less polite handles. But on a dry drive, when the cowboys were working the clock around to keep the steers moving

north, the cook kept open house all night long, with food and Arbuckles' to keep the waddies going; he knew that hardship is easier
to bear if the hands are well fed. And on more normal nights, when
the cook had put a lighted lantern on the tip of the wagon tongue
to guide the night crews back to the outfit, and pointed it towards
the North Star to provide bearings for the next day's drive, it was
easy to remember that the wagon was home, and the chuck wagon
cook—ugly and irascible though he might be—was in some ways
the heart and soul of the outfit. Jack Thorp said a bunch when he
wrote, "When it came to serving up ample and good-tasting food
under unfavorable conditions, I never saw anybody to beat the average cow-camp cook." Without him the roundup, the trail drive,
and the cattle industry could never have been—and even with the
distortions of fact that Hollywood provides, his lore lingers on, relic
of a bygone day. (215–25)

When the country was too rough for a chuck wagon, the cowboys had to
pack the grub on horses or mules. Jack Hittson, ranching at Palo Pinto, described these camps as unbearable—the food was always wet. Wild animals
would come and help themselves while the men were out with the cows. Their
utensils were one skillet and a beat-up bucket for making coffee. A potato
baked in ashes or a steak pan-broiled was a rare treat for these men. Hittson
had an old uncle whose herd grew to such size that he had two crews—and
two camps. He had a skillet, a big iron job with long tapered handles made by
a blacksmith. The men called it "old rat-tail." The men grew violent about
which crew would get "old rat-tail." But the old uncle, with the "wisdom of
Solomon and the patience of Job," managed to settle the controversy amiably;
possibly neither crew got "old rat-tail." To these men, going on a drive with a
chuck wagon sounded better than life in an uptown hotel (38–39).

A Chinese chuck wagon cook took his shotgun one morning and shot
some squirrels. He cooked them up for the boys.

When they came in for dinner, one asked, "What is this?" The smiling
Chinaman answered, "Kitty Labbit."

At that, the boys put their tin plates down and sent that Chinaman
packing. They'd not eat *cat!*

Frank X. Tolbert thought the chuck wagon cooks learned about Sonofabitch Stew from the Plains Indians. The Comanches did not have greens to
speak of on the Staked Plains; their diet was mainly meat, but they preferred
this stew, made of vital organs, probably because of the Indian belief that
eating the organs of an animal will endow the eater with all that animal's
power.

Butchering on the range. *Courtesy Erwin E. Smith Collection of the Library of Congress, on deposit at the Amon Carter Museum.*

Bringing a side of beef to the cook. *Courtesy Erwin E. Smith Collection of the Library of Congress, on deposit at the Amon Carter Museum.*

Tolbert wrote that the stew must have at least a yard of marrow gut, called margut, brains, all the sweetbreads, half the heart, some liver (he says to go easy on the liver else the stew will be bitter), all the meat behind the ribs, half the gland behind the floating kidney (called the melt), several cups of rendered kidney suet, the oxtail soup bone (which has to be boiled first until the meat comes off it), the calf's tongue (if you have time and will go to the trouble of skinning it), and several pounds of stew meat. All of the ingredients are cubed or cut even finer. The stew is seasoned with salt and sage, a lot of black pepper, and even more red pepper. Never add onions, tomatoes, or potatoes. Simmer slowly until done. It takes a while.

The heart and the tongue must be boiled first as they are toughest, and the brains are added during the last half hour of cooking, or they will cook away.

The essential ingredient for the flavor the cowboys found so delicious is margut. This is the long tube connecting the two stomachs of the calf and is edible only if the calf has not been weaned. It is considered such a delicacy that sometimes it is put on a stick for roasting, or it may be cut into rings, dipped in flour, and fried (*A Bowl of Red*, 131–33).

> "They call their coosie Jesus,
> 'E turns bread into stones."
> —Paul Patterson

In Fort Worth, Mac McDaniels is the coosie for Texas Trails Bar-B-Q. Mac was a range cook for many years. "The last old-timey chuck wagon in use," he said, "was on the 6666, but it was retired in 1966." These days he and his wife, Jalyn Burkett, give chuck wagon demonstrations and have a catering service. Sometimes they arrive for the occasion in their wagon drawn by a team of mules. Other times they have to hitch the wagon to a pickup because the mules are not always welcome at the entertainments.

In *Chuck Wagon Cooking* they give some authentic recipes:

COOSIE MAC'S RECIPE FOR STEAK

Build a fire and put on the meat.

SON-OF-A-GUN-IN-A-SACK

When the coosie wanted to return a favor to a cowhand who had brought in some dry firewood (or cow chips) off the range, or if there was a special occasion, he would make this boiled suet pudding. He would add raisins or dried apples if available. Some sources say it got its name because it was so difficult to make and others because it was so good.

2 cups flour

1 cup dried fruit such as raisins

1 tablespoon soda

1 cup bread crumbs

1 teaspoon salt

1 teaspoon ground cinnamon

1/4 teaspoon ground cloves

1/4 teaspoon ground nutmeg

1 cup ground beef suet

1 cup canned milk

1 cup molasses

Mix dry ingredients together. Add suet and mix well. Stir in milk and molasses until well mixed. Pour mixture into a cloth sack and tie with a string. Place in a large pot of boiling water, cover and boil gently for 2 hours. Serve warm with sweetened canned milk or cream if available.

> There was a cowboy named Zack,
> That wanted a wife in his shack,
> He said he didn't care about looks,
> Just as long as she cooks,
> Good Son-of-a-Gun-in-a-Sack!

DUTCH OVEN COBBLER

Cobblers and pies were not regulars on chuck wagon menus. In fact, if the boss was thrifty, they were nonexistent. But when they were served, stewed, dried fruits such as apples, peaches, or apricots would be baked with dough in a heavy Dutch oven.

1 cup butter or other fat

2 cups sugar

1 1/2 cups flour

2 teaspoons baking powder

1/2 teaspoon salt

3/4 cup canned milk

3/4 cup water

4 cups sweetened fruit with juice

Melt butter in Dutch oven over low heat. Mix sugar, flour, baking powder, and salt. Stir in milk and water and mix until well moistened. Pour into Dutch oven. Pour fruit on top. Cover with flanged lid and place a thin layer of coals on top. Cook until top of cobbler is lightly browned.

This may be cooked in an oven at 350 degrees, 35–45 minutes.

One-fourth cup of sourdough starter may be added at the same time the milk is added if desired.

The cowboy has many fanciful names for his food: "mountain oysters"; "dry land oysters"; "heifers' delight," a meat stew; eggs, "shanghai berries"; molasses, "lick"; rice, "moonshine"; butter, "cow salve"; cake frosting, "calf slobber"; biscuit, "terrapin" or "sinkers"; bakers' bread, "gun waddin'"; coffee, "alkali water." Bacon is called "Ned" (according to one cowboy explanation it got its name from a picture in *McGuffey's First Eclectic Reader* where the pig was named "Ned"); prunes are "nigger toes"; "dog bread" is the name applied to bread made of water and baking powder without shortening except tallow, wrapped around a stick and then baked over the coals; whiskey is called "road shortenin'," and a bottle of whiskey is a "bottle of barbed wire." On a long ride the crowd would stop to "wood up" or take a drink (Lomax, 17).

J. Frank Dobie quoted an old Texan as saying, "Try to get your beefsteak three times a day, fried in taller. Taller is mighty healing, and there's nothing like it to keep your stummick greased-up and in good working order."

The following range recipes were gathered by Donna Koch and Helen Vaughan of El Paso for the John O. West Collection of Texas Folklore:

SOURDOUGH STARTER

Mom says only a person raised in this age of refrigeration would ask where to get the yeast for sourdough starter. The air is full of yeast, she says; we refrigerate to keep yeast from spoiling our foods. To get a "starter," mix equal amounts of flour and water to a soft paste and set in the sun in hot weather, and it will soon begin to ferment and rise. Also any other food or fruit juice will ferment faster, I believe. If it's cold outside, put the dough in any warm place. It will ferment. Sourdough starter is just that—sour dough— and in the good old days Mom talks about, if baking was delayed too long it would be so sour only a small part would be mixed with fresh flour and water for a new starter or bread would taste sour too.

ABOUT SOURDOUGH

A small wooden keg was usually used by the old roundup cook, in which to keep his sourdough. The first batch of batter was merely to season the keg. After fermentation was well started, it was poured out, and enough new batter mixed up to fill the keg.

Each day it was put into the sun to hasten fermentation, and each night it was wrapped in blankets to keep the batter warm and working. Some cooks even slept with their kegs.

After several days of this treatment, the dough was ready to use; from then to the end of the season, the dough was never cleaned out. Every time the cook took out enough dough for a meal, he put back enough flour, salt, and water to replace it. In this way, he always had plenty of dough working. His biscuits and hotcakes were light as feathers.

MORE ABOUT SOURDOUGH

If your sourdough bread raised slowly, here are some hints to help: Use plain salt, never iodized salt. To keep your bread from sticking to your hands, use animal fat to grease them such as butter, lard, or bacon grease. And always remember not to use too much flour or your bread will be heavy and slightly soggy.

SOURDOUGH BISCUITS

2 cups flour
1 tablespoon sugar
1 tablespoon baking powder
3/4 teaspoon salt
2 cups prepared sourdough starter
3 tablespoons fat

Mix flour, sugar, baking powder and salt. Add starter and stir to make a soft dough. Pinch off pieces of dough the size of eggs. Melt fat in heavy preheated Dutch oven. Place dough balls close together, coating tops with a small amount of fat as they are placed in oven. Set oven on coals. Cover Dutch oven and place a thin layer of coals on top. Cook until browned.

SQUAW BREAD

Use sourdough biscuit dough. Pinch off enough dough so that when it's rolled or patted out you will have a patty about the size of a pancake, that is, an 8-to-10 inch one. Cut a 2-to-3-inch "X" in the middle to let the air get through so they will cook in the middle. Fry in a skillet until brown on each side.

CAMP BISCUITS

I have a recipe for biscuits used by the sheepherders and trail drivers. It is interesting, and I keep it in my recipe file box just for laughs.

Take a good deal of flour, more or less, according to the number of campers and the dimensions of their appetites, to which add salt to taste and baking powder to raise. Mix with water into a soft dough, bake in a Dutch oven, frying pan, or whatever utensil may be at hand—using a flat stone if nothing else can be found. Serve hot on a tin plate or piece of bark, garnished with pine cones and field daisies.

COWBOY CAKE

On roundups and cattle drives, the cook often had no eggs or butter, and so baked a cake similar to this:

Cook 1 cup raisins or cut-up dried peaches or apricots in 3 cups water for 15 to 20 minutes. Drain and save juice. To 1 cup hot drained juice, add 1 tablespoon shortening and allow to cool. Then add 1 teaspoon soda, 1 cup sugar, and spices as you may have on hand, to taste. The cowboys liked cinnamon and nutmeg, which were sometimes available.

Also add a pinch of salt, 2 cups flour, and the fruit. To the remainder of the juice, add a cup of sugar, a little shortening and allow to come to a soft ball stage. Beat slightly and pour on top of cake. The frosting may be gooey, but that's the way the boys liked it. Bake in Dutch oven as for biscuits about 30 minutes.

ROCKY MOUNTAIN OYSTERS

After castrating the calves, the men would throw the "rocky mountain oysters" into the fire, dirt, hair, and all. When they became crisp and began to crack open, the cowboys had a feast. That's the story cowboys like to tell. Usually they took them to the coosie who would clean them, drop them in hot grease and fry them to a crisp brown.

COWBOY GRACES

"Eat the meat and leave the skin
Turn up your plates and let's begin."

•

"Yes, we'll come to the table
As long as we're able,
And eat every damn thing
That looks sorter stable."

(Lomax, 23)

PART TWO

Texans Have More Fun
Celebrating the
Seasons

Geography has much to do with folks' eats. But, today, considering the mobility of people, the influx of ethnic groups, and other factors like the burgeoning shelves of Texas cookbooks, we have to look beyond locale to continue our folk history. The people had brought with them a culture rich with the traditions of the Old World. Some of these traditions they retained in spite of the exigencies of frontier life—or perhaps because they needed some links with the past. Others were altered by contact with cultures they found here or with their neighbors who, like themselves, were immigrants seeking "the land of milk and honey." And, along the way from open hearth cooking to the microwave, they originated new traditions, sometimes limited to family, sometimes community-wide. Seasonal celebrations, when traditions are most likely to be recalled, give the most complete picture of the folkways of Texans as revealed by their foodways.

Spring Delights

COME SPRING, Texans may think of raising a garden. They envision the delights of fresh English peas, leaf lettuce, green onions, and strawberries. Later, new potatoes, radishes, carrots, squash, cucumbers, okra, tomatoes, cantaloupes, watermelons, and string beans, called green beans when they are bought in cans and snap beans by folk who have forgotten how they grew in their grandmothers' gardens.

Beans were often planted along the corn rows. The vines caught hold of the cornstalk and used it as a bean pole to climb up into the sun. Or four plants were spaced around a six-foot pole and heavy strings run up from the plants to the top. The beans grew so rank that the strings were tied from one pole to another, five feet or so away, like a clothesline. Is this the reason they were called string beans? Not really. When the cook prepared beans for the pot, she had to snap off the tip and pull off the seam string that runs the length of the bean.

In the old days, February was the time for swappin' seeds, and the women eagerly anticipated the garden. It was an extension of parenting, and the whole family became involved.

Charles Linck tells about a time when his dad plowed the garden:

> Daddy had bought an army horse to go along with a blind horse we had. Mother held the plow as Daddy drove the horses. At the end of a row, he shouted, "Whoa, whoa, whoa!" The army horse just kept going, the blind one along with him. Finally in desperation, Daddy yelled, "Halt! You son-of-a-bitch!" The army horse stopped.
>
> We've had many a laugh about that. We would tease Daddy about what might have happened if he had said "Charge" with Mother at the other end of the plow.

Then there's planting, watching the seedlings burst forth, and weeding. The gardener hoes the weeds, pulls out the weeds, chops the weeds. Whatever hands lie idle are given the hoe. Charles says a story about his eighty-some-odd-years-old grandpa, who wanted to be useful. He was told, "Go chop the weeds." He did. He cut out all the watermelons that had been planted between the rows of corn. "Grandpa knew what he did," Charles says. "He disappeared. When he finally decided to return home, he explained his absence by saying he had gone to town to buy some tobacco. No one ever mentioned hoeing to him again."

The gardener is plagued by varmints: cutworms, army worms, grasshoppers, tomato worms, aphids, rabbits, and birds. One year, Charles says, the robins would not leave the strawberries alone. Not even a scarecrow kept the pesky things away. One day he was alarmed to hear the sound of gunshots. Running to the house, he found his mother standing on the back step, banging away at the robins with a .410. "Mother wasn't a very good shot. We didn't have many strawberries that year. We did see lots of fat robins."

> "What do you put on your strawberries?"
> "Horse manure."
> "Oh? I put sugar and cream on mine."
> —Willard Scott on the *Today* show

STRAWBERRY SHORTCAKE

Gently wash about 2 pints of strawberries. Drain and hull. You may want to set aside a few to garnish with. Slice the berries and add a cup of sugar, stirring the berries very carefully. Set the berries aside and keep them cool.

Some folks prefer a sweetened biscuit dough for shortcake. A sponge cake is also popular:

1 1/4 cups flour, sifted
1 1/2 cups sugar
1/2 teaspoon baking powder
1/2 teaspoon salt
6 eggs, separated
1 teaspoon cream of tartar
4 tablespoons water
1 teaspoon vanilla

Preheat oven to 350 degrees.

Sift flour, 1 cup of the sugar, baking powder, and salt. Beat the egg whites until frothy. Add cream of tartar and beat until the whites are stiff but not dry. Mix the other 1/2 cup of sugar into the egg whites gently.

Mix the egg yolks, water, and vanilla. Add the dry ingredients. Beat well until lemon-colored and smooth. Fold this mixture into the egg whites. Pour the batter into an ungreased 10-inch tube pan.

Bake for 45 minutes or when cake springs back when lightly pressed with fingers. Let the cake cool by inverting it on a rack before removing it from the pan.

To serve, cut the cake in half. Spread the bottom half with butter. Spoon half the berries on this part. Top with the other half of the cake. Spoon the rest of the berries on top. Spread a half cup of cream, whipped, which you have flavored with a teaspoon of vanilla, over the berries. Garnish with whole berries. Serve immediately.

GARDEN WISDOM

If you plant beans while a norther is blowing, they will never cook soft.

Onion's skin very thin, mild winter coming in; onion's skin thick and tough, coming winter cold and rough.

When the okra pod sheds its seeds, do not burn the pod, or there will be a drought.

Redheaded farmers raise more carrots than anyone else and the hottest red peppers.

It is corn planting time when the leaves on the oak trees are as big as a squirrel's ear.

If you plant parsley on Good Friday, you will have a good crop until fall.

Plant root vegetables in the dark of the moon.

Plant corn when the dogwood is in bloom.

Sweet basil planted on either side of your doorstep will bring good luck.

Plant peas on Valentine's Day,
potatoes on St. Patrick's Day,
green beans on Good Friday.

Plant potatoes in the dark of the moon,
corn when there is a full moon,
fruit trees during a new moon.

Although Texas has a long growing season, it was necessary to lay by a store of canned goods for the "six weeks want" during winter. Good pickings in the garden meant hours of hot work in the kitchen. A family with ten or so children would have better than five hundred jars of vegetables and fruits. Beans, corn, tomatoes, okra, peaches, pears, preserves, and on and on, were taken to the dugout, the storm cellar, for storing. Also, the cellar provided a cool place for potatoes, onions, turnips, pumpkins, and what have you.

"Obviously, not the least of the storm cellar's uses was one of life or death consequences in a storm," says Faye Leeper of Midland. She remembers an iceman's tale about two mature maiden sisters, active in temperance causes, frugal and upright in every way. One stormy night they were forced to go to the cellar, some paces from the house. There among the jars that told of summer's plenty, they saw several jars of vintage juice that had popped their lids. Not wishing the juice to go to waste, they tried to drink it all. They must have passed out. But when they awoke the next morning, they resumed drinking the stuff. Later, the iceman missed them at the house when he made his rounds. He knocked on the cellar door. He was shocked when they staggered out, greeted him affectionately, and—what else?—offered him a shot.

In the spring, roast beef disappeared as the choice viand for Sunday dinner. There was, instead, a spring fryer. In the days before processing, someone in the household had to wring the chicken's neck. Martha Emmons of Waco faced this trial once. Her mother was sick. She called to Martha and said, "Martha, I'd surely like to have some chicken soup. Do you think you could make some for me?" Of course, Martha agreed and really wanted to do anything to help her mother get well. But she had to wring the chicken's neck! She tried to get her courage up. Time passed. "Martha," her mother called, "are you cooking my soup?" About that time, the postman came by. "Mister," she said, "my mother is sick and wants some chicken soup, but I can't wring the chicken's neck. Can you help me?"

"And do you know," Martha concludes, "that nice man put down his pack, went around to the backyard, caught a chicken, and wrung its neck. I can still see it floppin' around in the dust."

"After that," she adds, "I always thought postmen some of the best people I ever knew."

HOW TO MAKE CHICKENS TENDER

Take them out of the hen-run. Pursue the chickens into open country, and when you have made them run, kill them with a gun loaded with very small shot.

The meat of the chicken, gripped with fright, will become tender. This method is infallible even for the oldest and toughest chicken.

Chris Elliott of Cash tells that her father made a living for his family during the Depression by selling frog legs to fancy restaurants. He would work at catching the frogs from early spring until late fall:

> He had a cap like a miner's cap with a carbide light attached to the front. He would put on his hip waders and go out along the edges of the lake or creeks by night, with his light shining. The light would mesmerize the frogs so that Daddy could just reach down, pick them up by the back, and throw them in his tote bag. When he returned home, he put the frogs in a "holding pen," which was a wooden frame covered with wire and having a trap door. This way, the frogs did not have to be killed and cleaned until desired. This was extremely important because these were pre-refrigerator days. That's why Daddy never gigged the frogs.
>
> But one time he wished he had. He had a big frog immobilized by his light and reached down for it. But when he picked it up, a big cottonmouth snake came up too. The snake had the back half of the frog in its mouth. That's one frog Daddy did not throw into his sack.
>
> Later on, Daddy "frogged" for our own family's eating pleasure. By then I was old enough to help clean them. I was told that the frogs were cold-blooded and it did not hurt to kill them, but I'm not so sure now. Anyway, I would cut off the heads and feet and skin them. The skin slipped right off. Then I would quickly slit them down one side and clean out the inside.
>
> Some people throw away everything but the back legs. We didn't! The meat from the front legs and body is really the "sweetest" meat. If a frog is quite large, the back legs may be tough. We cooked the whole frog as one unit. Of course, we snipped the tendon on the back legs. Then the frogs couldn't jump out of the skillet. That's just an old tale, but they will jerk around in the hot grease unless the tendons are cut.

ONION AND GARLIC LORE

Hang a string of onions in the entryway to absorb evil spirits. Don't eat the onions.

If you burn the skin of onions, you will receive money.

Onions will make you smell strong (body odors) as well as cause cancer.

If you put a half-onion on a shelf, all who reside there will remain healthy.

Onions on the back of the neck will stop nosebleed.

A piece of onion on a wasp sting will stop pain and prevent swelling and infection.

Onions will induce sleep.

Garlic worn around your neck will ward off colds.

To keep from crying while peeling onion, put a little bit of onion skin (the outer layer) on the top of your head.

Hold a piece of bread in your mouth to keep from crying when you chop onion.

Drink milk as you peel the onions and you will not cry.

Garlic clears a muddled brain.

Apply a poultice of mashed onions to the stomach, armpits, soles of the feet, and palms of the hands to get rid of a fever.

Cut an onion in quarters and place one quarter in each corner of the room to cure typhoid.

Chopped onion will cure boils.

Rub onion and skunk oil on the chest for a chest cold.

For earache, boil a mixture of onions and tobacco in water. Drop the juice from the mix into the ear.

For earache, tie a string to a pod of garlic, place the garlic pod in the ear, and wear it for three days.

Red onions boiled with sugar are given to children for colds.

Carry an onion in your pocket to ward off fits.

Easter

Easter marks the resurrection of the spirit and strengthens mankind's bond with nature. It also marks our release from the harshness of the winter months and the return of the earth's bounty.

To children, Easter is a plush bunny and colored eggs to seek, to roll, or to crack. In Texas, where competitive games are king, the one who finds the most eggs *wins*; the one whose egg rolls down the hill first *wins*; the one whose egg cracks the least when two players knock them together *wins*. And when the games are over, eggs are to eat.

Minetta Goyne of Arlington, whose family were early settlers at New Braunfels and Comfort, writes about Easter eggs:

> When I was very small, I would go to look for colored eggs at the Grandparents Altgelt's home, and I remember that my grandmother was inclined to hide them among the aromatic plants of which she was so fond. The eggs themselves were not especially distinctive. Mother, on the other hand, had the inspired idea of having us two younger children (the others were too old by the time I came along) prepare what she called "Easter nests," because at this time of the year the weather was often unsettled and the dew heavy in any case. We would (on Saturday before) line a tin pie pan with fresh grass that we cut in the neighbor's yard (our yard was mostly crushed stone, since that is what my father produced for a living and it was therefore cheap for us; New Braunfels always had and still has many such yards). Around the top edge we would then make a woven wreath of wild flowers (usually bluebonnets and paintbrush, because they were relatively durable) that we got from my grandfather's farm near town, where the grandparents by then no longer lived. We would put these "nests" in a sheltered place (my favorite was under the gas meter), and—miraculously—the next morning it would be filled with eggs and, occasionally, some candy eggs or a chocolate rabbit or hen. Weather permitting, there would also be colored eggs to look for under the shrubs and among mother's perennials.

Children like cakes and candies and chocolates shaped like rabbits, chickens, or eggs. Though they do not know it, eating the animal confections is a reenactment of the sacrifice of a symbol of fertility to the gods of agriculture.

In Fredericksburg the Easter Fires Pageant combines the holy day celebration with folklore and history. In 1847 John Meusebach had met with the Comanche chiefs Buffalo Hump, Santana, Old Owl, and some lesser chiefs to attempt to pacify them. They had become hostile the year before when another group of German settlers had attempted to move onto their land, but Meusebach was able to draw up a treaty that satisfied them. To let the settlers waiting in Fredericksburg know that the negotiations were successful, he built great fires, the prearranged signal that all was well.

This bit of history is central to the pageant, but there are also ancient rituals, Indian lore, and the observance of Easter to give the entertainment more meaning. Little children, dressed like bunnies, hop across the field with their baskets of eggs: both rabbits and eggs are old fertility symbols for human and agricultural prosperity. The Germans long ago had lighted new fires at dawn on Easter. From Indian lore, there is the story of a Comanche maiden who is about to be sacrificed to appease the rain god so that the earth may be refreshed. Though the rituals are greatly modified, the lesson of the pageant lies in its ties to agriculture and the renewal of the life cycle.

EGG LORE

Eggs set in a nest by a woman will hatch out pullets; by a man, cocks.

To set a hen in May is useless because none of the chicks will live.

To remove a baby's birthmark, rub the mark every day for nine mornings with a fresh egg. On the ninth day bury the egg under a doorstep. A goiter may be removed the same way.

If you dream of broken eggs, you will quarrel with your lover or a friend, or be involved in a lawsuit.

If you dream of eggs not broken, you will have good luck, get some money, or find a sweetheart.

If you dream of eggs, someone is going to tell lies about you.

If you dream of a lapful of eggs, you will become very rich.

If you find a soft-shelled egg, throw it over the house, thus throwing away your bad luck.

Don't bring eggs into the house or take them out of the house before sunset.

If you find two yolks in one egg, it is fortunate for the one who eats it and he must make a wish.

Eat eggs on Easter Day for good luck.

Don't throw away the eggshells until after the cake is baked. It may fall.

When my sister was sick, we wrapped her in a sheet and laid her in the dirt. My mother took an egg and made the sign of the cross on my sister's body while she was saying her prayers. Then she broke the egg and put it in a glass of water near my sister and left it there for 14 hours.

To remove particles in the eye, boil an egg for one minute. Place the white of the egg on a clean white cloth and apply to the eye.

Brown some eggshells, crush them, put sugar on them, and eat them. This stops bed-wetting.

The night before Easter put out a plate of celery and carrots and a bowl of water for the Easter bunny.

To dye Easter eggs, boil the eggs in grass for green, beets for red, and onion skins for yellow.

If you make ice cream without cooking the eggs first, your chickens will lay rotten eggs.

Eggs should be allowed to breathe for several hours before cooking for flavor and to make them easier to peel.

Break a fever by cracking an egg over the bed of a sick person.

Eating raw eggs when you are young will make you grow up to be strong.

Texans of English descent will eat hot cross buns, symbol of the sacramental bread, after four o'clock on Good Friday. The buns are marked with a cross cut in the dough before baking. In Texas cooks will make a cross of powdered sugar-butter icing on top of each bun. It is said the cross lets the devil out.

Ham is the traditional meat for an Easter dinner. A country ham will be only as good as the food the hog has eaten. In the old days, a hog might get fat on acorns, peanuts, peaches that had fallen to the ground, and what was thrown to it. Noah Smithwick and his friends, on one of his expeditions where food was scarce, found and killed a "hawg" and cleaned it. Their mouths watered for fresh ham—that is, a pork roast. But unfortunately their hog had fattened itself on cotton seeds. It was inedible.

Before commercial refrigeration, ham would be rubbed amply with salt to retard bacteria, then hung in a smokehouse. These two steps were taken right after butchering in the winter. Usually, the wood for smoking was hickory to give the ham a particular flavor, but whatever wood could be found in the neighborhood served the purpose. Cajuns preferred pecan; West Texans, mesquite. After the hams were smoked, they were taken down and put in a barrel of salt for further preservation.

Because of the salt, this country-cured ham would have to be soaked in water for most of a day before cooking and would be better boiled for 25 to 30 minutes per pound, then baked, they say. It was (and is) often served with a raisin sauce.

RAISIN SAUCE

1/4 cup brown sugar (packed firmly)
1 1/2 tablespoons cornstarch
A pinch of salt
1 cup apple cider
1/2 cup raisins
8 whole cloves
1 stick cinnamon

Combine the sugar with the cornstarch so it will not lump. Add the other ingredients. Cook and stir for 10 minutes. Add a tablespoon of butter. Remove the spices. Serve hot.

Bread pudding is also traditional at Easter with some people because of the religious significance of bread.

EVE'S PUDDING

If you want a good pudding, mind what you're taught:
Take of eggs six in number, when bought for a groat—
The fruit which "Eve" her husband did cozen,
Well pared, chopped and cored, at least *half a dozen;*
Six ounces of currants, from the stems you must sort,

Lest you break out your teeth, and spoil all the sport;
Six ounces of bread (let Moll eat the crust),
And crumble the rest as fine as the dust;
Six ounces of sugar won't make it too sweet;
Some salt and a nutmeg will make it complete.
Three hours let it boil, without any futter,
But "Adam" won't eat it without wine and butter.
— *The First Texas Cook Book,* 115

Juneteenth

This account of Juneteenth is from "The Texas Experience," published by the Texas Committee for the Humanities in commemoration of the Texas Sesquicentennial:

On June 19, 1865, Major General Gordon Granger . . . announced the freedom of more than 200,000 black captives and nullified all state laws enacted during the Civil War. This action enforced the Emancipation Proclamation signed by President Abraham Lincoln on January 1, 1863. . . .

Colloquially known as "Juneteenth," June 19 became the occasion for Afro-Americans in Texas to celebrate their emancipation from captivity, historian Melvin Wade says. . . .

The granting of citizenship to blacks ushered in an era of jubilee, Wade recounts. The pervasive mood of optimism was reflected in black music and dance of the Reconstruction period. While they varied from community to community, Juneteenth celebrations usually consisted of four segments: a mid-morning parade, a noon commemoration service, a picnic and recreation in the afternoon, and an evening party. It was common for family members to return from far away on Juneteenth.

Initiating the elaborate festivities, the parade usually marched through the heart of town, concluding at the commemoration site, a church, school, or other public meeting place. . . . Large crowds of spectators of all races and ages gathered to observe the brass bands and the accompanying marchers.

Austin's *Daily Statesman* in 1892 described the events this way: "The festivities of the day were started by a grand street parade forming on East Avenue and thence marching up Pecan Street to Brazos, down Brazos to Fourth and up Fourth to Congress Avenue and then up the Avenue to the Capitol where a grand review took place. . . . After leaving the Capitol the crowd repaired to Wheelers Grove in every conceivable style of conveyance. Oxcarts, country wagons, buses, carts, buggies and hacks were all brought into play, and during the remainder of the evening the vehicles were constantly on the go, carrying eager picnickers to the grove, and bringing those who were tired out back to their homes."

The commemoration service reminded the community of the significance of emancipation. . . . Prayers sought the blessings of God for the living and the recently dead. The songs of jubilee, "Free At Last" and "In That Great Gettin' Up Morning," recreated the joy of attaining freedom. Patriotic songs, "The Star Spangled Banner," for instance, were also sung, affirming newly won citizenship.

A minister's sermon or a speech by a community leader recognized Lincoln's contribution, praised the Union, or advocated a community project. It was customary to publicly read General Granger's declaration of freedom. But the highlight of the service came in testimonials by former captives about their life under bondage and their deliverance.

Recreation time generally featured competitive baseball games, horse racing, stunt riding, and sometimes rodeos. . . . But the preparation and sharing of food was the main attraction. In keeping with convention men barbecued the meat, and women prepared the remainder of the food. Usually meeting several nights before the picnic, the men inventoried their resources—meat, wood, personnel—and established a work schedule. Pits were dug; wood was cut and hauled; and the cooking was monitored. . . . Women prepared fried chicken, potato salad, greens, sweet potato pie, and peach cobbler. Homemade ice cream, "glassade" (a blend of shaved ice, sugar and fruit syrup), and red and orange soda were also served. While the meat was communally shared, other food was shared by relatives and close family friends.

At many of their celebrations, the blacks had a cakewalk, which they originated. A cake was given to the person who did the best walking. The contestant was supposed to walk stiff and erect as he balanced a bucket of water on his head. Whoever walked the straightest and proudest and did not spill a drop of water would get a cake. There were variations of the cakewalk, even a dance by that name, in which the dancer folded his arms across his chest, arched his back, threw his head back and, posturing grotesquely, pranced across the floor.

The cakewalk became a favorite way among church groups, both white and black, for making money. A person pays for a ticket, gets a number, and then walks in a circle. At a given time, a caller stops the walkers and calls out a number. The person having that number on his ticket wins the cake. Or there can be numbers painted on the floor. When the caller calls "Stop" and draws a number from a hat, the person standing on the lucky number takes the cake. Of course, the white Protestants would have no dancing or prancing in their walks.

A Juneteenth parade, Bonham, c. 1910. *Courtesy Erwin E. Smith Collection of the Library of*

Congress, on deposit at the Amon Carter Museum.

127

In his poem, "The Party," Paul Laurence Dunbar "mentions jes' a few things" that blacks liked to feast on:

. . . well, we scrambled to de table,
An' I'd lak to tell you 'bout it—what we
    had—but I ain't able,
Mention jes' a few things, dough I know I
    hadn't orter,
Fu' I know 'twill staht a hank'rin' an' yo'
    mouf'll 'mence to worter,
We had wheat bread white ez cotton an' a egg
    pone jes' like gol',
Hog jole, bilin' hot an' steamin' roasted
    shoat an' ham sliced cold—
Look out! What's de mattah wif you? Don't
    be fallin' on de flo';
Ef it's go'n to 'fect you dat way, I won't
    tell you nothin' mo'.
Dah now—well, we had hot chittlin's—now
    you's tryin' ag'in to fall,
Cain't you stan' to hyeah about it? S'pose
    you'd been an' seed it all;
Seed dem great big sweet pertaters, layin' by
    de possum's side,
Seed dat coon in all his gravy, reckon den
    you'd up and died!
Mandy 'lowed "you all mus' 'scuse me, d'
    wa'n't much upon my she'ves,
But I'se done my bes' to suit you, so set
    down an' he'p yo'se'ves."
Tom, he 'lowed: "I don't b'lieve in
    'pologizin' an' perfessin',
Let 'em tek it lak dey ketch it. Eldah
    Thompson, ask de blessin'."
Wish you'd seed dat colo'ed preachah cleah
    his th'oat an' bow his head;
One eye shet an' one eye open,—dis is evah
    wud he said:
"Lawd, look down in tendah mussy on
    sich generous hea'ts ez dese;
Makes us truly thankful, amen. Pass dat
    possum, ef you please!"
Well, we eat and drunk ouah po'tion, 'twell
    dah wasn't nothin' lef',

An' we felt jus' like new sausage, we was
mos' nigh stuffed to def!

Stories about food are rife in the black tradition. These stories are retold from a collection of "Richard's Tales." Richard Smith was a dairyman for most of his life in LaVernia:

In the old days, after butchering, a head could be bought for a dime or fifteen cents. There was a lot of meat on a head. A lady bought a sheep's head, and, as was her custom, she put it to cook while she went to church. Just before she left, she put the dumplings into the pot.

"Girl," she said to one of her chilluns, "now you watch this. Don't you let it burn or bile over. When it cook long enough, you take it off'n the stove."

The woman went off to church. The little girl and her brother went out to play. After a time, the little boy came back to the kitchen because he knew his little sister was forgetful. Sure enough, the dumplings had "kicked out." Away he went to the brush arbor where the singing was going on.

"Momma, momma, come quick," he yelled. "That old sheep's done butted all them dumplin's outa the pot!"

Another of Richard's stories is about a man who hunted often to feed his children. One day he wanted to take home something different, so he helped himself to two of Ol' Massa's piglets. He had them in the pot boiling when the master came by.

"What you got in the pot?" he asked.

"Jes a couple little ole possum."

"Let me see."

The black man lifted the lid of the pot a little and peeked in. "Well, jes' look at this. Them possums done turned to little pigs."

During the sixties, the term "soul food," made popular in the North, for a time replaced "jus' plain ol' cookin'," "down-home cooking," "home cooking," or "country cooking." Such food is appreciated by blacks and whites alike who want simple good food. Take cobblers. Whether they are called pandowdy, buckle, slump and grunt, or deep-dish pie, they will fetch a man to the table. There is a Texas story about a farmer of the white trash kind who left his wife seven times but had to come back every single time for more of her peach cobbler.

PEACH COBBLER II

Make up your favorite pie crust, or use this one:
3/4 cup vegetable shortening
2 cups sifted flour
1/2 teaspoon salt
1 tablespoon sugar

Cut shortening into flour, salt, and sugar until the consistency of meal. Add just enough very cold water—2 to 3 tablespoons—to hold the dough together. Handle as little as possible. Roll out on floured board very thin. Line the sides and bottom of a 2-quart baking dish. Cut small pieces from the rest of the dough—about an inch or so square.

Peel and slice 8 to 10 fresh peaches. Put a layer in the dish, dot with 2 tablespoons butter and 1/4 cup sugar. Lay half the pastry squares on top. Make another layer of peaches, butter, and sugar. Place the remaining squares on top. Sprinkle with sugar.

Bake at 325 degrees for about an hour. The crust should be slightly browned on top and around edges. Serve with cream.

Weddings

It is tradition that weddings take place in June, the time for ritual celebrations of the renewal of the life cycle. Though there may no longer be an awareness of the meaning of a springtime marriage, some of the outward signs remain. The orange blossoms in the bride's bouquet are a promise of fruitfulness. Sometimes a couple will be said to be enjoying their salad days.

Noah Smithwick recalled the early-day weddings in the Hill Country. The settlers, he said, never turned anyone away, once the Indian threat was over. When there was a wedding, everyone was invited. A table would be set up outside and loaded with vittles of all description. The following day, the relatives of the groom would give an "infair," a second outdoor dinner for everyone to partake of. But such free-for-all dinners had to be discontinued, for hungry hordes would descend from all over and, having satisfied their hunger, would fill their pockets and baskets and wrap in their kerchiefs enough meat and pies and cakes to feed the family for several days (234).

Having the right foods for the wedding celebration is quite as important as the bride's dress. In olden times, the cake was a thin loaf of wheat bread that was broken over the bride's head. Guests carried off the crumbs for good luck, for the bread stood for hearth and home. Later the wedding cake was a fruitcake, heavy with fruits and nuts, a portent of fertility.

In Texan culture, the cake is a white cake. The bride must not be engaged in making the cake. She and the groom hold the knife together to make the first cut. On a separate table is a groom's cake, often chocolate. Folklore has not attempted to explain why the bride's cake is light and white—like angel food—and the groom's is devilishly dark. Pieces of the bride's cake are given to the young unmarried girls to put under their pillows so that they will dream of the man they will marry. Some weddings have more unusual symbols. At a spring wedding of one of the Peacock cowboys in Albany, the bride's cake was decorated with frosted grapes. Now the grapevine is a sign of harmony, the grapes of fecundity. But the groom's table had a real Texas theme for a center-piece: his cowboy hat and lasso. The decorations would seem to imply that the Marlboro man has not disappeared after all! The signs would also seem to spell out the roles this couple plan to play in their new life.

As they leave the wedding scene, the bride and groom are showered with rice, symbol of plenty. With the rice goes the wish, "May your pantry always be full." Many weddings today omit rice and use herbs, but what herb carries with it a wish as practical as does the rice?

DO'S AND DON'TS ABOUT SPRING FOODS

Don't let a pregnant woman pick strawberries. If she should sit down on a berry, the baby will have a red birthmark on its backside.

Don't eat two green vegetables at the same meal. The results could be terrible.

Do eat carrots. They improve your sight. This was folklore among the slaves.

Do boil potatoes and leave them in their skins. After you boil them, put them on and around your feet when you have a cold. After they are cooled, you can peel them and make potato salad.

Do feed a baby with crossed eyes carrots while he is very young. The eyes will uncross.

Do eat brown eggs. They are more nutritious.

Don't eat cabbage, broccoli, brussels sprouts, and other members of this vegetable family in large amounts. Your skin will become rough and thick.

Don't feed babies new potatoes in the spring else they will have diarrhea.

Do place cucumber peelings around the door and windowsills to keep out bugs.

Do rub a tomato on your feet and then on your throat to cure a sore throat.

Do boil pokeberry roots and bathe an itch in the water to cure it.

Do drink sassafras tea in the spring for the blood.

Don't cook your vegetables in aluminum utensils or you will get cancer of the stomach.

Don't eat sun-ripened tomatoes picked off the vine or you will cause brain fever.

Don't eat the peeling of a tomato. It will stick to your stomach and cause cancer.

Don't eat tomatoes. They are poisonous.

MORE DO'S AND DON'TS

Don't eat tomatoes with anything else or you will have high blood pressure.

Don't leave tomatoes or potato soup overnight in aluminum pans. The tomatoes and the pan will turn black and the potatoes will be poisonous.

Do use the juice from the hulls of green black walnuts for ringworms.

Do make a paste of ground raw potato and hold it on a burn to relieve pain.

Do apply a wilted cabbage leaf to bring a boil to a head.

Do walk barefooted between corn rows if you are pregnant. It helps the woman and also the corn.

Do stick a pin in a wart until it bleeds, then stick the same pin into a corn kernel and bury it in the ground. As the corn germinates, the wart will grow out of your skin.

Don't eat cucumbers while you are pregnant. You will miscarry.

Do take a few doses of rhubarb and a dose of quinine at night for hay fever.

Do place an ear of corn in the sack where you have put the cat for a move. The corn will undo the evil that comes from moving the cat.

Do save the chicken wishbone. Break it with a friend. The long end of the pulley bone brings good luck or makes your wish come true.

Do eat chicken gizzards. They will make a girl have large breasts.

Do eat chicken gizzards. You will be pretty.

Do eat the peel off a potato; hair will grow on your chest.

Do eat spinach. It will make you strong, like Popeye.

Do eat fat to thicken the blood for winter.

Do eat raisins to keep mosquitoes from biting you.

Eats for Keeping Cool

BY THE TIME of the summer solstice, about June 22, Texans have settled into hot, hot weather. The farmer watches his crops mature and ripen. Most summers he will pray for rain and watch for snails to climb the fence posts, a sure sign that rain is coming. He and his neighbors may even bring in an Indian rainmaker.

In town, before air conditioning, there would be cold watermelon in the backyard, homemade ice cream on Sunday afternoon when friends came to visit, and picnics in the park.

WATERMELON LORE

Children must not swallow the seeds, else watermelons will grow out their ears. Watermelon-seed-spitting contests are encouraged to avoid such disasters.

If you eat the pulp, you will have a fever.

Eat watermelon juice for smallpox.

A tea made from watermelon or pumpkin seeds is good for kidney ailments.

For sore eyes, get some watermelon vines and leaves and boil them for a few minutes in a little water. Then thicken it with cornmeal or wheat bran. Put the mix in a thin white cloth. When it gets cool, apply it to the eyes.

White seeds in a watermelon, if eaten, will cause malaria.

Lay a straw across a watermelon. If it turns, it is yellow meat. If it does not turn, it is red.

Never eat watermelon until after Juneteenth.

Cutting melons for a watermelon-eating contest, Athens, Texas.

PEPPERMINT ICE CREAM
Cal Porcher, Fort Worth

1/2 gallon whole milk

1 7-ounce package of peppermint candy (Cal prefers peppermint twists)

1 can sweetened condensed milk

2 tablespoons vanilla

Mix milk, sweetened condensed milk, and vanilla. Crush peppermint candy and add to milk.

Freeze according to instructions for your ice cream freezer. Makes 1 gallon.

Cal's ice cream is always served with his wife Hobby's brownies:

BROWNIES

4 squares unsweetened chocolate

2/3 cup butter or margarine

2 cups sugar

4 eggs

1 1/2 cups flour

1 teaspoon baking powder

Watermelon-eating contest, Athens, Texas.

1 teaspoon salt
1 cup broken nuts (optional)

Melt chocolate and margarine over hot water or low heat, stirring to mix. Add sugar and mix well. Add eggs and mix well.

Sift flour, baking powder, salt together and add to chocolate mixture. Stir until flour is well blended and then stir briskly for about 25 strokes. Spread in well greased 13-inch by 9-inch pan.

Bake at 350 degrees for 25 to 30 minutes. The top will have a dull crust and a slight imprint will be left when it is touched lightly with finger. Cool before cutting.

Icing (optional):

1 cup sugar
1/4 cup cocoa
1/4 cup butter
1/2 cup milk
2 tablespoons light corn syrup
1 1/2 cups sifted confectioners' sugar
1 teaspoon vanilla

Mix sugar and cocoa in saucepan. Stir in butter, milk, syrup. Bring to a full boil. Boil for 3 minutes or until spoon is coated when dipped in mixture. Stir occasionally.

Remove from heat and set pan in cold water.

When you can hold your hand on the bottom of the pan, the syrup is cool enough to add confectioners' sugar and vanilla. Stir the frosting until thick enough to spread. If frosting is too thin, add more sugar; if too thick, add a little more milk.

VANILLA ICE CREAM
Jenny Hanby's Prize-Winning Recipe
State of Texas Homemade Ice Cream Freeze-Off
Sulphur Springs

4 eggs
2 1/2 cups sugar
3 to 4 cups whole milk
4 cups whipping cream
1 tablespoon vanilla
No salt, no flour

Beat eggs. Add sugar gradually. Beat until it is like custard. Shake the carton of whipping cream, then add it and the milk to the egg mixture. Add the vanilla.

Freeze the cream 4 to 5 hours in advance of eating. This makes one gallon.

Jenny likes to make ice cream for her friends, and she will always have some left over. But it will not keep properly in the refrigerator freezer unless you put it in while it is still frozen hard.

The Terrys' Fourth of July Barbecue on Carter's Lake

On the highest point above Carter's Lake, near Karnak, in a setting incredibly beautiful with Spanish moss draped from oaks, cypress, and pines, where the Caddoes must surely have camped, Dr. William Seth Terry's father built a one-room cabin on land he had inherited from his father's acreage. These are Julia Terry Templeton's memories of good times at Carter's Lake:

The house is special. My grandfather built it as a one-room hunting cabin and for years it was just that—one room with a fireplace where the men ate and slept, and no doubt told all kinds of hunting and fishing yarns. Later the other rooms and porches and dogtrot were added, with the kitchen being added last, during my childhood by my parents. They also panelled the bedroom, added a closet and bathroom and the small bedroom. Before the bathroom was added

Dr. W. S. Terry's wife, Lucille, welcomes guests for the Fourth of July Barbecue at Carter's Lake near Jefferson.

we had to go to the outhouse and take showers in an outdoor shower stall with a water tank above our heads. Also, the electric pump was added sometime about then, too, 'cause we finally had running water inside the house. Until then we had to prime the pump to get any water.

And the water—it tasted awful! And it still does. However, the water at Zilphie's house was delicious and cool on the hottest days. We hauled our drinking water from there except when our relatives came from El Paso and they brought big bottles of distilled water with them. The water from our well was good for cleaning fish—or our bodies—and that's about all. And that's still true!

Zilphie and Edgar lived on the place as caretakers, but they also farmed the fields and fished and he was a guide on the lake. They had a wonderful old horse and buggy they used to go to church in and sometimes they would let me go along with them. Edgar always kept the yard around the house swept and did general fix-up chores and tended the boats. Zilphie cleaned the house, and whenever we were there she cooked all our meals. She was the daughter of Ole Joe, one of his many children. Ole Joe lived across the lake. We would stand on the porch and blow a horn to signal him to come over. Ole Joe was part Caddo Indian and told us many stories of Indians and wild animals and the like. He taught my daddy to fish when Daddy was a little boy and then he taught me. He insisted that we respect nature and catch only what we intended to eat. Further, he made us learn to clean the fish we caught. I remember him as an old, old man with snow white hair and kind of stooped. He was patient with me, but very strict about safety.

We used the flat-bottom boats—wooden ones back then—and would go out early in the morning so we'd be in our best "fishing spots" by daylight. If Daddy was along, the boats were always fully loaded with all sorts of fishing gear and seat cushion/life vests and extra paddles and gasoline for the motor and, of course, a water jug and snacks in case we got hungry. It's a wonder the boat didn't sink with all the junk and us. If it was just Ole Joe and me, we had only our fishing poles, a can of worms, and paddles.

Ole Joe had several sons. One of them was called Preacher Man, and he was one of the best fishing guides on the lake. When our relatives would come from El Paso to stay a month at the lake, Ole Joe and Preacher Man were around all the time. When the grown-ups weren't out fishing, Ole Joe and Preacher would let me sit with them on the pier and catch bream. They'd even bait my hook although Ole Joe didn't really approve of that. He thought I should do it myself if I wanted to fish.

Mornings at the lake were always special because of the way the lake smelled and the animal noises and the bob-o-link calls—and, maybe, because the sun came up in our eyes. Before the running water, early morning meant washing hands and face in basins filled with the cold, cold water poured from the pitchers on a shelf outside on the front porch. Somehow even summer mornings seemed cooler at the lake.

Breakfast was always a treat prepared by Zilphie: eggs and bacon or sausage and toast smeared with mayhaw jelly. This fare was served even on the morning of July 4th no matter how many mouths there were to feed. And Zilphie was strict! She and Edgar didn't have children and I often thought she didn't even like children. However, Robert Connor wasn't afraid of her one bit and he would dare to enter the kitchen while she was cooking and swipe hush puppies and French fries while she wasn't looking. Of course, she knew he was there and that he was sharing with me. When we were older, she said she couldn't fry them fast enough to keep us satisfied.

The Fourth of July celebration always began with July 3rd, and in the old days we would go to the lake on July 2nd in the afternoon or early the morning of July 3rd. The blacks who worked for the family for years and years did the cooking. They would build a fire down by the barbecue pits and start it burning around noon on July 3rd. About dark they would put the chunks of meat into boiling

Parboiling the meat.

The meat is placed over coals.

water over the open pit fire using huge black iron kettles (like old-fashioned washpots). This was the parboiling step of cooking the barbecue. About midnight they would transfer the meat to the pit for the slow cooking process that turned it into real East Texas barbecue.

Using the coals which they had accumulated from the fire that they had been burning all afternoon, they would line the large rectangular pit with hot coals. Chicken wire over pipes supported the hunks of meat—goat, beef, and pig. Once the meat was all on the pit the men would baste it with a special barbecue sauce (yellow, NOT red)—baste and turn—all night and all the morning of July 4th. During the night the men would tell jokes and stories and generally entertain each other. If we had behaved ourselves and stayed out of the way earlier, they'd allow us kids to listen 'til Mama made us go to bed. My Uncle Dick would sleep in the back of his pick-up truck under mosquito netting, which I remember thinking must be the greatest adventure.

The July 4th celebration was always fun, too, because so many old and dear family friends came to share the festivities. The Northcutts from Longview came with their two boys and the Connors always came with their children and the Golemans from Dallas and the Lucases from Shreveport. Cousins from Atlanta and from all around the countryside came, too. Some spent the night and others just came for the evening. Mama and Daddy always let me invite anyone I wanted to from town and we'd often end up with twenty kids sleeping on pallets on the floor in the dogtrot and bedrooms—that is, we slept after we had told lots of ghost stories. I'm told that in 1987 some of the children of those friends of my parents and mine and my brothers were back again with their children. My husband says I'm always homesick on July 4th, more so than at any other time of the year—even Christmas—because that whole scene is such a vivid and very special memory and I am so far away.

About the July 4th day itself, the barbecue has always been served at 12 noon after a prayer given by a local minister (usually Methodist, but sometimes Episcopal or Baptist). Daddy presides over the meat but I think that Gene may have taken over that responsibility in the last few years. There are long wooden tables set up under the huge old cypress, oak, and sweet gum trees. The tables are covered with white butcher paper and laden with all manner of wonderful goodies from the tables of our talented Jefferson and East Texas cooks. Anything you can imagine could be found on those tables, but for someone with a sweet tooth like mine it was simply heaven. The grown-ups didn't tell us what to eat and not eat. We could just help ourselves. And my plate would always be full of Olive King's baked beans, Becky McCasland's fruit salad, and some of everything chocolate plus Becky McCasland's lemon pie. It was a true feast for the glutton! The barbecue itself wasn't something I'd eat that day—we'd have plenty of that as leftovers in the days ahead. I preferred sampling all the other things.

Back in the old days I remember the visiting going on under the trees 'til late afternoon and then the people would begin loading up for the long ride back to town. Those of my town friends who had been there the night before usually went home with their parents, and the place would be left to the few out-of-town guests who were staying over another night. Mostly, we kids would be so tired and stuffed we would be ready for bedtime by the time dark came around and, having been up most of the night before, even the ghost stories wouldn't keep us awake long.

I must tell you that the July 4th barbecue is traditional not only with the Terry family, but with several other local families, too. I guess the DeWares and Terrys have been going to the lake together forever. One of the things I remember most vividly is the sight of Duma DeWare sitting in the little rocking chair on the front porch. The rocking chair was purported to be my own grandmother's favorite sitting place when at the lake. Anyhow, I remember sitting at Duma's feet watching her rock and listening to her talk with my father's older sister, Madge, who was like a grandmother to me. They told about trips to the lake in wagons over muddy roads. They told about getting stranded at the lake and having to stay there 'til the rains stopped and the roads dried out so they were passable. My father's other sister, Dorothy, says she got stuck down there one time and couldn't get back to town and for years she refused to go anywhere near the place.

On July 5th we'd begin the "breaking camp" routine. As a little child this just meant "stay out of the way," but as a teenager, it meant load the cars and stack the mattresses and pick up the mess in the yard and bring up the paddles and fishing poles from the pier.

The memories are so numerous I can't begin to tell them all: happy days and evenings of eating, fishing, boating, hunting, card-playing, reading quietly, just soaking in the beauty and peace of East Texas and Carter's Lake. It is truly a very special "place of the heart."

A happy guest.

OLIVE KING'S BAKED BEANS

The very best! You'll never have better anywhere! She always made a *huge* pot of these for the Fourth—but also provided them for my houseparties at the lake and later for my brother Gene's parties.

2 large (#2 1/2) cans pork and beans—any brand
1/2 pound bacon
1 cup brown sugar
1/2 bottle catsup (small)

Open and drain beans in a colander; wash canned juice off with cold water. Fry bacon crisp; crumble. Empty beans into dish and stir bacon into them. Add sugar, catsup and bacon grease. Bake in moderate oven (350 degrees) for 30 to 45 minutes, uncovered.

MAMA'S PIMIENTO CHEESE

I never remember going to the lake without a batch of Mama's pimiento cheese—the very best ever!

1 pound mild or sharp cheddar cheese, grated
1 to 2 tablespoons sugar
2 tablespoons sweet pickle juice
1/2 cup Miracle Whip
1 4-ounce container pimiento, chopped

First grate your cheese and then let it sit until it is quite soft. Then mix in all the other ingredients, adding more Miracle Whip if necessary to make the mixture spreadable. Remove to refrigerator container and chill thoroughly. This can be served right away, but is much better if the flavors are allowed to blend for several hours.

MAMA'S POTATO SALAD

6 large potatoes, pared and boiled and drained (cook potatoes to the
    degree of doneness your family prefers)
1 cup sweet pickle relish
1/2 cup sweet pickle juice
1 1/2 tablespoons sugar
2 tablespoons prepared mustard
3 hard-boiled eggs, chopped
1/2 cup chopped celery (more if you prefer)
1/2 cup shredded carrots
1 cup Miracle Whip Salad Dressing
2 teaspoons salt
1 teaspoon pepper
1 tablespoon Durkee's Famous Sauce

Place drained, cooked potatoes into a large mixing bowl while they are still hot. Stir in all the other ingredients, adding more Miracle Whip if necessary for the consistency you prefer.

Transfer to a container that can be covered tightly or to a bowl that can be covered tightly with plastic wrap and chill until ready to serve. Just before serving, garnish with paprika.

MISS BURMA'S FRESH LEMON CAKE

Miss Burma Bramlett was a patient of my dad's, and this was a cake she brought to our house as a treat for him. Of course, we ate it with vigor and he often had only a piece or two.

Batter:
2 sticks butter or margarine
2 1/2 cups sugar
4 eggs
2 1/2 cups sifted all-purpose flour
1/4 teaspoon salt
1 cup buttermilk with 1 teaspoon soda dissolved
1 teaspoon vanilla

Cream together the butter and sugar until light and fluffy; add the eggs, one at a time, beating after each addition. Add dry ingredients alternately with milk. Blend in the vanilla.

Grease and flour 3 9-inch layer pans. Divide batter equally into the three pans and bake in a preheated 350 degree oven for about 25 minutes. Cool the layers.

Filling:

1 1/2 cups sugar
1/2 cup whole milk
1 stick margarine
Scant 1/3 cup lemon juice (or juice from 3 lemons)
2 eggs, beaten
2 tablespoons cornstarch
1 tablespoon water
1 teaspoon fresh lemon zest, finely minced

Put all ingredients except lemon juice and zest into a saucepan and bring to boil. Cook to soft ball stage (240 degrees on candy thermometer). Set off heat and slowly add the lemon juice and zest. Stir until smooth. Spoon over layers while syrup is still hot, piercing layers with toothpick or fork to make them absorb more of the syrup. The filling recipe makes about 1 3/4 to 2 cups syrup. It should be thick and translucent, but it won't be as thick as, for example, 7 Minute Icing or cold molasses.

GLADYS MEISENHEIMER'S CUSHAW

Cushaw is a large, squash-like vegetable. It is native to areas like Jefferson, very common in Louisiana. Peel the cushaw and cut it into small pieces; cube it if you like but you don't want it so small it loses its shape in the cooking. Simmer gently until it is tender in lightly salted water. Drain. Sprinkle the top with ample amounts of butter, sugar, and nutmeg. Place it in the oven until pleasingly browned. Do not let it dry out.

ZILPHIE'S COLE SLAW DRESSING

. . . always served at Terry's Camp with fish caught that day, French fries, and hush puppies. Zilphie always claimed she couldn't fix enough to fill Robert Connor and me up and still have any to serve the adults.

1 quart Miracle Whip Salad Dressing
1 10-ounce bottle Durkee's Famous Sauce
3/4 cup sweet pickle juice
1/2 cup granulated sugar

Mix all ingredients together until well blended. Add additional sweet pickle juice or vinegar to make consistency of a "runny" dressing.

Pour into a large container and refrigerate until needed. It will keep for several weeks, covered tightly, in a refrigerator. To make Zilphie's cole slaw, thinly slice a medium-size head of cabbage and toss with the dressing. Delicious!

Note: This recipe makes enough dressing to toss with 3 large cabbages and serve about 25 people. I like to serve it with fried chicken or fish, and hush puppies of course.

CADDO LAKE RELISH A LA HAGGARD

2 gallons green tomatoes, rough chopped
2 quarts onion, rough chopped
1 quart green hot peppers, chopped
6 cups sugar
1 cup salt
2 quarts vinegar

In a large soup pot, bring the sugar, salt, and vinegar to a boil; then add vegetables; bring contents of pot to a boil and boil for 2 minutes (timed). Remove to sterile canning jars. Process in hot water bath for 10 minutes.

Serve either chilled or at room temperature with fried fish or any other plain meat.

Note: In East Texas this delicacy is served along with hush puppies, French fries, cole slaw, and fried fish at the commercial fishing camps on Caddo Lake. Make a batch of it at the end of the tomato season with your green tomatoes and serve it on a cold winter evening. Guaranteed to warm you all the way to your toes!

About Barbecue

Barbecue, barbeque, bar-b-q, and BBQ are all variations of the Haitian word *barbacoa*, which meant a framework of sticks for smoking or roasting meat. The planters in South Carolina, who had bought slaves in great numbers from traders out of Haiti, found the succulent pork roasts cooked over the *barbacoa* pleasing to their refined palates, and they began to serve them to their guests. By transference, the Haitian word came to mean both the meat and the social gathering where it was served.

The word barbecue has also come to mean meat that has been smoked in a pit. At the annual late summer XIT Rodeo and Reunion held in the Texas Panhandle, a two- to three-hundred-foot trench, about five feet deep and four feet wide, is dug. Covered over with sheet metal, then dirt, the pit holds the coals of fifteen cords of mesquite on which are laid as much as 12,000 pounds of beef to feed up to 10,000 people. After the meat has smoked for thirty hours or so, the ranch hands bring in a front-end loader to scoop off the dirt, then lift off the sheet metal and take the meat from the coals. With beans, cole slaw, pickles, a slice of bread, and a tall glass of iced tea, Texans think of themselves as "livin' high on the hog."

In 1937, H. P. Allen and W. J. Erwin, old-timers in Honey Grove, recalled their Fourth of July barbecues for the local *Citizen:*

> We do not remember when they [the celebrations] were first adopted, but evidently in the early fifties; before that period there were scarcely enough settlers to get together and make a very large gathering for celebrating this national day.
>
> Those large gatherings and matchless dinners were more social than political demonstrations. One or two speakers would be engaged before the Fourth and a speaker's stand erected and decorated with the national flag, and while there was no brass band to be had, there would be three or four as good old-time fiddlers as could be found to furnish music for the occasion.
>
> It was no trouble to get donations for the dinner. Some men would offer a whole beef steer; others a quarter or half, and others would give a mutton or two, others a pig or two, and others baked and fried chickens. A Mr. Tate, a Kentuckian, who lived a few miles from town, was an expert in barbecuing meat, and could be had on most occasions. The grounds for holding the celebration would be where there was a well of good water and plenty of shade trees, and the necessary preparation was cleaning up the grounds and digging two pits about 20 or 25 feet long, 3 or 4 feet wide and about 3 feet deep; then have hauled a good supply of dry wood—not crooked limbs and brush, but practically straight poles, with some good sized logs. Most all of this preparation was contributed free of cost.
>
> Mr. Tate would come on the grounds the day preceding the dinner and take charge of everything. By noon he would start the fires in the pits, so as to have huge beds of coals and practically no smoke, by sundown. After laying green sticks, preferably split hickory, across the pits, he would lay the meat to be cooked on them and he, with one or two assistants, would be attending to the cooking by turning the pieces and changing them over. He would have a bucket of liquid seasoning in one hand and a long-handled mop in the other, and would frequently go over all the meat, applying the seasoning, doing this all through the night and until 11 o'clock the next day, when it was cured, ready for the tables. Practically every family brought a box or basket well filled and turned it over to the

table committee. By 12 o'clock the speakers were notified that dinner was ready, and in an orderly manner the several hundred persons present found room at the tables and found far more than they could eat. Every family who possibly could came, for they knew that everybody else would be there.

These dinners were kept up till about 1862, when so many men were in the army the fashion was discontinued and never taken up after the war was over, for valid reasons.

The Tucker Family and Emblem Community Gathering on the Fourth of July

"Y'all come! Y'all come!" is the invitation to a Tucker family gathering, as some of the Tuckers load up the black washpot, onions, potatoes, and tomatoes in their pickup and go driving around the rural roads in a five-mile radius of Emblem, in East Texas, "settin' on their horns to alert folk that the day looks good for fishin' and it's time to put the fat to heatin' and a stew to cookin'." By the time they get to the creek, there will be a caravan of trucks and cars following.

Among the small fry are sixth-generation Texans, the Tucker family having settled in Austin very early. Like other Tennesseans come to Texas, they enjoy the tradition of dinner under the bright cloudless summer skies, no matter the sun. The East Texas Tuckers have a grove of oaks on their place to provide welcome shade.

By the thirties it had become custom for the Tuckers and folk of the whole community to gather for a Fourth of July fish fry. This is a fixed date. Other times of the year they will gather on short notice for squirrel stew, or rabbit, or whatever is in season.

The men grappled (some say "went muddin'") for their fish in old days. Along the banks of the South Sulphur, near Talco, they would wade into the river, moving along the banks to find the big holes where the catfish get trapped when the water is low. Or they would swim underwater to find holes in the bank where the big fish lie. Then they would reach into the hole, ram a fist into the fish's mouth, grabbing hold, and wrestle the fish out of the water, where they could get a rope around it. The fishermen—Glendale and L. C. Tucker, Tommy Sanderson, and Harold David Finley—like to talk about their glory day when they pulled a forty-two-pounder out of a huge sycamore stump that had partly fallen into the water. The fish swam up through the hollow into the part of the tree that lay on the shore. The men made a hole in the tree, reached in, pulled out the fish, and roped it. In the same stump they found a twenty-eight-pounder. Then, farther upstream in a bank, a thirty-nine-pounder and a thirty-four-pounder. A funny thing happened. One of the boys startled a fish: It "kinda ran over him, made a big wide circle and swam right up on a sandbar. All we had to do was go over and pick him up."

When you opened up one of those big fish, did you ever find a fish that had swallowed a fish that had swallowed a fish that had swallowed a fish?

No, that's just biblical stuff. But frogs and snakes will swallow things bigger than themselves.

Aren't you afraid of snakes when you're out there grapplin'? Isn't it dangerous?

Sure, but not from snakes. The big cat eat snakes, so they stay away. Oh, you get your hands and arms skinned up. Once a fellow got his cat roped and was drug under. But if you do it real often you don't notice danger.

Couldn't you get your fish by trotline?

No sport in that, but we used to seine for them if the water was high.

Have you ever heard that if you eat onions before you go fishing, you will have good luck?

No, we can wait and have onions in the stew.

Have you heard about the Mexicans in West Texas who rope their fish? They make a noose, dangle it in the water, lie back on the bank, and wait for the fish to swim into the loop.

Well, it seems they don't have a lot of hungry folks waiting for their feed.

Do you believe that to spit on your bait will help you catch a fish?

No, that may work for old Festus in *Gunsmoke*, but the men around here don't fish thataway.

Frying the fish and stirring the stew at Tuckers' gathering.

The Tucker men clean and fillet the fish in the creek nearby, and when the fat reaches the rolling point, the pieces are salted, dipped in cornmeal, dropped into the pot a few at a time, and fried to golden crispness. Whoever can take the heat gets to fry the fish.

While the Tucker men fish, the women have had a fire going under their old washpot and a stew bubbling in case the men don't have luck that day. When the men get back, the stew is ready. And even if they bring back fish, they can stand around the fire having a bowl of stew while they dry out.

In the early days there were only fish and stew. Through the years some of the men took over cooking the stew. At least three to four hours in advance of eating time, they put on meat and chicken with plenty of onion and chili powder. After a couple of hours they add potatoes and tomatoes. "Some folks," says Tommy Sanderson, who took turns cooking with Glendale Tucker,

Iced tea for a hot Texas summer day.   Garden-fresh foods.

"like to put in garden things, celery and peas and stuff like that. Look here, someone has thrown in some okra. But we like it best with the real things—just 'mate', onion, potatoes, and tomatoes."

When all the ingredients are combined, the men hand over the stirring stick—a one-by-four-inch board—to the taster, Odell Tarpley, daughter of the Tucker matriarch, Evalee, who in her day determined when the stew was just right. Now Evalee sits in the shade as her daughter begins to shake lots of salt and black pepper and chili powder into the stew. This was the procedure in Tennessee before the family migrated to Texas, and even today on the Fourth of July, Odell says, those other Tuckers and the ones who have gone to Alabama are having a family gathering just like this and cooking stew just like this.

She continues:

> Some woman who liked to put on airs, you know the kind, said
> to my mama once, "Only pore folks put all their eats in one pot."
> She just didn't know what is good.

Those people down at the Hopkins County Stew Cook-Off tell some story that the stew got started in the Depression days when hoboes rode the rails through here, and when they got thrown off, they'd start a fire and boil anything that could fly or run or crawl—and that includes a calf that might come near their fire, or some chickens roosting in nearby trees, or even rattlesnake. They'd run off other drifters, claiming their meat was still moving around in the pot.

But this stew is the real Tennessee thing. Over there in Sulphur Springs they have a big fuss about whether the original stew was made with chicken or beef. Now this stew started out with some brisket and chicken too.

On a twenty- to thirty-foot flatbed gooseneck trailer, the women spread other foods, mostly whatever the garden affords: cabbage, carrots, summer squash, corn, cucumbers, green beans, radishes, tomatoes, berries, watermelons, and cantaloupes. And plenty of iced tea.

The Tucker women have a long tradition of good home cooking in the family. Evalee came from Austin in 1919 as the bride of Harley Tucker, who had a cotton farm in the Willow Oak Community in Hopkins County. She cooked on an old-fashioned wood-burning stove.

She told James Conrad, archivist at East Texas State University: "Breakfast usually consisted of ribbon cane syrup, peach or pear preserves, ham or bacon, eggs, milk, corn meal mush or grits, coffee, biscuits, and gravy; while the main meal of the day—dinner—might include boiled vegetables, sweet potatoes, hominy, baked pies, and the famous Hopkins County stew (made of chicken, tomatoes, potatoes, corn, onions, and seasonings), or fried chicken, or chicken and dressing. . . . Supper might be only corn bread crumbled in milk."

> What are the kindest vegetables?
> (Answer: *Cabbage and lettuce because they have such big hearts.*)
> What has eyes but can't see?
> (Answer: *Potatoes.*)

GRANNY SWIFT'S SQUASH SOUFFLÉ

In a covered saucepan, cook 2 pounds of sliced yellow or white summer squash in 1/2 cup of boiling salted water until tender. Drain well and mash. Melt 1/4 cup of butter or margarine in skillet; sauté 1/2 cup of chopped onions in the butter. Combine squash and onion. Salt and pepper to taste. Add 2 teaspoons of celery seed, 1 small jar of pimiento, 1 cup of grated American cheese, and 2 eggs well beaten.

Pour into a greased shallow baking dish. Top with 1/2 cup fine bread crumbs mixed with 1/2 cup grated cheese. Bake in a moderate oven (350 degrees) for 30 minutes.

Serves 8.

MARINATED DILL CARROTS

Cut carrots into sticks 1 or 1 1/2 inches long. Have 3 cupfuls. Boil until just barely tender. Drain. Mix with dressing made of 1/4 cup Green Goddess dressing, 1/4 cup Wishbone Italian dressing, 1/4 teaspoon salt, 1/2 teaspoon pepper, 1 teaspoon dill seed, 1/4 cup grated onion, and 1 teaspoon parsley flakes.

Marinate overnight. Serve hot or cold.

GRANNY SWIFT'S OUT-OF-THIS-WORLD EGGPLANT

1 medium eggplant, peeled and cubed
2 eggs, beaten
1 small onion, chopped
1/4 cup milk
Salt and pepper to taste
3/4 cup corn bread crumbs
Sage to taste
3/4 teaspoon butter, melted
Grated cheddar cheese
Buttered crumbs for topping

Boil eggplant until tender, drain, and mash. Add eggs, onion, salt and pepper, milk, corn bread crumbs, sage, and butter. Cheese too. Mix well. Put into buttered casserole. Sprinkle top with buttered crumbs and more cheese. Bake at 350 degrees for 25 or 30 minutes.

Serves 6–8.

To finish their meal, the Tucker men cut up lots of cantaloupes and watermelons, all sweet, all just right.

How do you know when they're ripe for picking?

That's easy. On a cantaloupe there's a little pigtail curl at the end of the cantaloupe. When it dries up, the melon is ripe. It's harder to know a ripe watermelon. You can turn it to see if the ground side is white. Anybody can tell by color, but that doesn't always work. The best way is to thump it for sound. Of course, you have to know what the sound is. I've heard you can put a broom straw on a watermelon, and if it begins to turn, the watermelon is ripe. Don't ask me if it works!

What is red and white and green all over?
(*Answer: A watermelon.*)

•

Mark Twain on watermelons: "It is chief of this world's luxuries. . . .
When one has tasted it, he knows what angels eat. It was not a Southern
watermelon that Eve took. We know it because she repented."

MARCILLE TUCKER'S BLACKBERRY COBBLER

Boil fresh or frozen blackberries for 10 minutes. Have 6 cups of
berries. Strain to remove seeds. Add 2 cups of sugar or whatever
amount to taste, 1 stick of real butter (margarine will do). Reheat
the blackberries to melt the butter and the sugar.

Take 1 dozen large flour tortillas. Brown them on a cookie sheet
and crumble them into the mixture while it is hot. Pat or press the
tortillas down, letting the juice come up. Let stand for an hour or
two. It needs no more cooking.

GRANNY SWIFT'S FRUIT PIES

Dough:
1 tall can Pet milk
2/3 cup Crisco
1 teaspoon baking powder
1 teaspoon salt
4 teaspoons sugar
1 egg
4 cups flour

Cut Crisco into flour, salt, sugar, and baking powder. Add milk
and eggs. Work together well and chill in refrigerator. It will keep
for two weeks. Pinch off pieces the size of a walnut and roll out.

Filling:
1 package dried apples, peaches, or apricots
2 1/2 cups water
1/4 teaspoon salt
1 cup sugar

Bring fruit and water to a boil and cook for 30 minutes on simmer.
Add sugar and stir until sugar is dissolved. Put 1 heaping teaspoon
of filling on top of rolled-out dough, pinch sides together and fry in
medium hot fat until brown on one side. Roll over and brown other
side. Drain on paper towels.

Old Settlers' and Family Reunions

Family reunions in Texas are rather recent—Texans had to wait several generations for families to multiply—but there were Old Settlers' Reunions. Nearly every town had a designated place for the reunion: in the Granbury-Glen Rose area, it was the east end of Mile Long Mountain. Great slabs of limestone served as paving where some of the settlers have left their names and a date scratched into the surface. This had been a lookout point for the Comanches, and it also served as a gathering place for Confederate veteran reunions.

Jack Homer Hittson remembered Old Settlers' Reunions and Fourth of July picnics near Palo Pinto at Lovers' Retreat, where there was clean water. These were the horse-and-buggy days when there would be barbecue, baker's bread, and Arbuckle coffee made with sweet limestone water in a clean washpot. The barbecue—goat, beef, and shoat—was furnished by the neighbors and swabbed with a sauce of vinegar, red and black pepper, and water; it was fit for a king!

These socials would last up to three days, so there was time for much entertainment. Sometimes there would be a speaker, someone known for his oratorical skills to keep the audience laughing at his jokes and comments. There would always be bronc riding and roping, fiddlers and square dancing, and tournaments. The horsemen who took part in the tournament had short cues, much like billiard cues, made to look like the lances of medieval knights. They would ride at terrific speed toward goal posts at the end of the field, each post having a piece of two-by-four from which hung a short iron strap with a hook to loosely hold a 2 1/4-inch ring. The rider who caught up the most rings with his lance was the winner (26–27).

The Black-Eyed Pea Festival at Athens

In July the green black-eyed peas are ready for picking. But the people of Athens don't go to the fields to celebrate the harvest. Instead they have an annual festival where they hold black-eyed pea eating contests and watermelon eating contests, and they sell armadillo drumsticks for a dollar.

The armadillo drumsticks are turkey legs, as it turns out, and a man, speaking loud enough to make sure he is heard, says, "Armadillo legs are real good, and don't let no one tell you no different. They're especially good if you singe the hair off real good. Like pork. Sure, people ate them—during the Depression. We called them Hoover hogs."

Black-eyed peas were originally used as feed for the cattle—and called cowpeas. Hungry folks during the War of Northern Aggression took the peas from the barns and put them on their dining tables. It is said the Yankees destroyed all the crops but left the peas because they considered them unfit to eat. Some Southerners are still convinced they would have won the war had a trainload of the peas on their way to the boys in gray not been blown up.

The Athenians are ingenious. They have reci-peas for Jeepers Pea-pers, Pea-tini, Pea Puppies, Gazpeacho, Pea-males, Jala-Pea-No-Pie, Peasagne, and Pea-culiar Pie, to name a few. But most Texans will take just plain old peas for good eating—and good luck.

The peas are easier to shell when they begin to dry. Take a pea shell, or pod, that is filled out well, open an end, and run your thumb down the inside. If there are nine peas in a pod, you are going to have very good luck. When your thumb gets sore, use the other thumb. The peas are ready for shelling if the cheeks of the pea are fat and almost blushing and the eye seems about to wink at you.

MICHAEL FIELDEN'S
"JUST PLAIN OLD GOOD OLD PEAS"

Shell and wash 1/3 bushel of black-eyed peas. Put in a Dutch oven and cover with water by two inches. Liberally season, according to taste, with Lawry's Seasoned Salt and Lawry's Lemon Pepper (approximately 2 teaspoons each). I like to do this much in the evening and set them, covered, in the refrigerator overnight. Then I start cooking them at 8:30 the next morning and they are ready for lunch.

Three and one-half hours before you want to eat them, put the peas on a medium heat and add 1/3 cup fresh bacon drippings. Cover. Every half hour, stir and add water as needed. After two hours, liberally season with seasoned salt and lemon pepper (approximately 2 teaspoons each) again. Turn heat to low. Cook another hour, stirring occasionally and adding water as needed so you have plenty of pot-likker for your corn bread!

Serve with your favorite tomato hot sauce and your favorite onions.

BILLY ARCHIBALD'S BLACK-EYED PEAWHEELS
(Grand Champion 1985)

1 15-ounce can black-eyed peas
1/2 stick butter (or margarine)
1 dash garlic
2 dashes cayenne
1/4 teaspoon Lawry's Seasoned Salt
2 3-ounce packages cream cheese
2 packages imported ham
8 green onions

Heat peas in melted butter. Add garlic, cayenne, and seasoning salt. Simmer for 15 minutes. Cool and mix black-eyed peas and softened cream cheese together in food processor until mixture is creamy and well blended. Spread mixture onto each slice of ham. Roll green onion lengthwise in ham. Chill and cut into 1/2-inch peawheels. Serve these delicious Black-eyed Peawheels as appetizers any time of the year.

LINDA MARTIN'S "EYES OF TEXAS" SALAD
(First Place 1982)

1 1/2 cups black-eyed peas, drained
1 cup chicken, boned and chipped
1/4 cup celery, chopped
1/2 teaspoon salt
1 cup cooked rice
1/4 cup onions, chopped
1/4 cup mayonnaise
1 teaspoon pepper
1 dash hot sauce

Blend above ingredients and pack in mold. Let set for one-half hour.

Ice with topping:
1 avocado, mashed
1/2 cup sour cream
1 teaspoon garlic salt
1/2 cup mayonnaise
1/2 teaspoon Worcestershire sauce
1/4 teaspooon salt
1/2 teaspoon lemon juice

MARY KING'S PEAS 'N' BREAD
(Grand Prize 1973)

1 cup cooked black-eyed peas
1 cup white cornmeal
1/2 cup flour
1/2 teaspoon soda
1 teaspooon salt
2 eggs
1/2 cup corn oil
1 chopped onion
2 chopped jalapeños
3/4 cup creamed corn
1 pound browned and drained hamburger meat
1/2 pound grated cheddar cheese

Mix all ingredients together. Add cheese last. Pour into greased pan and bake at 350 degrees for 45 minutes.

Laura Hamner told this story of the lowly pea on the frontier:

The cook of the Carter outfit on the Pecos preferred black-eyed peas to all other foods. The boys liked them too. They had peas for dinner, for supper, and sometimes for breakfast. Ellen Carter hated the peas, wished a blight would destroy all the peas in the entire world.

One day, while cleaning the dugout, she looked up to see a polecat, waving its lovely tail at her. She screamed. The cook came running and chased the cat into the storeroom, where it took refuge on top of a hundred-pound sack of peas.

As Charlie the cook slipped around carefully to move the cat toward the door, Mrs. Carter saw her chance. She snatched his gun from its holster, fired at the skunk—and clapped her hand over her nose.

Charlie was disconsolate. The peas were ruined. Then he had an idea. He would take the sack of peas to the river and let it float there until the peas would come clean enough to eat.

Now Ellen was disconsolate. Her plan to get rid of the peas was not working. As Charlie left with the sack of peas on his back, she called to one of the cowboys and instructed him to go to the river, and when Charlie had left, to cut the sack so the peas would wash down the river.

For the next few months, she happily ate red beans. Fall arrived. One day a cowboy rode up with his slicker full of black-eyed peas. The little seeds had washed down the river, spread over a flat in an overflow, and produced a good crop, "enough for folks in the Pecos Valley for a year." Ellen was whipped. She was doomed to continue dining on black-eyed peas (146–49).

Threshing

> Out on the hill there is an old bull.
> You feed him and feed him and he never gets full.
> What is he?
> *(Answer: A threshing machine.)*

The threshing season, though it meant hard, hot work for the entire family, was a memorable time. Audrey Parker Brooks of Moran recalls:

My dad was a grain farmer. His specialty was oats. He grew cotton but he probably would have been better off, money-wise, if he hadn't. He did know the ins and outs of growing oats. The late

"The threshing machines were sights to see." *Courtesy the John Black Collection, East Texas State University.*

C. C. Ballard, another transplanted San Saban, reminded me more than once of my dad's 100-bushel-per-acre oats.

Harvesting has come a long way since the days of my father's oat growing. All the way from horse-drawn equipment to air-conditioned super combines.

The first thing I remember about the grain harvest season are the huge "thresher dinners" served to the threshing crew. Those dinners had to be big ones. The crew following the thresher was always large and there always were the hangers-on—the moochers who went from farm to farm to stuff themselves with good country food. They always were there and no farmer was so inhospitable as to turn the bums away. Of course if his wife had been consulted, said freeloader might have departed with an empty stomach.

These noon dinners were not one-woman jobs. It took nearly as big a crew to prepare the food as it did to thresh the grain. The food spread out on an oilcloth-covered table was equal to a Christmas feast. In some cases those dinners exceeded the ones at Christmas.

The threshing dinners didn't just happen. They were thought about—and dreaded—for weeks before the thresher moved in. They were collaborative projects by women of the community.

The one I remember the best wasn't even at our house. I have no idea why I remember it because I certainly wasn't very old at the time. The thresher was at our nearest neighbors in Shaw Bend—the

Taffs. I recall the long table loaded with food in the Taff dining room. There were several kids there. Our job was to take a dish cloth and wave it back and forth above the food. No, we weren't trying to fan the vittles. The cloth waving was intended to discourage the landing of flies on the food. There were no screen doors. Looking back this scene seems almost like a dream in black and white. There was some kind of food picture on a dining room wall. I remember it in shades of gray, black and white. I wonder how accurate my memory really is?

I can't actually recall a single item of food on that table but I think I can say without a doubt that there were mashed potatoes and/or potato salad, fresh green beans and fresh corn, probably cooked on the cob. I'm reasonably sure there were platters stacked with fried chicken. The parts of the chicken not fried were, most likely, used to make chicken and dumplings. I'll bet there was blackberry cobbler for dessert. Or maybe peach. Could have been both. And for drinking there would be the rarity—iced tea! That iced tea didn't always "set well" with the thresher hands. They drank too much of it and when they went back to work in the hot sun the results weren't always pleasant. But by the next day's big dinner, they would have forgotten the experience and ask for seconds, thirds, fourths and maybe fifths when the iced tea was passed.

The threshing machines were sights to see. They were powered by steam engines attached to them with wide, racing belts. The oats—the grain always was oats when I was a kid—had been cut and bundled with a horse-powered reaper several weeks earlier. Field hands following the reaper gathered the bundles and placed them in shocks. A "shock" was several bundles of oats stacked together on end to dry for threshing. Occasionally the shocks were "capped" with a bundle placed on top to protect them from weather.

A number of bundle wagons followed the threshing machine from farm to farm. Each wagon had a driver and a hand who pitched the bundles on the wagon. Each bundle was carefully placed so that the wagon could be stacked high with bundles before turning the team toward the thresher. At the threshing site the wagons lined up awaiting their turn to unload. When it came, the bundles of oats were speared on a pitchfork and tossed into the gullet of the separator. After proper chewing the steam-powered machine spat out bushels of oats and masses of straw. The oats were caught in sacks by a threshing hand designated as "the sacker."

The masses of straw grew taller and taller and became a straw-stack—a once familiar sight on every farm of any size. Those old strawstacks helped many a farm animal make it through the winter. During the cold winter months, cattle, horses and mules surrounded the strawstack, munching away at the bucolic smorgasbord. During the winter the animals ate their strawstacks into toadstool-like designs. The huge pile of straw usually was sufficient for a winter's feeding.

Strawstacks have an undeniable fascination for kids. My brothers and I were no different from the average farm kid. We wanted to climb the strawstack just as soon as the thresher moved on to the next farm. My dad was not in agreement. Strawstacks were not elevated playpens in my father's opinion. But we did climb the strawstack when Papa was somewhere else. When we reached the top of that forbidden pile of oat straw, we had the elation of a mountain climber atop mighty Mt. Everest.

Strawstacks vanished with the advent of the combine. No longer do horse- or mule-drawn bundle wagons trail a ponderous steam-powered machine that separated the oats from the straw. Gone too are those massive threshing dinners! That is progress with a capital "P"! (*Albany News*, June 25, 1987)

Dinner on the Grounds

Chorus:
It's a Homecoming Sunday and dinner on the ground
They're comin' to the country from miles around
It's an all-day singin' when they all gather 'round
And we sing our sol-re-do.

When I was just a little boy, summer in the country
We all went to singin' school
Everybody took a lunch, we stayed all day
We learned the old Stamps-Baxter way.
   Chorus

Sopranos on the right, altos on the left
Tenors and basses behind
Get your pencils and your paper, watch the blackboard
We're gonna learn to count basic time.
Now, four-four goes "One, two, three, four"
Two-four goes "One, two"
Three-four's always like a waltz
Six-eight's just like two-four.
   Chorus

Do-sol, do-sol-do, sol-sol-sol-re-do
   do-sol, do-sol-do, sol-sol-sol-re-do

Sol-fa-mi-re-do, do-ti-la-sol-fa,
  sol-fa-mi-re-do-sol-sol-re-do
Sol-fa-mi-re-do, do-ti-la-sol-fa,
  sol-fa-mi-re-do-sol-sol-re-do
(Sol-fa-mi-re-do-sol-do-sol-la-fa-do-la-sol-
  do-la-sol-la-sol-sol-fa-mi-re-do)
Chorus

—"Homecoming Sunday,"
Aileen and Elkin Thomas

Esther Huckaby has memories not of the old Stamps-Baxter way but of Sacred Harp singings on Homecoming Sundays, family reunions, and cemetery cleaning with dinner on the grounds:

I remember those times out of my childhood held in little churches far out into the country, in Rusk County, near Henderson and Mt. Enterprise. We would go to Liberty, where the Crawfords, my grandfather's people, were buried and to Zion Hill, where the Burkses, my grandmother's people, were.

On cemetery days, the families cleaned around the graves, pulling weeds, raking away brush, sometimes bringing plants to put out around the simple stones, and sometimes bringing plastic flowers, usually roses or lilies.

I was taught a kind of graveyard etiquette. I was never to be rowdy in the cemetery nor to walk on a grave. The latter admonition was essential. Grave markers for our family were small and flat and the graves were hardly discernible. However, displays of sentimentalism or dramatic grief were not appropriate. Occasionally, a voice might break in speaking of a dead friend or family member, but the speaker quickly regained composure. People died, often after terrible suffering, and in our family, they went to heaven. Of course, they were missed, and that was that. Memory, yes, histrionics, no, and absolutely no superstition.

The gathering was ostensibly an occasion for cleaning the graves, a necessity if the cemetery was not to be taken over by the vegetation that thrived in the red clay and sand. However, it also served as a family reunion and community homecoming (virtually one and the same, since almost all members of the community were in some way related; my father, for example, had over 100 first cousins, most of whom would have called either Zion Hill or Liberty "home").

At these gatherings, the women cleaned the graves and prepared the lunch, which would be served promptly at 12:00, after a blessing. The food was put on weathered boards set up on sawhorses and covered with cotton tablecloths brought from home. You can guess the menu: fried chicken, of course, barbecue, chicken and dressing,

Church picnic at a lake near Clifton. *Courtesy Amon Carter Museum, Fort Worth.*

and chicken and dumplings, all served at whatever temperature it happened to arrive at by noon. Very generous families brought food in enamel or aluminum dishpans. Most of the chickens had without a doubt been killed no earlier than the afternoon before, killed, plucked, cleaned, and cooked without benefit of indoor plumbing. Chicken did not keep, and although most rural homes had electric lights, many did not have electric refrigerators until after World War II. Mashed potatoes seasoned with fresh milk and butter, now tepid. Pickled beets and peach pickles. There were also corn bread, some fried hot water dodgers, and others containing egg, baked in a skillet and called "egg bread." Town dwellers brought "light bread" (sliced store-bought bread left in the wrapper), deviled eggs, potato salad (in East Texas, the potatoes were left in chunks, not mashed). The potatoes were literally new potatoes, fresh-dug, the onions just pulled, the pickles homemade, the eggs fresh-laid. Black-eyed peas and fresh green beans (called string beans) with new potatoes, seasoned, of course, with salt pork and very well cooked. Apparently, crispness was not the quality most desired in a vegetable. Sliced fresh tomatoes, cantaloupe, cucumbers, warty and blessedly unwaxed. Watermelons arrived in pickups, either as they were, still dusty from the patch, or floating in washtubs with chunks of ice. Paper plates were offered at some tables, and some families ate from blackened pie tins with corrugated bottoms. There were peaches and wild blackberries, usually prepared in cobblers, the pastry made with real butter and sprinkled with granulated sugar. Defying ptomaine, I sought out banana pudding, that legitimate and worthy descendant of the English trifle, and chocolate pies topped with peaks of meringue leaking brown bubbles. Every summer people sickened and died from eating potato salad or barbecue from a washtub at a family reunion. We children were shown the newspaper clippings and warned and warned again never to eat from a washtub. To this day, I have never done it.

Iced tea (usually a lot presweetened) was served in Mason jars, a practical rather than a clever solution. Those with more money than we had brought washtubs of cold drinks—sody, sody water, or sody pop, never soft drinks. At Zion Hill, I walked from the church down a deep path worn in the red clay narrowly walled with small pines and white oaks and maples. There, at the bottom of the hill and still surrounded by woods, a spring rose up from a bed of white sand, and there a pottery churn without a bottom had been sunk to provide a little cistern of clear, ice-cold water. There, since the days of my great-grandmother and before, people had come from the church to drink, and there children of my age still liked to gather. Among them were handsome country boys with coloring that in some way seemed to me rustic; the color of their skin appeared to be a lighter version of the color of their hair. Materializing from the woods, they would claim to have been hunting muskeydines, and, jostling one another and laughing and drawling, would tell the girls that they were sure we were all some of those kissin' cuzzins.

As the years passed after World War II, everything became less down-home, as did the cooking. Hot dogs appeared, and angel food cakes made from mixes, using electric beaters. Potato chips. German chocolate cakes. Paper cups and plates became the rule.

The all-day singing with dinner on the ground was Sacred Harp. First-time hearers are likely to notice several differences between it and more familiar religious music; they note the minor sound, the lack of instrumental accompaniment, parts sung so strongly that a central melody is hard to find, and, strangest of all to them, the singing of musical syllables as a prelude to singing the words of the song. Listeners might also notice the choppy rhythm and the leader's shouting out the first word of each verse, resulting in a sound not entirely reverent. They would be surprised to learn that Sacred Harp music was not sung at regular church services.

The singers would sing through the morning, take a long break for lunch, and sing again until four or so. Some of the people sat on old bedspreads or quilts spread under a tree, most people sat on car fenders, on tailgates, in lawn chairs, in cane-bottom chairs brought from home. There were babies everywhere, usually very fair and fat and suffering badly from prickly heat. Some were in playpens. Others rolled irritably on the quilts.

The singing was carried out decorously. It always was, and it still is. The benches were arranged in a U shape. "Cousin Dennis, sound the note," my grandfather would say, and then announce his song. If Dennis Jones was not there, someone else might strike a pitchfork. Occasionally, a woman would lead; less frequently, a child, who proceeded without any cuteness, exactly like an adult.

The singing sessions opened and closed with prayers. Almost invariably, the prayers referred to dear departed ones and to singing the old songs. Just before the benediction, the last leader would announce one of the traditional closing songs, "Blest Be the Tie" or "Parting Hand." It was here, rather than at graveside, when tears flowed, quietly, privately, as the singers remembered not only the long-dead people buried in the churchyard, but also the singers who had died just since the last gathering. I saw old people weeping, and guessed that they remembered their own mortality.

Harvest Time

Back to School

In the old days, school started when the crops were in. The children were sent off with lunches usually made up of whatever was left over from the night before. Lee Ann Sewell of Richardson recalls her mother speaking with relish of her favorite school sandwich: a slice of onion between the pieces of last night's biscuit. Audrey Parker Brooks has written about her school lunches:

> All morning the kids looked forward to the noon hour. Then girls went one way and boys another to open their lunch buckets or paper sacks. Some of the pupils brought their lunches in tin lard buckets. With the lard removed of course. Some of them used the navy blue and silver striped Rex Jelly buckets. And some used brown paper bags. My brothers and I carried our lunches in store-bought lunch pails as did many of the Live Oak bunch.
>
> The girls always looked forward to my lunch. Not especially for the lunch itself but for the napkins Mamma put in the pail. She always bought flowered napkins, and each day I would give the napkin to one of the other girls. The napkins didn't impress me so I gladly gave them away. Our lunches usually included a boiled egg with salt and pepper, wrapped in wax paper. Sometimes Mamma deviled the eggs my brothers and I took for lunch. My mother made delicious pimento-cheese sandwiches from scratch. It was mixed with Mamma's own homemade salad dressing. For variation she sometimes placed slices of cheese on the homemade light bread, topped them with marshmallows and placed the bread in the oven of her wood-burning stove for a few minutes. The boys and I loved

Honey Grove public school teachers picnicking, fall 1910. *Courtesy the John Black Collection, East Texas State University.*

the cheese-marshmallow sandwiches. Fried cold sausage between biscuits was standard fare for nearly all of us. More than likely our sausage patties would be between light bread slices because Mamma made so much bread (*Albany News*, September 3, 1987).

A TONGUE TWISTER

Peter Piper picked a peck of prangly prickly pears
Did Peter Piper pick a peck of prangly
    prickly pears?
If Peter Piper picked a peck of prangly
    prickly pears,
Where's the peck of prangly prickly pears
    Peter Piper picked?

William A. Owens, author of *This Stubborn Soil*, at Hopkins County Stew Cook-Off.

Harvest Festivals

The ancient rituals of celebrating harvest may not be conscious in the minds and hearts of Texans, but the spirit is still there, as Texans swarm to all kinds of outdoor activities and merrymaking before the northers start blowing in.

Tumbleweed Smith has said, "One time a Yankee told me, 'Texans have more fun than anybody else.' I think so." The fall festivals bear him out: the Kolache Festival at Caldwell, Hopkins County World Championship Stew Cook-Off at Sulphur Springs, the World Championship Barbeque Cook-Off at Pecos, the Peanut Festival at Grapeland, the Turkeyfest at Cuero, the Rice Festival at Winnie, the Shrimporee at Aransas Pass, the Pinto Bean Cook-Off at Ballinger, the East Texas Yamboree at Gilmer, and the Original Terlingua International Frank X. Tolbert-Wick Fowler Memorial Championship Chili Cook-Off.

The East Texas Yamboree in Gilmer

The Yamboree is one of the earliest of fall festivals, originating in the early thirties. In early days, when Texans spoke of potatoes, they meant sweet potatoes.

Everything in Texas is higher, longer, deeper, wider, taller, and bigger. One old tale is about the woman who set before the traveler who had just dropped in some of the biggest potatoes he had ever seen. He commented on their size. "Oh, these are not so big. Had one a while back so big all them kids made their dinner off'n it and left enuf to feed the pig."

The sweet potato is a pre-Spanish Meso-American vegetable. An early observer of food of the Rio Grande Valley, Captain John G. Bourke of *On the Border with Crook* fame, gave highest praise to the *chalupa*, a sloop—really a sweet potato, a *camote*, hollowed out like a little boat, fried in syrup, and filled, as he wrote, "with a cargo of slices of the same material. It is very palatable and much relished by the Mexican *muchacho*, into whose good graces I have on several occasions forced my way by a diplomatic presentation of a mouthful" (103).

Sarah Greene, editor of the *Gilmer Mirror*, likes to tell that after only four years of festivities, the Yamboree achieved national recognition. RKO Pictures released *Carefree* with Fred Astaire and Ginger Rogers just two months before the 1938 Yamboree. In the picture, Astaire and Rogers danced the "Yam" dance, which promised to take the place of the "Big Apple." A telegram from Hollywood extended congratulations to Gilmer, saying "Carefree Yam is now known in every section of the country and we wish as much for the Texas Yam—Long may the Nation Yen and Yowl for it."

There is a song for all the visiting bands to play in the parade and Gilmerites to sing with fervor:

MARCH YAM

East Texas is the home of Yamboree,
A great festive show, where each one should go . . .
Who loves our hills, our lands, our pines, our yams,
The best place on earth to be.

We ask you all to join our happy throng,
And come on with us, where you all belong . . .
Among our hills, our lands, our pines, our yams,
Our Yam . . . Bow . . . Reeee.

The popularity of the yam brought along in its wake a possumology (possumolatry is a better word). Beginning as a spoof, Rhonesboro entered its float in the annual parade, promoting roasted possum with sweet potato pie as a delicacy to tempt the most discerning taste. Now Rhonesboro is the center for the serious study of the possum.

Sarah says there's an old country saying to children who have grown impatient for Sunday dinner to be served when the preacher was coming or some other such occasion: "Take a cold 'tater and wait." The cold 'tater would serve very well if it were a yam.

This brings up the question of the difference between a yam and a sweet potato. Palmer Olsen of Clifton has written:

> I'm nearly ninety-three years old. From about 1897 to 1910, I remember distinctly and most pleasantly the sweet potatoes my mother baked in the oven every day in late autumn and gave to us about 4:30 p.m. when the older children came from school. They were called Puerto Rican yams and were so sweet that sugar heavily coated the outside.
>
> About 1910 a plague struck these yams, and I have never seen one since. A law was passed prohibiting westward shipment of any type of yams past a line east of Waco. Of late years, we have had some fairly good sweet potatoes, but they don't even compare in texture and taste with the old Puerto Rican yams.

Sarah writes that there was a quarantine caused by a sweet potato weevil, and when it was lifted in 1935, Gilmer celebrated by organizing its Yamboree. But the word yam today is just a marketing device for sweet potatoes. It is possible that the sweet potato puzzle may continue—at least for those who still remember with Palmer the fat, red, sugary sweet baked potatoes, dripping with real butter.

SWEET POTATO PONE

- 6 medium sweet potatoes, peeled
- 2 cups brown sugar
- 1 stick (1/2 cup) butter or margarine
- 1/2 teaspoon cinnamon
- 1/2 teaspoon nutmeg
- 1/2 teaspoon allspice
- 1/2 teaspoon cloves
- 1 cup molasses
- 6 eggs, beaten
- 2 tablespoons flour
- 1 cup milk

Grate potatoes. Mix all ingredients. Cook in greased baking dish at 350 degrees until set and slightly brown on top. 6–8 servings.

Sarah Greene, editor of the *Gilmer Mirror*, plays the accordion for the "March Yam," 1972. *Courtesy the Gilmer Mirror.*

"Long may the nation yen and yowl for the Texas yam." *Courtesy the Gilmer Mirror.*

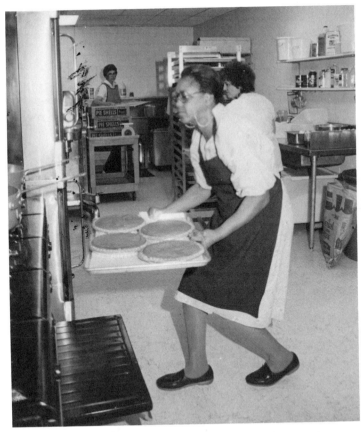

Sweet potato pies are baked by Gilmer cooks for the Folklife Festival in San Antonio. *Courtesy the Gilmer Mirror.*

SOUTHERN SWEET POTATO PIE

1 cup brown sugar (packed)

3 beaten eggs

1 cup mashed sweet potatoes (*sweet potatoes are better when they are boiled in their skins*)

1 teaspoon cinnamon

1 teaspoon nutmeg

1 teaspoon allspice

1/4 cup lemon juice

1/2 cup bourbon (optional)

1 cup cream (or 1 cup canned evaporated milk)

1/2 teaspoon salt

 Mix well. Pour into unbaked pie shell and bake at 350 degrees for 45 minutes or until knife, when inserted, comes out clean.

YAMS BAKED IN ASHES

In this method, the sweetness and piquancy of the yam is brought out in a manner not obtainable in any other way. Cover the yams with warm ashes to a depth of four inches; upon this, place live coals and hot cinders; let bake slowly for at least two hours. Remove the ashes with a soft brush and serve yams with butter while hot.

YAM ICE CREAM

2 quarts milk
1 1/2 cups sugar
1/2 cup yams, boiled, mashed, and strained
2 cups cream
2 eggs
1/4 teaspoon salt

Boil yams, mash, and strain; add sugar and salt. Scald milk in top of double boiler; meanwhile add egg to yam and sugar mixture, then add scalded milk to mixture gradually while stirring constantly. When cold, add cream. Put in ice cream freezer with ice and salt, 8 parts ice to 1 part salt.

YAM BISCUIT

4 cups flour
2 cups mashed sweet potatoes
1 tablespoon lard
1 teaspoon sugar
1 cup sour milk
1/2 teaspoon soda
1 teaspoon baking powder

Boil yams until quite soft. Mash thoroughly, add salt to taste and lard while hot, and if not sweet enough, add a little sugar. Dissolve soda in the milk. Mix baking powder in the dry flour. Gradually mix the yam and milk; add the flour. Knead into a smooth dough, make into biscuits, and bake in a hot oven. Potato biscuits are better and sweeter when the dough is kept over a day or so in a cool place.

GOLDEN STICKS

Peel and cut the yams in sticks a half-inch in thickness. Drop sticks into fat a half-inch in depth and smoking hot. When sticks are golden brown, lower the flame and cook until done, testing with a fork. Sticks may be rolled in powdered sugar and spices.

BAKED YAMS A LA ROXY

Select small, uniform yams and parboil until the skin slips off easily. Roll in finely chopped pecans and place in a buttered baking dish. Sprinkle lightly with sugar, dot with butter, cover, and bake 30 minutes.

Original Terlingua International Frank X. Tolbert-Wick Fowler Memorial Championship Chili Cook-Off

Lord God, You know us old cowhands is forgetful. Sometimes I can't even recollect what happened yestiddy. We is forgetful. We just know daylight and dark, summer, fall, winter, and spring. But I sure hope we don't never forget to thank You before we is about to eat a mess of good chili.

We don't know why, in Your wisdom, You been so doggone good to us. The heathen Chinee don't have no chili, ever. The Frenchmens is left out. The Rooshians don't know no more about chili than a hog does about a side saddle. Even the Meskins don't get a good whiff of it unless they stay around here.

Chili eaters is some of Your chosen people. We don't know why You so doggone good to us. But, Lord, God, don't ever think we ain't grateful for this chili we about to eat. Amen.

—Bones Hooks, a popular cook
of West Texas, delivered his chili prayer
at a cowboys' reunion in
Amarillo (Tolbert, 205).

The first chili cook-off was in 1967 when H. Allen Smith, then living in New York, challenged Wick Fowler's claim as the chief cook of the Chili Appreciation Society International. The affair was arranged for Terlingua, so far away that few people were expected. However, 209 chapters of the Chili Appreciation Society sent representatives, Frank Tolbert reported in *A Bowl of Red*. Some flew in in jets, some came in prop planes, some in DC-3s. There were smaller planes, there were autos. There were school buses from Alpine.

After puttering over their pots for two hours, the contestants pronounced their chili ready for judging. Judge Hallie Stillwell, who discovered that H.

Allen Smith was her cousin, voted for the New Yorker's. Judge Schneider, who was next, gobbled Wick's. The third judge, Mayor Witts, took one taste of Smith's chili, seemed to go into convulsions, his face red and contorted, and fell to the floor. It was impossible for him to cast a vote. His taste buds had quit functioning. It was decided to have a run-off the next year, but that never came to pass. Smith came down with a case of the hives (86).

The cook-off continued, however, becoming bigger and bigger, with musical groups moving in for part of the fun. Too many free spirits, too many liquids to wash the stuff down with, and too few johns led to a bit of trouble.

Things have changed now. There is plumbing. And there are rules.

Lyndon Johnson suggested chili be named the state food of Texas. The chili cooked at the LBJ ranch was made by this recipe:

PEDERNALES RIVER CHILI

4 pounds chili meat
1 large chopped onion
2 cloves of garlic
1 teaspoon oregano (wild marjoram)
1 teaspoon ground cumin seeds
6 teaspoons chili powder
2 16-ounce cans of tomatoes
Salt to suit you
2 cups hot water

Put the meat, onion, and garlic cloves (finely chopped) in a large skillet and sear until light brown. Add the other ingredients, bring to a boil, lower the heat, and simmer for an hour with the cover on the skillet. Skim off the grease. This will serve 12. (Tolbert, 14–15)

Tolbert wrote that the original Texas chili never had vegetables in it except for the chili peppers and the spices. There were no tomatoes or onions added—and never beans. The chili was made with bite-size or coarsely ground meat—beef or venison or both (but never veal) cooked slowly with oregano, comino, and chopped garlic.

Contrary to popular thinking, chili is not an authentic Mexican dish. It was sold on the square in San Antonio in the last decades of the nineteenth century, but prior to that there are no accounts of such a dish. Tolbert seemed to think it originated with poor folks who hashed their meat for stew and threw in some chilis. To the Mexicans, chili means the pepper, not a bowl of red.

Alexander Sweet, in his 1885 column, "Texas Siftings," would surely have provoked a response from Tolbert with his observations about eating chili in San Antonio:

During the broiling heat of the mid-day sun, the Military Plaza is as deserted as a lemonade stand at a Kentucky fair. It is no exag-

Market Plaza, San Antonio, 1878–79, by Thomas Allen. *Courtesy San Antonio Museum Association, San Antonio, Texas.*

geration to say it is as vacant as the mind of a man who does not read newspapers. It is as destitute of people as a green watermelon is of hair.

But it is not so after the shades of night have begun to fall. The visitor who strolls around that ancient Plaza, that has so oft resounded to the clash of arms between Spanish cavaliers and the Indian hordes, will observe campfires. He will see an array of tables and benches, and he will be assailed by the smell of something cooking. At the fire are numerous pots and kettles, around which are dusky female figures, and faces that are suggestive of "the weird sisters" whose culinary proclivities were such a source of annoyance to MacBeth.

These are the *chile con carne* stands, at which this toothsome viand is sold to all who have the money and inclination to patronize them.

Chile con carne is a dish, which literally translated means "pepper with meat." . . . There is nothing hotter than these little red *chile* peppers with which the Mexican seasons everything he eats. After these *chile* peppers have been kept on ice a week or so, they still retain sufficient heat to blister the mouth of an Alaskan river. . . .

The innocent stranger who takes a mouthful of *chile con carne* never inquires what the other ingredients are. His only thought is how to obtain the services of the fire department to put out the fire in the roof of his mouth. The incandescent glow is almost as heated as is the language he uses after his mouth has sufficiently cooled down to enable him to use it for conventional purposes. . . .

To relish *chile con carne* when eaten for the first time, it is indispensable that the would-be junketer have his throat lined with some uncombustible substance, and a ceiling of fire-proof bricks inserted in the roof of his mouth. (187)

A traveler, feeling under the weather, stopped by a cabin where he was offered a toddy "garnteed" to make him forget his ailment. In good faith, the sick man gulped down the drink. His insides broke into flames. When he gained enough breath, he asked what he had drunk. It was whiskey strained many times through red hot chili pods.

Hallowe'en

All peoples set aside a time for commemoration of the dead toward the end of the year. Custom and costume attest to the endurance of a centuries-old story of a pilgrim who, as he was returning from the Holy Land, came upon a hole in the earth from which he heard the groans of the dead. Frightened, he sought solace from the holy fathers who at length set aside the first days of November for a religious celebration of the life/death cycle.

November 1 was named All Saints' Day; November 2 All Souls' Day, and the night of October 31 was All Hallow Even, or Holy Evening. Witches and evil spirits were abroad on that evening but had to leave before the advent of All Saints' Day. Traditionally children have costumed themselves as spirits and played pranks on Holy Evening, now called Halloween. After the merrymaking, there is a party, where dipping for apples or catching one suspended from a string with one's teeth is traditional—and comes from a divination ritual of the ancient Druids.

Halloween is the time for revelry. *Courtesy the Southwest Collection, Texas Tech University.*

The jack-o'-lantern had its origin in the Will-o'-the-Wisp, the phosphorescent light that hovers over swampy ground on autumn nights. The light was thought to lead travelers astray, into bogs or over cliffs. Will, the folk said, was an elf bearing the soul of a dead man and carrying a lantern to help him find a place of rest. The practice of making a jack-o'-lantern by hollowing out a pumpkin, cutting a face in it, and placing a candle inside for keeping spooks away could have originated in the Southwest, where the native pumpkin grows to plumpness in the fall and is last to be harvested, along with the corn. Pranksters on the prowl for friendly people to fill their trick-or-treat bags with goodies look on the pumpkin face as an invitation to come knocking.

Though apples and pumpkins are important to Halloween celebrations, these are not the refreshments. Hot dogs, soda pop, and marshmallows roasted over a bonfire—to keep away the witches—are the popular fare.

A numbskull thought his pumpkin was an ass's egg. He threw it into the bushes. It broke. A frightened rabbit ran out of the bushes. "Oh," said the numbskull, "look at the ass's colt."

Apples by the barrel in time for Halloween. *Courtesy John Black Collection, East Texas State University.*

APPLE LORE

An apple a day keeps the doctor away. This is a modern version of "Eat an apple going to bed,/Make the doctor beg his bread."

One rotten apple ruins the barrelful.

An apple-shaped birthmark may be removed by frequent rubbings with an apple.

An apple for the teacher is a token of respect.

An apple is a love charm.

An apple before you retire will give you uninterrupted sleep.

Apples are the fruit of the gods.

Apples insure knowledge, eloquence, and perpetual youth.

Eating an apple will clean your teeth.

•

RIDDLE

An apple with worms is bad 'tis true;
But what is worse than that to you?
(*Answer: Half a worm in an apple.*)

Día de los Muertos—almost picnic time. *Courtesy John O. West, El Paso.*

Among the Mexican population in Texas, *El Día de los Muertos* is one of the most important of Mexican religious observances. The Mexicans accept death as part of life. Their philosophy is pre-Christian: life goes on, the cycle continues. Surely there is fear of death, and to satirize the figure of death and joke about death may be their way of ingratiating themselves with the Grim Reaper.

It is important to remember, however, in talking about Mexican customs, that what is true in Brownsville may not be true of customs in Laredo. There are, it is said, some fifty-nine different ethnic groups in Mexico, and those coming into Texas bring many variations of their festivals.

On November 1, the Mexican people will prepare altars in their homes for the *angelitos*, the little children who have died. Little toys, paper dolls, candies children like, foods, and flowers will be offered before the altar, for it is believed the spirits of the dead will come back on that day and they should be fed. Even if they cannot eat, they can inhale the odors of the offerings.

November 2 is the day for adults. There are prayers of gratitude for the gift of life and for talents ancestors have bestowed on their descendants. On the altar there will be fruits, tamales, tortillas of blue or red corn, sweets, chocolate, *alote* (a corn flour drink), and *pan del muerto*, a special bread. Sometimes the breads have particles on top to represent bones and the whole loaf is covered with sugar.

All of the foods will be extraordinary, not everyday food: *molé* for example, and pumpkin cooked in molasses, and ornate candied skulls. The candies are made of a sugar almond paste (basically egg whites, refined sugar, and lemon beat together to the texture of a paste), molded in the shape of a skull or miniature animal, and decorated with vegetable coloring.

Following the ritual before the home altar, the celebrants will take the offerings in a processional to the cemetery, where everything is spread on the graves for the dead. When the ritual ends, the people eat the foods. Joe Graham of Kingsville says the entire ritual, with the trip to the cemetery, can be observed in the Big Bend area and around Presidio.

Tailgating

Tailgating, an autumnal ritual practiced one to two hours before another rite involving the manipulations of a pigskin ball among Mustangs, Longhorns, Cougars, Owls, and Horned Frogs, has become Texas tradition. Although there is no recorded history of the tailgate tradition, it appears likely that eating at the site of a football game prior to its start has a practical reason behind it. Traffic around a stadium at game time is thick. Since it is a good idea to arrive early enough to beat the traffic, fans find a way to pass the time until the game starts.

A meal can be spread on the tailgate of a station wagon or pickup truck with everybody eating buffet style and standing around to eat. Vans that have a back opening and cars with a commodious trunk serve as well. The meal may be prepared by one person, or several families may contribute a dish or drinks or eating equipment and "spread" together.

A typical Saturday at the stadium at Texas Christian University in Fort Worth revealed styles of tailgating. Some spread purple cloths on picnic tables which the university scattered under trees in order to accommodate tailgaters. Others opened up trunks to distribute the food and used hoods as tables. There were folding tables and lawn chairs at several cars. The smells wafted on the breeze caused the neighborhood dogs to stand at the perimeters and smile as hopeful dogs smile. Food ranged all the way from a sack of McDonald's taste treats enjoyed by a young couple sitting on the hood of their sports car to barbecue sandwiches purchased from a catering truck to the full-scale Football Orgy of baked beans, potato salad, fried chicken, sandwiches, sheath cake, cold drinks, iced tea, and grilled-on-the-grounds hamburgers and steaks. You name it, people were eating it. Then, wearing big smiles of contentment, the crowd went inside the stadium and watched the Horned Frogs beat the hell out of the Brigham Young Mormons—in a Christian way, of course.

The recipes and menus for most tailgating parties are not out of the ordinary and may be found in any good cookbook. It is the "extra" dishes, sometimes out of the ordinary but never trouble to make, that make the menu special. Here is one from Ann Gibson:

CORNED BEEF BISCUITS

1 12-ounce can of corned beef, unchilled
2 cups sifted all-purpose flour
3 teaspoons baking powder
1/2 teaspoon salt
1/4 cup shortening
2/3 cup milk
1 cup grated cheese

Flake the corned beef. Sift the dry ingredients; stir in corned beef and cheese. Drop in the shortening and mix up. Add milk and blend. Turn dough out onto lightly floured board and knead for 1/2 minute. Pat dough out to a 1/4-inch thickness. Cut with a biscuit cutter or into bite-sized squares. Bake on a greased sheet at 450 degrees for 12 minutes or so. Freeze. Before the game, heat in oven or microwave. Put hot biscuits in foil and put in an insulated food tote.

Thanksgiving

Agricultural peoples have always had communal religious celebrations and feasts to mark the final gathering of the crops. Such old rituals are still observed among Rio Grande Pueblo peoples, such as the Tiguas in El Paso. The autumn equinox is the time for the Winter Chief to take over. There is a dance lasting the better part of a day, or perhaps for several days, and ending with feasting. The costumes for this ritual dance have red ribbons or yarns to ward off cold, and the dancers wear silver jewelry, their symbol of the cold. The dance is a procession with two lines of men and women stomping lightly in place to put the earth to sleep. These are solemn, religious occasions with only the sound of the drums and chanting to break the silence. The entire village attends, and the women prepare food for the feast that follows.

Other Texans celebrate Thanksgiving, along with the rest of their countrymen, by having a traditional dinner with turkey and trimmings to commemorate the story of the Pilgrims and to pray for continued good fortune. Then they fall to gorging and drinking—this, too, an old custom predating modern refrigeration: eat all you can while there is plenty.

Still other Texans have their own way to celebrate, what with their obsession with football. It seems the religious origins of the day are lost as football fans gather for a different kind of autumnal ritual. But it is interesting that throughout the Southwest there are prehistoric ball courts among the ruins where it is believed the Indians held competitive games along with their seasonal rituals. And just as praying and feasting were part of the ball games, so the sport-loving Texans have their tailgate parties, take their places in the stands, and solemnly bow their heads in prayer a moment or two before the whistle blows for the line-up.

Returning thanks. *Courtesy Otha C. Spencer, Commerce.*

After Grandpa had thanked the Almighty and had blessed everybody, living and dead, he looked around the table and said sternly, "God bless everything on this table except the dishrag." Grandma jumped up in shame to remove it.

—Charles Linck, Commerce

•

The preacher had been invited to dinner. Everything was on the table and the family and guest sat down, making room for the four-year-old blonde cherub. In the pregnant pause before the meal began, the child spoke out loud and clear: "God damn, we haven't asked the blessing."

—Anonymous

•

The War Between the States still rouses emotions among Southerners. My grandfather, who saw his father shot down by a Yankee during that war, lived to see his favorite daughter married to an outsider from the North. At Thanksgiving dinner, where all the family had gathered, he delivered his usual lengthy blessing. Then, just as everyone anticipated his "Amen," he burst out vehemently, "And God bless everyone at this table—except the God damn Yankee."

—Sam Sewell, Richardson

•

A slightly slurred blessing: Thank you for this food that we are bowed to eat in your many blessings. Amen.

Emily Thom, formerly of Houston, calls the family traditional Thanksgiving dinner "a true groaning board." She says, "It makes me think of the many long hours of preparation before and the cleaning up after dinner." But then she adds, "The memories of many wonderful meals with family all around make it all worthwhile." This is her menu:

Salted Pecans   White Wine
Roast Turkey
with
Corn Bread Dressing and Giblet Gravy
Waldorf Salad
Relish Dish
with
Pickled Onions, Pickled Okra, Sweet Pickles and Dill Pickles
Chilled Cranberry Sauce, sliced
Green Beans Supreme
Mashed Irish Potatoes   Southern Sweet Potato Casserole
Buttered Homemade Rolls with Honey/Apricot Jam
White Wine
Southern Pecan Pie
Old-Fashioned Mincemeat Pie with Brandy Hard Sauce
Pumpkin Pie with Whipped Cream
Coffee

SALTED PECANS

Spread pecans on a cookie sheet. Salt to taste. For a pound of pecans, use up to 1/2 pound of butter, melted. Pour the butter evenly over the pecans. Put into a slow oven (200–250 degrees) and bake for 20 minutes or until the pecans are lightly browned. Stir them every 3 to 4 minutes as they will burn easily.

ROAST TURKEY

Allow a pound per person when you purchase the turkey. Let it thaw in the refrigerator. This will take several days. Turkey spoils easily, so do not let it stand on your drainboard or immersed in water for thawing. When it is thawed, wash it thoroughly with warm soda water. Dry the turkey with a cloth. Rub the inside with salt: a good measure of salt is one-half teaspoon per pound of fowl.

Truss the bird so that the wings are bent behind the back and the legs are close to the body. Now place the bird in a large roasting pan with the breast up. Brush the bird with melted butter or cover it with bacon strips. Cover it with a cloth.

Leave the pan uncovered and roast in a slow oven (300 degrees) until tender. It is better to use a meat thermometer; as you want to serve turkey well done, you should let it reach a heat of 185 degrees. This will take about 20 minutes per pound. Baste the bird often with pan drippings so that it will not dry out. When it is half cooked, salt the outside with another half-teaspoon per pound. Remove the cloth for the last 30 minutes of roasting time so that the turkey will be nicely browned.

CORN BREAD DRESSING

Baked corn bread
Stale light bread
Onions
Celery
Bell pepper
Bacon drippings or butter
Jalapeño peppers or Tabasco sauce
Poultry seasoning
Red pepper
Sugar
Eggs
Milk
Turkey or chicken broth

Use equal parts of corn bread and stale light bread, the amount depending on size of turkey and number of people to be served.

Crumble the breads together in a large mixing bowl. For about 8 cups of crumbs, chop 3 onions, 6 ribs of celery, and 1 bell pepper, fine. Sauté in about 4 tablespoons of bacon drippings or butter (drippings add to flavor) until onions are clear.

Mix with crumbs and add salt and black pepper to taste. Add about 3 teaspoons of poultry seasoning, about 1 tablespoon of jalapeño pepper chopped fine (or 3 dashes Tabasco). If you like the taste of sage, you can add it, too, according to your taste. Also add about 2 teaspoons of red pepper and 1 tablespoon sugar. Stir all this together well. Beat 4 eggs and stir them into the crumb mixture. Now add broth and hot water to moisten and then enough milk to make slightly mushy.

Pour into a greased pan and bake at 325 degrees for about an hour. The dressing should not be dry, but if you overcook it, pour some more of the turkey broth over the dressing to moisten.

It is better not to stuff the turkey because of the danger of spoilage.

GIBLET GRAVY

To prepare the stock, boil several cups of water with 2 ribs of celery, a carrot sliced, 1 small onion chopped, and several sprigs of parsley. Add the giblets (the heart, the gizzard, and liver) and the neck, also the wing tips if you have cut them off. Simmer all these ingredients until the liver is tender. Remove it. Continue cooking until the gizzard is tender. Now remove the meat and strain the stock.

Strain the drippings from the roasted turkey. Spoon off the fat. Heat 4 tablespoons of fat (use margarine if you want to avoid animal fat). Add 4 tablespoons flour. Blend. Stir in 2 cups of pan drippings and stock. Add stock until you have the desired thickness. Now add the chopped giblets. You may add some seasonings, but taste first.

WALDORF SALAD

2 apples, unpeeled, coarsely chopped
3/4 cup celery, chopped
1/2 cup walnuts, chopped
Sprinkle with:
2 tablespoons lemon juice
2 tablespoons sugar
2 tablespoons mayonnaise
Toss lightly and serve cold. *Serves 8.*

PICKLED OKRA
(canned in season)

Wash okra, leaving stems on. Pack into sterilized jars, taking care not to break the pods. In each jar place a chili pepper, 1 clove garlic, and 1 head fresh dill.

Mix a quart of cider vinegar with an equal amount of water, about a half cup of salt, 1 clove garlic, 1 chili pepper, 1 teaspoon celery seed, and 1 teaspoon dill seed. Bring to a boil and continue boiling for 5 minutes. Pour the hot liquid over the okra and seal. Process in hot water bath for 10 minutes. Remove and let cool.

GREEN BEANS SUPREME

2 cans vertical packed green beans
1/2 pound bacon strips, cut in half
1 cup bean juice
1/4 cup brown sugar
1/2 teaspoon allspice
Salt and pepper
Wrap half-slices of bacon around 8 or 9 beans. Fasten with a

wooden toothpick. Continue making bundles of beans wrapped in bacon until all the beans are used. Put the bundles in a shallow baking dish as close together as possible. Mix the bean juice with brown sugar and seasonings. Pour over the beans and bake at 400 degrees for about 25 minutes or until the bacon is browned. Turn and baste once during the cooking. Serve hot.

SOUTHERN SWEET POTATO CASSEROLE

1 cup sugar
2 eggs
1/2 stick softened butter
1 large can sweet potatoes
1 teaspoon cinnamon
1 cup milk

Mash potatoes and blend all other ingredients with them. Pour into a well-buttered casserole.

Mix until crumbly: 1/2 cup sugar, 1/2 cup flour, 1/2 stick butter, and 1/2 cup finely chopped pecans. Sprinkle this mixture over the top of the sweet potatoes.

Bake at 350 degrees for 1 hour, or until the potatoes are set.

BUTTERED ROLLS

Mix and bring to a boil 1 cup water, 1 cup shortening, 1 teaspoon salt, and 3/4 cup sugar. Set aside to cool to lukewarm.

Dissolve 2 yeast cakes in 1 cup warm water. When lukewarm, beat well and add 2 eggs. Mix well. Put all the liquids together in a warm bowl.

Gradually add 5 1/2 to 6 cups of unsifted all-purpose flour to the liquids. Let stand for 1 hour. Punch down.

Roll 1/2-inch thin and cut out, fold in half, and brush insides with melted butter. Arrange on pie tins or cookie sheets so sides will touch when they have risen. Let stand and rise for about 2 to 2 1/2 hours. For rising, room temperature should be around 80 degrees. The top of the refrigerator is a good place. Bake at 425 degrees for 10 to 15 minutes or until brown. Halfway through cooking, switch the pans on the top and bottom racks of the oven so they will brown evenly.

MINCE PIE

Buy prepared mincemeat packed in a glass jar, not the condensed cake kind. Use two cups. Add 1 1/2 cups unsweetened applesauce and 1/2 cup crushed pineapple, drained well. Fill an unbaked pie shell with this mixture. Cover it with a lattice top of pastry. Bake in a hot oven (450 degrees) for about 30 minutes.

BRANDY SAUCE

Beat 2 to 5 tablespoons butter until soft and add to 1 cup confectioners' sugar. Blend until smooth.

Add 1/8 teaspoon salt and 1 teaspoon or more of brandy. Beat in 1/4 cup cream and continue mixing until smooth.

EASY PECAN PIE

1 cup sugar
3 eggs
1 cup white Karo syrup
1 teaspoon vanilla
1 tablespoon liquid margarine
1 cup pecans (halves or pieces)

Stir eggs and sugar until well blended. Stir in remaining ingredients. Cook in unbaked 9-inch pie shell with high fluted edge, in a 350 degree oven for 45 minutes.

PUMPKIN PIE

2 eggs, slightly beaten
2 cups pumpkin (1 16-ounce can)
3/4 cup sugar (half brown if you like)
1/2 teaspoon salt
1 teaspoon ground cinnamon
1/2 teaspoon ground ginger
1/4 teaspoon ground cloves
1 can evaporated milk (12 to 13 fluid ounces) or 1 1/2 cups half-and-half
1 9-inch unbaked homemade pie shell with high fluted edge

Preheat oven to 425 degrees. Combine ingredients in order given. Pour into pie shell. Bake 15 minutes. Reduce heat to 350 degrees and bake about 45 minutes or until a knife inserted near the center comes out clean. Cool before serving.

Serve with whipped cream.

Laura Hamner told a story about pioneer woman Florence Harrington's Thanksgiving cake. The XIT boys had come before cold weather set in to clean the Harrington meadows of waist-high grass that was growing up to the door. Out of gratitude, Mrs. Harrington said, "Boys, if I had some eggs, I'd bake you a cake for Thanksgiving."

The boys couldn't let a chance like that go by. They showed up with four dozen eggs they had separated from their cook. Florence put the eggs in a box that had been nailed to the wall of a new room her husband was finishing up. He was outside nailing on some stripping. His hammering dislodged the box and the eggs smashed to the floor.

Florence was dismayed, but not for long. After all, the floor was new; it was clean enough. She scooped up the mess of eggs and proceeded to make the cake.

The XIT boys felt themselves well rewarded.

MAXIMS YOU SHOULD OUGHT TO KNOW
ACCORDING TO TEXANS

Don't lend or borrow salt or pepper; it will break up a friendship. If you must borrow one or the other, don't pay it back.

Don't drain a teakettle dry, as unlucky things will happen to you.

Bubbly champagne means the devil is in it.

If you pour tea back into the kettle, it is a sign of trouble.

Proteins and starches eaten at the same time will explode in your stomach.

Carbonated drinks will eat up your stomach.

Eating at irregular times causes stomach trouble.

When little bubbles appear in a cup of fresh coffee, that's money for you.

A stranger is coming if a tea leaf floats in a pot of tea. To stop the stranger from coming, butter the stem of the leaf and throw it under the table.

Tea will cause barrenness and sterility.

To forget to put coffee or tea in the pot is a sure sign company is coming.

Rub whiskey and salt on a baby's head to make his hair curly. The informant places great faith in this treatment; three of her six sons have curly hair.

Eating a chicken neck will make you pretty.

To make soup meat more tender, place the lid of a Mason jar in with the ingredients as they cook.

If you stir your milk with a fork, the cow will go dry.

Never tell a dream until you have broken your fast.

If you are working in the kitchen and a knife drops out of your hand, it's a sure sign you will quarrel with your husband.

If a girl eats from a frying pan, it will rain on her wedding day.

Diabetes can be cured by eating sauerkraut and vinegar.

For major burns, rub butter on the burn for five to ten minutes. Then brown 1/2 cup of flour and put it in a cheesecloth. Dust this on the burned place. It will help bring the color back.

For boils or stone bruises, use scrapings of homemade lye soap mixed with a tablespoon or two of sugar or molasses and apply as a salve or poultice.

For boils, make a poultice of bacon rind or of prickly pear.

You will dry up your blood if you eat a lemon a day.

A mixture of wild plum bark, sugar, and whiskey, boiled, will stop asthma attacks.

MORE MAXIMS

Asthma and T.B. can be cured with a syrup made by silkweed [milkweed] root, adding honey and pine tar in equal quantities. The mix must be taken at least three times daily until the person is well.

Kill a rattlesnake and boil in a wash pot. Skim oil from the top and drop warm into the ear. The oil can be kept in a bottle for future earaches.

Make a small cloth sack and partially fill with salt. Warm the sack on the stove and place in the ear for earaches. The salt holds the heat.

Use rattlesnake oil to cure corns, calluses, bunions, and hard skin on the heels.

After the birth of a baby, a mother must abstain from all acidic foods (oranges, lemons, etc.); otherwise she will not conceive again.

Children should not eat mustard, because it makes their feet stink.

If a baby's navel protrudes, bury a hen egg on the southeast corner of the house with a little part of the egg out of the ground. When the egg rots, the navel will go down.

For a burn, apply soda and molasses or linseed oil.

Soda and vanilla extract paste is good to relieve the pain of burns.

For cold, cough, or sore throat, take mullein tea, turpentine and sugar, horehound tea, or honey and whiskey, or hot lemonade.

Yerba de la vibora [snakebite plant] is also good for colds. Boil this weed with two drops of turpentine. Drink the mix while it is hot.

Honeycomb chewed every day for one month before hay fever season will prevent an attack or make it milder.

Drinking a mix of honey and vinegar before going to bed each night will help make you fertile.

If you wash your face with buttermilk before 6:00 a.m., your freckles will go away.

To keep healthy, use this liniment: 2 pounds hog lard, 1 pound rosin, 1 pound beeswax, 1 pound cayenne pepper. Melt together over a fire. Take from the fire and stir until you can bear your finger in it, then add 1 ounce of sassafras oil. Stir until nearly cold.

For heart trouble, boil a roadrunner (paisano) and eat it.

Put cow's milk in a fruit jar nearly full of water and watch it. If it clears up fast, you can expect a mild winter. But if it stays cloudy and foggy for a long time, there is going to be a bad, cold, wet winter.

End of the Year Chuck

Christmas on the Range

So that I may raise corn,
So that I may raise beans,
So that I may raise wheat,
So that I may raise squash,
So that with all good fortune I may be blessed.
PUEBLO INDIAN WINTER SOLSTICE PRAYER

Between Thanksgiving and Christmas a ranch cook had some time to demonstrate his culinary prowess. He would roast wild turkey. Or he would dig a pit and, over sweet mesquite coals, lay steaks across the branding irons for broiling. When the cook finally got a portable stove, he could prepare mince and pumpkin for holiday pies:

MINCE PIES

Boil and chop very fine 4 pounds of lean beef and 2 pounds fresh beef suet. Add 2 pounds brown sugar, 2 ounces ground spices, grated rind of 6 lemons, 1 pint brandy, 1 pint wine, 2 pounds raisins, 2 pounds currants, 2 pounds citron. Chop the raisins with 6 apples; add the other fruit to the mixture. Add 2 teaspoons of salt. Stir all together.

Bake as needed for two-crust pies.

MOCK MINCE PIE

1 cup sugar
1 cup corn syrup or molasses
3/4 cup vinegar
1 cup chopped raisins
1/2 cup melted butter
1 cup nuts
2 or 3 apples, chopped fine
4 crackers, broken up, over which pour a cup of boiling water
1 pinch salt
1 teaspoon cinnamon
1 teaspoon cloves
1/2 teaspoon allspice
Mix and bake in pie shell.

> Spell pumpkin pie:
> P-U umpki umpkin, I
> P-U umpkin,
> Pumpkin pie.

PUMPKIN PIE

Wash and cut a pumpkin crosswise. Remove the seeds and what you can of the strings. Place it in a pan shell side up, and bake in a moderate oven (325 degrees) until it begins to fall apart and is tender. Scrape the pulp from the shell and put it through a ricer or strainer.

For two pies, use 1 1/2 cups pumpkin. Mix with 2 egg yolks, 2/3 cup brown sugar, 1/2 teaspoon ginger, 1/2 teaspoon cinnamon, 1 1/2 cups milk, 1/2 cup cream, and 1 teaspoon vanilla.

For a different flavor, add the juice and rind of a small lemon or 2 tablespoons of brandy.

Whip two egg whites until stiff with 1/2 teaspoon salt. Fold them into the pumpkin mixture. Fill the pie shells and bake for 15 minutes in a hot oven (450 degrees). Lower the temperature to 350 degrees and bake for another 30 minutes or until the custard is set.

Not all the cowboys would be so fortunate, as S. Omar Barker wrote in "Bunkhouse Christmas":

'Twas Christmas Eve out on the ranch, and all the winter crew
Was settin' 'round the bunkhouse fire with nothin' else to do
But let their fancies wander on the thoughts of Christmas chuck,

And what they'd like the best to eat if just they had the luck
To set down to a table where the feast was laid so thick
That all they'd have to do was reach to take their choice and pick.

Young Sleepy Kid, the wrangler, claims he'd love a stummick-ache
From stuffin' steady half a day on choclit- frosted cake.
"A slab of turkey breast," smacks Pete, "and good ol' punkin pie!"
"I'd reach for oyster dressin'!" Lobo Luther heaves a sigh.
"It ain't no Christmas feed for me," says little Charlie Moss,
"Without brown turkey gravy and some red cranberry sauce!"
"Mince pie!" avers ol' Swaller-Fork. "The kind my ma could make.
It beats your punkin forty ways—and also choclit cake!"

So each they named their fancy, till their chops begun to drip,
Then ol' Pop Williams gives a snort and rubs his crippled hip.
He hitches to the window, sorter sizin' up the night.
"Well, boys," he says, "it's Christmas Eve, and if I figger right,
That snow's too deep for travel, so before I hit the hay,
Upon the subject now in hand I'll have my little say.
It ain't what's in your stummick that's the most important part.
It's the feelin's of your gizzard, or in other words, your heart.
A-doin' others kindness is the road to Christmas cheer,
But that, of course, ain't possible, the way we're snowbound here.

It looks like all that we can do for our good Christmas deed
Is hustle all the livestock in and give 'em extry feed.
To hungry cows an extry fork of hay will seem as nice
As when a hungry cowboy finds a raisin in his rice.
And as for favorite Christmas chuck, I'll name mine now, to wit:
It's beef and beans and biskits—*'cause I know that's what we'll git!*"

(146)

If Barker's cowboys had lived in or around Motley County, their story of
"what we'll git" would have been quite different. Pioneer woman Lizzie Campbell held the first Christmas celebration in Motley County at the Matador
Ranch in 1880. She had waited weeks for the freight wagon to bring fixin's,
but the freighter failed to come in time. Laura Hamner told what Lizzie did:

What was Lizzie to have for Christmas dinner unless the freighter
came back with tame turkeys, fattened for the season, and cranberries? Wild turkeys were lean and their meat was hard and tough and
brown at this season, but she had two killed anyway. Years ago some
tame hogs had been turned loose in the thickets along the Pease
River and had grown fat on acorns. Two were killed and strips of fat
were laid on the stringy turkeys so that the grease would soak in and
season the turkey meat. Hams of the hogs, venison steak and ante-

lope stew with "sinkers," as the cowboys called dumplings, provided enough food for the boys to enjoy on Christmas day and to take home to the several line camps. Rich dressing was baked in the turkeys which were thus made into a luscious treat for Christmas. Wild plum jelly took the place of cranberries. Rice and canned corn were the only vegetables and apple pies, made of dried apples, served as dessert.

Lizzie had brought popcorn with her when she came that spring. Strings of popcorn, combined with colored leaves and berries from the breaks, formed the decorations for the tree. The walls rang with cries of joy when Lizzie came in with a big tin pan filled with pop-corn balls, the greatest treat for the cowboys.

One of the boys had been down in the state on a visit and had brought home a sack of pecans on his packhorse. He gave them to Lizzie. On Christmas afternoon, she let the boys play hull gull with them, pocketing their winnings for future enjoyment.

The first Christmas celebration in Motley County, Christmas of 1880, was a success, even though the decorations for the tree did not arrive until the following March. (130)

Christmas as described in this letter from a settler on the South Plains would indicate that the freight wagons were making regular runs toward the end of the century. There was no waiting until March for fixin's, as Nellie Witt Spikes has reported:

Emma, Texas
Summer, 1895

Dear Annie:

We made preparations for Christmas early this year. The boys got a nice cedar tree from the brakes and I did my baking several days ahead.

Wish you could have seen the table Christmas day! I used my yellow and white checked cloth with the fringe and set the tables with my blue dishes. The children polished the bone handled knives and forks in the sand several days before. There were six different kinds of cake, coconut, pound cake, fruit cake, whipped cream cake, pecan and jelly cake, cheese-apple and fried peach pies, egg custards and a cobbler made from wild green grapes. For meat we had baked prairie chicken with dressing, beef and antelope, and some nice quail. Also potato salad, six kinds of pickles and relishes, grape and plum jelly, salt rising bread and sour dough biscuits.

You may wonder where we get the milk and butter as I wrote you we never had any in the winter, but last summer we put up plenty of butter in brine and were fortunate to find a cow last fall with a young calf.

Hoping you are all well
Margaret

Christmas Customs Then and Now

Christmas in Texas has remnants of much of the folklore and religious customs of Europeans. In olden times the celebration took place on Christmas Eve and centered on the crèche. Later the Germans originated the custom of having the Christmas tree and gifts from Saint Nicholas on Christmas Day. The French began their celebration on Christmas Eve and continued through January Sixth, the feast and giving of gifts to coincide with the arrival of the Wise Men in Bethlehem.

Today children will leave a plate of cookies, some candies, and a glass of milk for Santa Claus. This is like an old Swedish custom of setting out a meal for the spirits to enjoy while the family is away at church.

The Reverend W. M. Elliott and his family enjoy Christmas dinner, Colorado City, 1952. *Courtesy the Southwest Collection, Texas Tech University.*

The custom of having roast pig—a meat popularized recently in Texas university communities, where a Feast of Carols is presented along with a traditional English Christmas feast—is derived from the Scandinavian countries. Brought into the great hall garnished with an apple in its mouth, it was an offering to the Norse Goddess Frey to induce successful crops for the coming year.

The Christmas tree too was a sacrificial token. The family would select a fruit tree during the bearing season, the most beautiful and bountiful tree in the fields. It would be marked and, for Christmas, cut, brought into the house, and decorated for the festivities. Today we have fruit-like ornaments for the trees. And an orange in the stocking is a symbol of nature's bounty when the gods are appeased.

Oranges in early Texas were a rare treat—hard to come by and costly. There might be no gifts under the tree, but a luscious, juicy orange for each child was a piece of gold in the toe of a Christmas stocking.

The fruitcake is yet another offering to the gods of fertility to insure good harvests. The more fruits, the more pleasing to the gods. And there must be currants, for the grapevine is a sign of peace and plenty.

After the gifts and the midday feast, there is visiting. People of English heritage will say that for every cake tasted in a friend's house on Christmas Day, a month will be added to your life.

Denise Anderson of Austin tells about the fruitcakes her mother made:

CHRISTMAS FRUITCAKE

Mother started preparing for her Christmas fruitcakes in watermelon time. After we had eaten an especially plump and sweet melon some July afternoon, she would take the rinds and make preserves. One good melon would yield about 4 pounds of rind.

The outer green skin and whatever was left of pink flesh were cut away. The rind was then cut into 1/2 inch cubes. The cubed rind was soaked in lime water (1 tablespoon to 1 quart of water) for an hour. Then it was drained and allowed to stand in fresh water another hour, drained again, boiled for 1 1/2 hours in fresh water, and drained again. This process was for crispness.

Now that the rind was prepared, she boiled 2 lemons cut into thin slices for 5 or so minutes in about 1/2 cup water. Then she took 4 quarts of water (less the 1/2 cup used for the lemons) and 4 pounds of sugar and boiled the mixture until it made a syrup. The watermelon rind (and some ginger root if desired) was added, and the whole pot was put to boil until the syrup was thick and the melon clear. This had to be stirred frequently to avoid sticking. The preserves were then placed in sterilized jars, sealed by processing for 5 minutes in a boiling water bath, and put away for cake-baking time during the Thanksgiving holiday.

This was her cake recipe: she creamed 2 pounds of sugar and 1 pound of butter until light and fluffy, then added 10 eggs, well beaten. Next she put in 1 pound of flour, 1 teaspoon of baking powder, and 1 tablespoon each of ground cinnamon, mace, nutmeg, and cloves, which had been sifted together. Last she worked in 2 pounds of raisins, 2 pounds of currants, a pound of citron sliced fine, some of the drained watermelon rind preserves, whatever candied fruit she had, like cherries and pineapple, and a pound of chopped pecans, all dredged in a little flour so that they would not sink to the bottom of the cake as it baked.

Some cooks will add a glass of brandy, but my mother, after baking her cakes in a slow oven (250 to 300 degrees) for 2 to 3 hours, wrapped the cakes in cheesecloth and kept them moist until Christmas by spooning bourbon over them quite often.

She made big cakes, small cakes, round cakes, and square cakes. Then she had special gifts for special friends when the holiday lights went on.

CHRISTMAS FOLK SAYINGS

If you eat too much and get indigestion, wear a penny around your neck.

If you have eaten so much your stomach is upset, turn your medicine glass upside down under the bed.

Enough is as good as a feast.

After dinner, rest a while; after supper, walk a mile.

If the sun shines through an apple tree on Christmas Day, there will be a good crop next year.

Edith Cashatt had a cafe on Dodson Prairie in Palo Pinto County. One week before Christmas Day, she would have her own celebration for friends and neighbors. She would get a cedar tree—it's hard to come by a well-shaped cedar tree because deer and cattle eat the limbs off—and she would make it "flossy" (Hittson, 31). She would serve barbecued venison, sometimes beef, and one year she had ham. This is her way to prepare the venison for pit barbecuing:

Take either the fore or hind quarters. Place the meat in a utensil large enough to hold it and cover it with vinegar and water, one part of vinegar to nine parts water. Marinate for several hours, making sure the meat is completely covered. Drain. Next peel off the fibrous membrane just under the skin. Let the meat marinate for another two hours in more vinegar and water. Then rinse it and dry.

Slice some apples and onions. Place the meat in the pit (or an oven if you prefer) and cook it covered with apples and onions. If the meat is to be turned, remove the apples and onions and then place them on the top side again. When the meat is done and tender, gouge it with an ice pick many times. Now pour a barbecue sauce over the meat and continue to baste with the sauce until you are ready to serve it. (Hittson, 64)

Edith also made a prune cake for her celebration, adapted from a recipe more than two centuries old, she said, handed down by Irish ancestors:

PALO PINTO PRUNE CAKE

1 cup sugar
3 eggs
1 cup Wesson oil
1 1/2 cups all-purpose flour
1 teaspoon each soda, cinnamon, nutmeg, allspice
1 teaspoon vanilla
1 cup buttermilk
1 cup cooked, pitted prunes, chopped with juice
1 cup pecans or walnuts

Blend sugar, oil and eggs. Mix dry ingredients and add to creamed mixture. Add milk and vanilla, then prunes and nuts. Butter the tube pan, set oven at 300 degrees. Bake one hour.

Cover with glaze:

1 cup sugar
1/2 cup buttermilk
1/2 teaspoon soda
1 tablespooon Karo syrup
1 stick butter
1/2 teaspoon vanilla

Bring ingredients to a boil. Stir and cook over medium heat until you have a thick syrup, about 12 to 15 minutes. Have glaze ready when you take the cake from the oven. Pour the glaze over the hot cake so that the cake is soaked.

> Year of snow
> Fruit will grow

Madeline Sullivan of Scatterbranch tells that when she was a little girl, her grandfather, James Monroe Bailey, whose place was at Garza (now Lake Dallas), would help her shoot her firecrackers every Christmas. He would put a firecracker under a can to make a loud explosion, and they would have quite a time, just the two of them together. And, without fail, during the years, he would tell her about the Christmas in 1883 when they had the firing (or shooting) of the anvils.

Christmas Day at the Bailey home was quiet, with just family. They had had their eggnog the first thing on Christmas morning and had exchanged their little homemade gifts from under the tree. Of course, the most delightful gift of all was the orange in the stocking, for Christmas was the only time they had oranges. And they always had hard rock candies shaped like little animals.

There were three boys in the family: Shelton Augustus Bailey (Madeline's grandfather), Randolph (better known as Dolly), and Willis Tanzy (known by Will). About eleven on Christmas morning the boys put Dolly up to asking their father to let them shoot the anvils. He had the community blacksmith shop in addition to his farm, so he had anvils of different sizes. Now firing the anvils did two things. It gave noise and excitement to the day's festivities, and it also provided a way of sending Christmas greetings to the neighbors.

The father agreed and the boys set up the anvils down close to the creek so that the noise could be heard several miles away. The boys put gunpowder in the hole of the anvil, making a trail of gunpowder down the side. Then they would place another anvil on top. After they put fire to the trail, they would run like everything and squat or lie down because the blast would shake the earth. The more gunpowder they used, the louder the boom. When they put a little anvil on top, it would go sky-high. A big anvil wouldn't go so high, but how the earth did tremor!

They had fired several times when the near neighbors arrived in their buggy with their kids. In a little while another came, and then another.

It was lunchtime. The first arrivals ate Christmas dinner—the regular feast—with the family. Then more and more came, bringing their jellies and preserves, their cakes and pies. The family's goodies had disappeared, but everyone got fed. The mother, Teesie (her name was Lucretia), would send the boys back to the smokehouse for more hams and would put on another pan of biscuits. Madeline's grandfather said he couldn't count the pans of biscuits Teesie made that day. They were big round biscuits, high and fluffy, which she made by her own recipe, that is, by the pinch.

By three in the afternoon, her grandfather said, they had fed over a hundred people. Everybody had a marvelous time. The older boys brought their rifles and shotguns, firing them just for the fun of it and having target matches. The little children played at their games. The men talked about the weather, their horses, and their crops. The women kept the tables piled with food, washed dishes, brought their handwork, and talked about who was sick and what was going on in the neighborhood.

It was, indeed, a Texas Christmas to be remembered!

Favorite Christmas Recipes

German families favor sauerkraut and turkey for Christmas dinner, along with other side dishes. Minetta Goyne of Arlington wrote about preparing pumpkin the way her mother did, especially for the holiday season:

The dish is a nice alternative to cranberry or apple sauce with the standard roast turkey.

Cut one medium-sized (or two small) pumpkins into one-inch cubes, after having removed the peeling and seeds. Steam in about two cups of water in a covered pot, checking and stirring from time to time, until it is possible to mash the pumpkin. Cook a bit longer to reduce the moisture, then drain in a colander. Return the drained pumpkin pulp to the pot and add the following ingredients. The proportions here are for 4 cups of pulp (1 quart). Add the ingredients a bit gradually, since tastes differ and you may prefer more sugar and vinegar, or less of both or either. To 4 cups of pulp I add 1 1/2 cups of granulated sugar, 3/4 cup white vinegar (the kind not diluted with water), and 1 teaspoonful of ground cinnamon or 2 cinnamon sticks. Stir thoroughly, then cook over medium heat for about ten minutes, stirring repeatedly to let moisture escape and prevent burning of the mixture. At the end, add 1 lemon sliced into thin slices. The lemon is not essential, but it does improve the flavor and the appearance of the dish. It is equally tasty served warm or cold and can be kept in a covered container for a long time in the refrigerator. I would suggest it not be kept more than ten days, however.

Incidentally, use an enamel or (to be more modern) "Silver-stone" pot. Otherwise, the vinegar will give the dish a disagreeable metallic taste.

Minetta is not certain where the traditional family recipe got its start:

My feeling is that somebody in Mother's family (whether Zesch or Coreth I do not know) originated the recipe, although Mother may have invented the recipe herself. In any case, it is quite old (she would now be 102 years old and started housekeeping before she was twenty, in Irapuato, Mexico, incidentally; she was from a ranch outside New Braunfels). It was traditional in our family. I have wondered many times whether by any chance the idea suggested itself to earlier kin because of the sound of the first syllable of pumpkin and its similarity to the French *pomme.* Apples do not thrive in south Texas, and I would imagine that Germans and Austrians missed this fruit that is so common in their cuisine. Logically, if they gave it further thought, the idea breaks down, though. The ending *-kin,* as you know, is a north German diminutive (like standard or south German *-chen*). The pumpkin is obviously much bigger than an apple! It recalls to my mind a story in one of my grade-school readers in which Robert Bruce, the Scottish king, sat beneath a tree and puzzled over why the Creator had put such a big fruit or vegetable as the pumpkin on a frail vine and the small apple on such a sturdy tree. Then an apple fell on his head, proving him less wise than the Creator beyond a shadow of a doubt. (I went to a parochial school, as you might guess from this parable.) I had not thought of that story in well over fifty years until I wrote down the gist of it just now.

Most families have a favorite food that has become traditional for them. Reverend Harry O. Ball of Hunt County makes this sweet for his invalid wife for Christmas:

CARAMEL

Open one can sweetened condensed milk and set it in a saucepan of water on a burner, low to medium heat. Let it stand for two or three hours.

After an hour put a table knife in it. When the milk is solid, lift the caramelized milk out of the can by lifting the knife.

Billy Couts Hutcheson of Fort Worth always has custard for his special Christmas treat—and for New Year's also. This is a fancy dessert his mother made and served instead of eggnog. It is almost thin enough to pour:

CUSTARD

Mix together 1/2 cup sugar and 1 teaspoon flour. Beat 2 eggs with the sugar and flour. Scald 1 quart of whole milk (it must be whole milk; 2% won't do). Very slowly add the scalded milk to the egg mixture. Cook over very low heat and stir constantly until the mixture thickens and coats a silver spoon.

Add 1 teaspoon vanilla and a little cinnamon and nutmeg, if desired.

If the mixture is lumpy, beat it or put it in a blender at high speed. It can be served warm, or chilled, even frozen and served as ice cream.

Elly Hutcheson's favorite treat for the holiday season is strips of grapefruit peeling, boiled in sugar and water syrup until tender, then dried.

CANDIED CITRUS

3 large thick-skinned grapefruits or oranges
Cold water
1 1/2 cups light corn syrup
Sugar

Peel and cut rind into long narrow strips. Cover rind strips with cold water and bring to boiling. Drain. Repeat process three times, draining well after last time. Pour corn syrup over rinds. Cook slowly until rind is translucent. Remove each piece and let excess syrup drain off. Roll in sugar and allow to dry. This makes one pound.

German Apple-Cheese Salad is the favorite dish for Thanksgiving, Christmas, and New Year's in Barbara Dittmar's family in the Emblem community. Everyone in the family competes to see who will make it, and she says it will be carried on, for her middle son now makes it for his own family for special occasions.

GERMAN APPLE-CHEESE SALAD

Take equal portions of apples (peeled, cored, and chopped) and medium sharp cheddar cheese, chopped into small pieces. Add enough salad dressing to moisten.

Reverend Roy Dittmar of Emblem makes this cake for an aunt who cannot eat eggs:

WACKY CAKE

1 1/2 cups flour
1 cup sugar
1/4 cup cocoa
1 teaspoon soda
1/2 teaspoon salt

Mix all dry ingredients, sift together, and place in a 9 × 9 cake pan.

Take 1 cup lukewarm water, 1/3 cup oil, 1 teaspoon vanilla, and 1 teaspoon vinegar. Make three holes in the dry mixture in the pan. Pour vanilla in one, the oil in another, and vinegar in another. Pour water over all. Stir all the ingredients together in the pan.

Bake for 35 minutes at 350 degrees. You don't mess up any other dishes. Frost if desired.

AMBROSIA

The Greek gods ate ambrosia to preserve their immortality. It is a melange of fresh orange segments or chunks, coconut, and sugar, served with pomp in a crystal dish. It was popular on Christmas Day at plantation dinners and became the custom in Texas. Pineapple, bananas, grapes, or whatever berries were at hand could be added.

Virginia Taylor of Commerce recalls why her family discovered an alternative to ambrosia:

PINEAPPLE SNOW

During the Depression, oranges were too expensive for us to have ambrosia at Christmas, but we could buy canned sliced pineapple. We had to cut it in chunks because it only came in slices. We added marshmallows, and we had to cut them up too with scissors dipped in water because there were no miniatures in the stores then. We folded it all in whipped cream, which we had plenty of.

We still have Pineapple Snow every Christmas.

Henry Spangenberg of Texarkana says his Aunt Nell always had eggnog on Christmas Eve for relatives and friends:

CHRISTMAS EGGNOG

Bring 4 cups whole sweet milk to a boil. Add 1 1/2 cups sugar and 1 teaspoon vanilla. Remove from fire. Cool.

Beat yolks of 8 eggs until lemon colored. Combine with milk and stir. Return and bring to boil but do not boil. Remove from heat. Cool again. Add 1 cup Mexican liqueur or 1 cup bourbon. Strain and serve in liqueur glasses.

And, of course, Christmas is a time for special cakes and candies:

MOIST JAM CAKE
Edna St. Clair, Klondike

1 cup sugar
2 cups flour
1 teaspoon soda
2 teaspoons baking powder
1/2 teaspoon salt
1 cup buttermilk
2 eggs
1 cup seedless blackberry jam
1/3 cup butter

Pour batter into three greased and floured round cake pans. Bake at 325 degrees for 25 or 30 minutes, or until a toothpick inserted comes out clean.

Filling:

2 cups sugar
1 cup blackberry jam
3 tablespoons flour
1 cup milk
Pinch of salt
1/2 cup black walnuts (or other nuts)

Cook over slow heat until very thick. Cool the filling but spread it while it is still a little warm. This is enough filling for two.

JAM CAKE
Florence Rowe, Richardson

5 eggs, beaten
2 cups sugar
3 cups flour (if cake flour is used, add 6 tablespoons more)
1 cup butter or shortening
1 cup buttermilk
1 teaspoon soda
1/4 teaspoon salt
1/2 teaspoon cinnamon
1 1/2 teaspoons cloves
1 1/2 teaspoons allspice
1 cup raisins or chopped dates (or 1/2 cup golden raisins and 1/2 cup
    chopped pitted dates)
1 cup chopped nuts (English walnuts are good)
1 cup jam (I use blackberry)

Cream butter and gradually add the sugar. Cream together until light and fluffy. Add well-beaten eggs. Sift flour before measuring and add to it the spices and the salt. Dissolve soda in buttermilk and add it and the flour mixture alternately to the egg-sugar-butter mixture and beat after each addition. Lightly dredge the fruit and nuts with extra flour and add. Next add the jam. Stir to get good distribution.

Grease and paper-line a 9-inch tube pan or two 9-inch round layer cake pans. Pour batter into prepared pan or pans. Bake at 325 degrees for 50 to 60 minutes. Ice with caramel icing or whatever you like.

CARAMEL ICING

2 cups brown sugar
1 cup cream or 1/2 cup butter plus 1/2 cup milk
3 tablespoons butter

1 teaspoon vanilla
Chopped nuts

Stir the sugar and cream until the sugar is dissolved. Cover and cook for about 3 minutes or until the steam has washed down any crystals which may have formed on the sides of the pan. Uncover and cook without stirring to 238 or 240 degrees.

Add the butter. Remove the icing from the heat and cool to 110 degrees.

Add vanilla.

Beat the icing until it is thick and creamy. If it becomes too heavy, thin it with a little cream until it is right for spreading. Top with chopped nuts.

AUNT ADDIE'S DATE CAKE
Gladine Coffey, Commerce

1 cup sugar
1/2 cup butter
1 slightly beaten egg
1 1/2 cups flour
1 cup dates, seeded and cut in half
1 cup boiling water
1 teaspoon soda
1 cup pecans, chopped

Mix the dates, boiling water, and soda until it is like mush. Use your hands. Set this mixture aside.

Cream the sugar and butter. Add the egg. Beat well. Add the flour, then the date mixture. Add the pecans last.

Line a bread pan with wax paper on the bottom. Grease the paper and the sides of the pan. Pour in the batter.

Bake in a moderate oven for 30 minutes, or until the cake is firm on top and light brown in color. Remove from oven and cool before slicing.

PEANUT BUTTER ROLL
Lee Ann Sewell, Richardson

3 cups white sugar
1/2 cup white syrup
1/2 cup water

Cook until it makes a hard ball in cold water and pour over 2 egg whites, stiffly beaten. Beat until stiff enough to spread on buttered wax paper. Spread with peanut butter and roll up like a jelly roll. Wrap wax paper around roll and cut into thin slices when cool.

New Year's Celebrations

On New Year's Day Texans watch football games. And eat snack food. Sometimes before the day is over, they will have a bowl of black-eyed peas. One can expect, some say, not just good fortune but a dollar for every pea consumed on that day. Such promise of fortune keeps one eating and counting. That means a mess of peas—not canned but dried peas cooked with ham hock for most of the morning.

Hoppin' John is a favorite recipe:

HOPPIN' JOHN

1 cup dried black-eyed peas
1/4 pound salt pork or hog jowl
1 green pepper, chopped fine
1 onion, chopped fine

Wash peas to remove all gravel. Soak overnight. Add the peas to boiling water with pork, pepper, and onion. Simmer the peas until tender.

Cook an equal portion of rice. When the peas are done and the water is low, add the rice with a tablespoon of butter, salt and pepper to taste, and as many pinches of cayenne pepper as it takes to keep John hoppin'!

Serve with onion slices and corn bread.

TEXAS CAVIAR

1 pound black-eyed peas
2 cups Italian dressing
1 cup diced green pepper
1 1/2 cups chopped onion
1 cup finely chopped green onion
1 small can chopped green chilies
1 2-ounce jar pimiento, chopped and drained
1 tablespoon chopped garlic
1/2 teaspoon salt
1/8 teaspoon hot pepper sauce

Wash the peas in several changes of water. Soak them for six or so hours. Cook them until tender. Mix with the remaining ingredients. Refrigerate.

This is good with chopped ham added before serving. Place the mixture on lettuce leaves. *Serves 10 to 12.*

BLACK-EYED PEA DIP

4 cups black-eyed peas, cooked and drained
5 canned jalapeño peppers
1 tablespoon jalapeño juice
1/2 medium onion
1 4-ounce can green chilies
1 clove garlic

Mix the above ingredients in a blender. Heat 1/2 pound sharp cheese with 1/2 pound butter. Add the blended mixture to the cheese mixture. Serve in a chafing dish with chips.

In the Hill Country, German families eat sauerbraten (marinated beef) and cabbage on New Year's Day. Some say it should be purple cabbage, but the good luck is to be returned in green money, so perhaps green cabbage will do.

In the late nineteenth century in Galveston, San Antonio, and perhaps some other places, New Year's Day calls were a debt society demanded of fashionable young men. To open their doors to the eligible bachelors in the interest of their daughters and also to maintain their social standing, ambitious matrons would hold elaborate receptions from noon until nine at night, all of which the young men were expected to attend. On January 1, 1877, the Galveston *News* listed thirty-three such affairs.

Alexander Sweet gave this account:

No doubt many of the ladies will have a great deal of curiosity to know how many previous calls each visitor has made, and owing to the different kinds of fruit-cake the caller takes at the different places, the caller himself is unable to furnish any reliable statistics. By comparing the remarks of the caller with the following time-table, as it were, a very correct idea may be obtained of the number of calls the visitor has already been guilty of:

First place—"A happy new year to you, Miss _____, a happy new year."

Next place—"Wish you a very happy new year, Mrs. _____, I wish you a hap' new year indeed; happy n'year."

Next place—"Mannam, wishu happy new year."

Next place—"Scuse me, Miss _____. Awful slipry—wizzu happy newer—wizzu great man' ofem."

Next place—"Begger par'n, mannam—wizzu yappy yawnear—splen' wine."

Next place—"Ello Mollie—izhoo—appy—wizzu—'lo, Molidy—washer mather you? Wiser heaper nopper—hisher happy hooyer, Molidy—lotsel' 'em."

Of course, the city authorities will see to it that the lamp-posts are duly propped and supported. A lamp-post can stand a great deal, but when five or six fashionable young men, strung together like so many ants, surge around a lamp-post, something has to give somewhere. A light house could not stand that very long.

Policemen will be very careful in identifying the occupants of the gutter. It once happened that a policeman lost his position by too much carelessness and lack of discrimination. He dragged the son of a prominent alderman to the lock-up by mistake. If a policeman is wise he will keep the caller as far off as possible while transferring him to the receptacle. There is a well-authenticated case of a hack horse getting the blind staggers from smelling the breath of a gentleman who had just made 854 calls that day. (149–50)

St. Valentine's Day

LORE FOR LOVERS

Put apple seeds on the stove and have someone else name each one. The first one to pop is the one you love best.

When hunting for a husband, tie a bunch of tomato seeds around your neck.

Love is crossed if you put cream or milk into the tea before the sugar.

If, after the table has been cleaned, there happen to be left a knife, some salt and bread, place these things under your pillow and you will dream of your wife to be.

Black and green olives will make you more loving.

You will have bad luck if you take the last portion of food. However, if you are invited to take it and you eat it, you will be sure to have a handsome husband or wife. If you are already married, you will receive something you want badly.

If the leaves of tea stay in the middle of the cup when you stir it, you will soon be married, or talk to a handsome stranger, or an absent friend will return.

February 14 is the day for baking heart-shaped cakes and making candies—especially chocolate. But don't make candy in damp weather.

FUDGE

2 cups sugar
6 tablespoons cocoa
3/4 cup milk

Cook very slowly to the soft ball stage. If you have a candy thermometer, the temperature will read 232 degrees. Do not stir the candy after it has reached the boiling point.

Remove from the heat and add 2 tablespoons of butter without stirring. Cool the candy at this point. Just let it stand. (Or put it in a pan of cold water if you want to hasten the process.)

When it is nearly cold, add 1 teaspoon vanilla. Now beat it vigorously until it is creamy and begins to lose its shine.

Add 1 cup of chopped nuts and pour onto a greased platter.

DIVINITY

2 cups sugar
2/3 cup water
2/3 cup light corn syrup

Cook these ingredients quickly to 238 degrees on your candy thermometer, or to the soft ball stage.

Whip until stiff 2 egg whites with a dash of salt. Pour the syrup over the eggs very slowly, beating all the time. When all the syrup has been added, place the bowl holding the candy over hot water, as in a double boiler. Beat the candy until it sticks to the bottom and sides of the bowl and will stand in peaks. Remove it from the fire.

Add 1 1/2 teaspoons vanilla and 1 cup chopped nuts. At festive times, add chopped red and green cherries.

DATE LOAF

3 cups sugar
1 cup milk
1 8 oz. package pitted dates
1 cup nuts
1/2 teaspoon salt
1 teaspoon vanilla

Cook sugar and milk together until it forms soft ball when dropped in cold water (238 degrees). Add chopped dates and continue to cook slowly for 5 minutes. Remove from heat and add chopped nuts, salt, and vanilla. Cook a few minutes, then beat until it thickens.

Form in a roll and place in a damp cloth. Chill and slice.

TAFFY

1 cup light corn syrup
1/2 cup sugar
1 tablespoon vinegar
1 teaspoon butter
Flavoring

Lightly butter a dish or platter. Combine syrup, sugar, vinegar, and butter in a saucepan. Boil until firm, 252 degrees on the candy thermometer. Pour onto the dish. When cool enough to handle, add several drops of whatever flavoring you desire.

Then pull it.

The secret to making good taffy is to cool it quickly and then pull it properly. Ideally, the pulling should be done by two people, one to hold his or her hands in the position of a hook, and the other to throw the elastic strip of taffy back and forth over them. The more delicately the candy is handled, the lighter it will become.

Never twist taffy as too much air is lost that way. Instead, fold it back straight after each pull. The object is to get a whitish, porous condition by carefully stretching the candy and keeping it folded back upon itself. Remember to butter your hands first, so the taffy won't stick to your fingers. When the mass is fluffy and full of air, it will no longer have a plastic feel to it. Fold it into a long oval shape and lay the taffy on a smooth warm surface. Start rolling the right side of the oval with the heels of the palms of your hands. Roll into a thin rope. Cut or pinch off bite-sized pieces of taffy. Work quickly before the taffy hardens. Wrap in waxed paper to keep the candy fresh and store in tightly closed containers until ready to serve.

Let Us Break Bread Together

Breaking bread together is a time-honored practice, not just as a reenactment of the Last Supper but as a proclamation of the community of brotherhood. In Texas this brotherhood is strongly fundamentalist—the buckle on the Bible Belt is said to be located around Waco—radiating far and wide to establish a strict moral code that is strengthened by social gatherings where the folk share their foods.

The frontier experience is still recent in the memories of some Texans. Many a person is removed only one or two generations from the life of folk who "had the go-yonders" as Paul Patterson says of his own father. And survival on the frontier prompted neighbors to share their food, their supplies, and whatever they had that another family needed.

More, the frontier offered little diversion, so church and school functions served a social need. It was civilizing to gather, to talk, and break bread. The womenfolk expected their menfolk to wash up and go to these affairs, and they considered it part of the children's education. It was easy to slip into careless habits at home, but at a church or school picnic, little boys and girls knew to say "Thanky-ma'am" and "Pleez."

TO MAKE BREAD
(From the 1904 Gold Medal Cookbook)

FIRST, mix a lukewarm quart, my daughter,
One-half scalded milk, one-half water;
To this please add two cakes of yeast,
Or the liquid kind if preferred in the least.

NEXT stir in a teaspoonful of nice clear salt,
If this bread isn't good, it won't be our fault,
Now add the sugar, teaspoonfuls three;
Mix well together, for dissolved they must be.

POUR the whole mixture into an earthen bowl,
A pan's just as good, if it hasn't a hole,
It's the cook and the flour, not the bowl or the pan
That—"Makes the bread that makes the man."

NOW let the mixture stand a minute or two.
You've other things of great importance to do.
First sift the flour—use the finest in the land.
Three quarts is the measure, "Gold Medal" the brand.

SOME people like a little shortening power,
If this is your choice, just add to the flour
Two tablespoons of lard, and jumble it about
Till the flour and lard are mixed without doubt.

NEXT stir the flour into the mixture that's stood
Waiting to play its part, to make the bread good.
Mix it up thoroughly, but not too thick;
Some flours make bread that's more like a brick.

NOW grease well a bowl and put the dough in,
Don't fill the bowl full, that would be a sin;
For the dough is all right and it's going to rise,
Till you will declare that it's twice the old size.

BRUSH the dough with melted butter, as the recipes say;
Cover with a bread towel, set in a warm place to stay
Two hours or more, to rise until light,
When you see it grow, you'll know it's all right.

AS soon as it's light, place again on the board;
Knead it well this time. Here is knowledge to hoard.
Now back in the bowl once more it must go.
And set again to rise for an hour or so.

FORM the dough gently into leaves when light,
And place it in bread pans, greased just right.
Shape each loaf you make to half fill the pan,
This bread will be good enough for any young man.

NEXT let it rise to the level of pans—no more,
Have the temperature right—don't set near a door.
Be very careful about draughts—it isn't made to freeze.
Keep the room good and warm—say seventy-two degrees.

NOW put in the oven; it's ready to bake—
Keep uniform fire, great results are at stake,
One hour more of waiting and you'll be repaid,
By bread that is worthy "A Well Bred Maid."

HONEY WHOLE WHEAT BREAD

2 packages active dry yeast
2 cups warm water
3 tablespoons honey
1/4 cup oil
2 teaspoons salt
1/2 cup bran (wheat)
1/2 cup wheat germ
3 cups white/unbleached flour
3 cups whole wheat flour

Dissolve yeast in warm water. Stir in honey, oil, salt, germ, bran, and white/unbleached flour.

Mix by hand or use a mixer to beat until smooth. Let rise 20 minutes.

Add enough whole wheat flour to make dough easy to handle. Turn onto lightly floured board and knead till smooth and elastic, 8 to 10 minutes.

Divide dough in half. Roll into a rectangle 18″ × 9″. Roll up and seal ends. Place seam side down in greased loaf pan 9″ × 5″ × 3″. Let rise until double in bulk. Makes two loaves.

Bake at 400 degrees for 35 to 40 minutes. To test for doneness, thump the bread. If there is a hollow sound, the bread is done.

The community of brotherhood can succeed beyond expectations. One informant tells that in East Texas, where she was reared, it was customary, after crops were planted, to set aside a day for cleaning the cemetery and having dinner on the grounds. But the townspeople from nearby would find out about it and come out uninvited to enjoy the food, saying, "Everybody knows country food is better than city food." The city folk became such a problem that the country folk now bring their own hampers and don't spread the food on a communal table.

Noah Smithwick wrote that camp meetings had become an institution where both the good and the greedy were welcomed in the Hill Country by the mid-1800s:

The hungry, both spiritually and physically, were freely fed at these meetings dispensing the stronger spiritual meat of fire and brimstone first and tapering off the feast with milk and honey, while outside at every camp long tables were spread, provided with comfort for the physical man, where all were welcomed. . . .

As other denominations took up the work, a regular chain of camp meetings every fall, with the incidental dispensation of free grub, induced many not overthrifty people to become regular camp followers, and most of them being quite forehanded with children, they became a heavy tax on the good brethren. (235)

BREAD LORE

It is commonly believed that a loaf of bread, weighted with quicksilver, will locate the body of a drowned person. Such a loaf is set in the water and travels towards the lost body and remains motionless over it.

When you make bread, you've got to be careful not to get hair in it because if you eat biscuits or bread with hair in it, the hair turns to worms in your stomach.

"When we said bread," a West Texas pioneer woman said, "we meant corn bread, not light bread. We called light bread 'wasp nest' bread—you know it has lots of holes in it. We thought people were lazy and no good if they didn't bake biscuits and corn bread. We never ate light bread until I was in my teens."

If you sing before making bread, you will cry before it is eaten.

If the loaf is upside down on the table, it means the devil is around.

If you have a cut, chew a piece of homemade bread with butter on it. Place it on the cut and it will heal.

If a bone is caught in your throat, eat a piece of corn bread and drink lots of water.

When buttered bread is dropped and falls on the buttered side, you will have bad luck and will be poor.

If you drop bread, pick it up and kiss it, and you will never be hungry.

Eating the crust of the bread will cause one's hair to grow extremely long and faster than usual, and it will be curly.

When bread or cake or pie burns in spite of you, your husband or lover is angry.

Save old bread until it gets mildew on it. Eat it to cure colds.

Pounding the Preacher

"It sounds pretty bad for the preacher," says Stan Allcorn, Baptist pastor in Commerce.

"But it is really very nice," quickly adds his young wife, Claudia. "I got so many things I would never have bought at the store." Then she says, "I especially liked jars of homemade preserves and relishes."

In the old days it was customary to bring a pound of sugar, a pound of flour, a pound of coffee, etc., to welcome the preacher and his family. But that has changed, though the staples and plenty of canned goods will be brought. Mary Jane Seigler, whose husband is part-time preacher at Klondike, says that she and her family receive poundings quite frequently. This is the way the community attempts to reward them for their services. One of the parishioners found that Mary Jane likes homemade fig preserves, so she can always look forward to a jar or two. Sometimes the people will have a paper pounding and the family will be supplied with all kinds of paper products.

When George Robson was printer of the *Frontier Times* at Fort Griffin in 1878 or thereabouts, he ran a little story about a new preacher in town. The people came for the pounding. But unfortunately too many brought biscuits. That preacher took quick measure of the town he had come to. He proceeded during the night to stack the cold biscuits on the fence posts around the parsonage and, by daylight, he was gone!

Some food gifts which might encourage the preacher to stay include:

CHOW-CHOW
Linnia Mai Wright, Commerce

These should be ground coarsely:
1 quart green tomatoes
1 quart apples, cored but not peeled
1 pint cabbage
Add:
1 teaspoon allspice
1 1/2 tablespoons cinnamon
1 teaspoon cloves
1 tablespoon salt
3 cups sugar
1 1/2 cups vinegar

Cook until tender, about 30 minutes. Pour in hot sterilized jars and seal.

Linnia Mai also recalls the pickled peaches her mother made from fruit in her own orchard. They were Indian peaches, a small cling-type and very, very red. The Cherokees claim that they are a wild peach that you can find growing in backwoods places now.

PICKLED PEACHES

Basic syrup recipe:

9 cups sugar

2 cups water

3 cups vinegar

Approximately 2 tablespoons each of allspice and cloves

Mix sugar, water, and vinegar. Bring to a boil. The spices are tied in a little cloth bag and dropped in the boiling syrup.

Peel peaches and place in boiling syrup. Cook until tender. Test by pricking peach with fork. When tender, place in fruit jar and cover with the boiling syrup. Drop two or three cloves down in the jar before sealing. Amount of syrup needed will depend on amount of peaches to be pickled.

BREAD AND BUTTER PICKLES
Thelma Erwin, Commerce

12 large or 15 medium cucumbers

5 cups sliced onions

2 teaspoons salt

1 teaspoon turmeric (up to 2 1/2 teaspoons if you like the flavor)

1 red pepper, chopped, or 1/2 teaspoon cayenne

1 quart vinegar

4 cups sugar

1 teaspoon nutmeg, grated

4 sticks cinnamon

(Instead of the nutmeg and cinnamon, you may use 2 to 4 teaspoons
  pickling spices.)

Sprinkle salt over sliced cucumbers and onions. Let stand for 1 hour. Drain well and place in a deep kettle with sugar, vinegar, and spices.

Cook slowly over simmer burner until sugar is dissolved. Turn flame on high and boil rapidly until slices begin to glisten. This takes about 20 minutes.

Pack in hot jars. Fill to overflowing with hot syrup and seal.

MESQUITE JELLY

2 1/2 quarts ripe mesquite beans

1 package powdered pectin

4 1/2 cups sugar

4 tablespoons lemon juice

The mesquite beans are picked just as they begin to turn brown. They should be tan and plump. Break the beans, pods and all, into small pieces. Don't ever try to shell the beans. Cover with water.

Simmer the beans. Take a potato masher and work the beans and pods until you have a yellow liquid. Strain. Continue to cook until there are 3 cups of juice.

Place the juice in a large kettle and add the pectin. Early housewives who could not purchase pectin would use the juice from some acid fruit (even apples have pectin). And they would cook their jelly longer.

Bring the juice to a full boil. Stir and boil for one minute or until the syrup sheets from a metal spoon. Remove from the fire. Skim off the foam. To give the jelly more color, a drop of red food coloring may be added. Pour immediately into hot, sterilized jars. Cover with melted paraffin or a tight-fitting lid.

Money-Raising Socials

Kathleen Roche Mottin, age ninety, told this story to Helen Vaughan in El Paso:

> We used to have box suppers all the time. We went to them both before and after we were married. Oh, yes, it was all right if someone else's husband bought yours. Everyone did it and understood. It was the custom. Every woman did her best to put good foods in her box. Her name was put on the box and they were kept behind a curtain or partition. The men would bid on them. The auctioneer would hold a box up and brag on it without saying whose it was. A man wouldn't know which was good unless someone had given him a secret word. The auctioneer would brag on the boxes, of course. Women who had a steady would tell him her box had so-and-so on it. And then some men sometimes got behind and played tricks and put signs on the boxes they wanted. There was many a fight over the boxes. They would bid and bid and bid. Often a man would know that another wanted a box and keep bidding until the boxes went as high as four or five dollars and then it might be the wrong one. It was a very great offense if you refused to eat with the man who bought your box. The money was raised for different things. Once I remember we had a box social to raise money to put a partition in Junction School and have two teachers instead of the one. (West Collection)

The cake walk and the pie supper are also popular for money raising. Virginia Walker writes that down by the Sabine the treat would be a syrup pie, as this area is known as sugar cane bottoms, while pecan pies would be made around Waterman, plum pies at Aiken, blackberry pies at Grigsby, and at

Lone Cedar peach pies. The people who lived a cut above the folk would bring some pie with a store-bought ingredient like raisins or coconut. (33–34)

APPLE PIE

Hobby Porcher, Fort Worth

6 to 8 medium apples, peeled and sliced
1/2 cup granulated sugar
1/4 cup light brown sugar (firmly packed)
3/4 teaspoon cinnamon
1/4 teaspoon nutmeg
1/4 teaspoon cloves
2 tablespoons lemon juice
2 tablespoons instant tapioca
    Combine all ingredients and pour into 9-inch unbaked pie shell.

Topping:

1/2 cup butter or oleo
1/2 cup brown sugar (firmly packed)
1 cup flour
    Cream butter and sugar. Cut in flour with pastry cutter (or you can use two knives) until crumbly. Pour over apples and bake 350 degrees 45 minutes or until crust is light brown and filling is bubbly.

CREAMY APPLE PIE

1 2-crust apple pie, baked and hot.
Prepare this creamy sauce:
2 eggs, slightly beaten
1/4 cup sugar
2 tablespoons lemon juice
1 package (3-ounce) cream cheese, softened
1/2 cup sour cream
    Combine the eggs, sugar and lemon juice. Cook over low heat until thick. Add cheese and cream. Let the pie cool for 10 minutes. Then open up the holes in the top of the pie a little and pour the sauce over the top so that it spills down into the apples.

CHESS PIE

Ella B. Robertson, Shiloh Community

4 eggs, well beaten
2 cups sugar
1 tablespoon flour
1 tablespoon cornmeal
1/4 teaspoon salt
1/4 cup milk

1/4 cup lemon juice

2 teaspoons grated lemon peel

4 tablespoons margarine

Combine the ingredients and bake in an 8-inch unbaked pie shell at 350 degrees for 1 hour. The top should be golden brown.

Winnie Kirkpatrick, who was reared in Leonard, says that her mother had eight children and made lots of pies. These were some of the favorites, as well as chess pie:

BUTTERMILK PIE

2 cups sugar

1/2 cup butter or margarine

3 eggs, beaten until fluffy

1 cup buttermilk

3 tablespoons flour

Dash of nutmeg

Cream sugar and margarine. Add eggs and then flour. Fold in the buttermilk and nutmeg. Bake in uncooked pie shell for 10 minutes at 425 degrees, then 35 minutes at 350 degrees or until knife, when inserted, comes clean.

OSGOOD PIE

1 cup pecans

1 cup raisins

1 cup water

1 small package dates

6 eggs

3 tablespoons butter

1 1/4 cups sugar

Grind pecans, dates, and raisins. Beat eggs; add sugar, water, and butter. Cook until thick; pour in baked crust. This recipe makes three pies.

Any of the molasses, raisin, chess, Osgood pies and their like—sticky, syrupy, often open-faced—could be called "shoo-fly pies," so called because of the worrisome winged visitors that came to the table uninvited. The children were given white cloths that they waved about to keep the flies off the food.

APPLE DUMPLINGS

Use 2 1/2 apples. Peel, quarter and core. Roll out pastry dough. Cut in rounds or squares large enough to wrap a quarter of an apple in each piece. Place in a baking dish upside down. Then mix in a pan:

1 1/2 cups sugar
2 cups water
1/2 stick butter or margarine
1 teaspoon vanilla
1 teaspoon cinnamon

Cook until butter melts. Pour over the dumplings. Bake for 30 to 35 minutes at 350 degrees, basting the dumplings frequently.

MUSTANG GREEN GRAPE PIE

Wild green grapes can be gathered, washed, stemmed, and drained well, then poured into an unbaked pie shell. Mix 2 cups of sugar and 2 tablespoons of flour. Sprinkle this mixture over the grapes. Pour 1 cup of cream (or evaporated milk, undiluted) over the sugar and flour. Bake the pie for an hour in a slow oven (325 degrees).

Just Ho'pin' Out

After a funeral in small towns a bounteous dinner is given to comfort the family. In the cities this custom is not so prevalent; people will simply take a dish to the family as a caring gesture.

Sandra Vlasin's sixteen-year-old son Keith, after going to a funeral in Roby and partaking of the feast, declared, "When I die, I want to be buried in Roby!"

"It looks like a holiday," says Sandra. "There's a real family feeling, and it is a real social occasion—like a wake. It is the American answer to the Irish wake. The feast serves to make the bond between children and family and community even stronger."

In former times the women of the church usually came into the home, set up some sawhorses and boards they kept for the occasion, and spread the food so that it was ready when the family returned from the cemetery. Nowadays they are likely to have the feast in the fellowship hall of the church.

Mary Jane Siegler in Klondike says they have dinners at the church. "In all the years Guille [her husband] has been pastor there, we have never had an unbalanced meal. Everything seems to work out right." That does not always hold true. One informant told about a time when her Sunday School class was having a covered-dish supper and nearly everyone brought sweet potatoes prepared in one way or another. How they laughed!

Often certain people will be known to bring a certain dish when ho'pin' out, whatever the occasion:

CHICKEN AND RICE CASSEROLE
Mary Jane Siegler, Klondike

Combine 1 package of dry onion soup mix and 1 cup uncooked rice in a baking dish. Place pieces of chicken on top of rice. Use a whole chicken cut up or use 6 to 8 chicken breasts.

Heat a can of mushroom soup with 1 soup can of water in a saucepan. Pour the soup over the chicken.

Bake covered, for 1 1/2 hours until tender in a slow oven, 325 degrees. Note: You may add jalapeño peppers, bell peppers, and onion.

CORN BREAD SALAD
Ora Bennett, Roby

4 cups corn bread crumbs
1 cup green onions
1 cup celery
1 cup green peppers
2 tablespoons chopped-up bacon with drippings

Mix all together with just enough mayonnaise to toss right before serving. Add 2 chopped tomatoes. It is wonderful!

MANDARIN ORANGE SALAD WITH GREENS
Penny Bigbie and Mabeth Abernathy, Lewisville

1/2 cup sliced almonds
3 teaspoons sugar
1/2 head iceberg lettuce
1/2 head romaine lettuce
2 whole green onions, chopped
1 cup chopped celery
1 11-ounce can mandarin oranges, drained

In a small pan over medium heat, cook the almonds and sugar, stirring constantly until almonds are coated and sugar is dissolved.

Mix the lettuces, celery, and onions. Just before serving, add the almonds and oranges.

Toss with dressing:
1/2 teaspoon salt
Dash of pepper
2 tablespoons sugar
Dash of Tabasco sauce
1/4 cup vegetable oil
1 tablespoon chopped parsley
1 tablespoon vinegar

GRANDMOTHER'S HOT CINNAMON ROLLS
Esther Huckaby, Fort Worth

3 cups all-purpose flour
1 tablespoon baking powder
1 teaspoon salt
1/3 cup lard or vegetable shortening
1 cup milk

Sift the dry ingredients together. Cut the lard into the flour mix. Add milk and mix until smooth. Roll out like biscuit dough on a floured board or pastry cloth. Spread with 3/4 cup butter. Sprinkle with plenty of sugar and cinnamon. Roll like a jelly roll. Cut into slices about 1 1/2" thick and place in baking pan. Pour boiling water over the top to cover the rolls. Sprinkle with more sugar and cinnamon.

Bake in moderate oven (350 to 375 degrees) about 1 hour or until the tops of cinnamon rolls are brown.

Serve with cream, plain or whipped. These are best served hot.

Emily Gregory, formerly of Houston, writes, "I always take these cookies to homes where there are children. My mother-in-law, Margaret Gregory, will take a big bowl of sliced and chunked fresh fruits with applesauce muffins":

SUGAR COOKIES

1 cup granulated sugar
1 cup powdered sugar
1 cup margarine (Fleischmann's)
1 cup cooking oil
2 eggs
4 cups plus 4 tablespoons flour
1 teaspoon soda
1 teaspoon cream of tartar
2 teaspoons vanilla
1/4 teaspoon salt

Cream sugars, margarine, and oil until fluffy. Add eggs and vanilla and mix well. Add flour and other dry ingredients one at a time. Form dough into walnut-size balls and flatten with bottom of glass dipped in sugar. Bake at 375 degrees for 12 to 15 minutes.

APPLESAUCE MUFFINS

1 cup butter or margarine
2 cups sugar
2 eggs
2 cups unsweetened applesauce

3 teaspoons ground cinnamon

2 teaspoons ground allspice

1 teaspoon ground cloves

1 teaspoon salt

2 teaspoons baking soda

4 cups flour

1 cup chopped nuts (optional)

Cream butter and sugar; add eggs, one at a time. Mix in applesauce and spices. Sift salt, soda, and flour. Add to applesauce mixture. Mix well and stir in nuts. Bake 15 minutes at 400 degrees or about 17 minutes if you have used margarine.

FOR COOKS ONLY

Put a horseshoe in your oven for success in baking.

Put nails in meat to make it tender.

Milk churned in the moonlight will curdle.

If you put a silver spoon in a pot of boiling mushrooms and it turns black, the mushrooms are poisonous.

Put a knife across a pan to keep the food from boiling over.

Birthdays

Forget the number of years, but don't let a birthday go by without celebrating. Birthdays mark the transition from one stage of development to another. As change can be dangerous and a source of fear, birthdays are times when good and bad spirits have the opportunity to influence the celebrants. The brotherhood of good friends and relatives is needed for protection from evil. Communal eating on this occasion strengthens the ties with the good fairies, just as the giving of gifts and good wishes by godmothers, relatives, and friends places the birthday boy or girl in the good graces of the benevolent spirits.

The birthday cake carries with it the same symbolism as bread: the protection of home and family. The candles that are placed on the cake must be blown out in one breath in order to have a secret wish come true. Also, as the last flame from the candles flickers out, the past is wiped out. A variation is to name the candles. The last candle to go out is the name of the person you will marry.

Whoever cuts the cake must not change directions or the birthday person will have bad luck. Sometimes good luck tokens are baked into the cake. If you get a dime, you will make money that year; if you find a tiny doll, there

The birthday cake is special because Mother bakes it. *Courtesy Otha C. Spencer, Commerce.*

will be a baby born into your family; if you get a ring, there will be a wedding in your family.

During the Depression, gifts were not expected. But a cake baked by the mother of the birthday child marked the day a special one. One family with several children made a game of allowing the honoree to do on that day whatever thing he or she most desired that was out of the ordinary—within reason, of course. The informant said, "My most memorable birthday was the time when I was ten. I decided that I would have—not my chair—but the stepladder at the table for my sitting place. It was wonderful to be on high, looking down at everybody else and having my fried chicken and mashed potatoes handed up to me."

Gifts pale beside the cake. One informant with a June birthday always had strawberry shortcake. Another, born in July, had a flag cake. A February child could celebrate with George Washington—but not Abraham Lincoln. Lee Dacus from Athens says, "My grandmother gave us no choice: 'The name of that man will not be mentioned in this house.'" But the June birthday child could have a Jeff Davis pie to commemorate the birthday of the Confederate president.

A Recipe for a Birthday Cake and a Short Play in One Scene

Narrator: Three significant, portentous, historical events rife with worldwide implications marked my early life and are responsible for all that I am today—a peaceful, satisfied, calm, optimistic individual. The events were the Great Depression of the 1930s, World War II in the 1940s, and My Birthday Cake, which first appeared in 1936.

The Depression was a delightful affair and was superseded only by World War II in its calming and reassuring remembrances. I lived in Jacksboro where we all had plenty of nothing in equal proportions, where we made our own entertainment and recreation, composed our own joy and sorrow and voted in favor of joy whenever we could. Although I was an only child, I believed that the entire town was kin to me and hold that place responsible even today for the peculiar way I turned out. All occasions of war and peace were shared together. I was enveloped in such an insular wrapping of loving, caring, sharing, and giving for so many of my formative years that it was a terrible shock to find out much later in my life that the history books considered both the Depression and World War II horrible and devastating occurrences. Only My Birthday Cake remains untouched by either the history books or someone else's opinion.

As I said, I was an only child, but even that is not significant necessarily. The Depression and World War II were at that time the most effective birth control devices ever invented, and there were many only children in my town. Not any only child, however, anywhere in the town or in the world had a cake like mine because it was *mine*. The cake could not have been baked except in an extraordinary place. The place was a kitchen. There was bright yellow linoleum on the floor. Brighter yellow curtains were at the windows. Everything else was white, bright white. The cookbook stood out in black relief on the table, giving depth and perspective to white on yellow. Texture was added by rough woolen coats and mittens, wintertime textures thrown over the kitchen chairs. The room was, however, merely a setting, a stage, until the central presence entered the kitchen—Mother, Leading Lady.

It was the day before my birthday, December 17, 1944. (Curtain up; lights up on Mother and Joyce Ann at the kitchen table, center; other lights dim on set.)

Mother: Dust the pans, Joyce Ann. That's all you have to do. It's your job, birthday or not. Wash your hands first. Wash your hands! Read me the recipe.

(Joyce Ann reads the recipe, but Mother is already pouring ingredients into a large mixing bowl, obviously familiar with the procedure.)

Joyce Ann:

DEVIL'S FOOD CAKE

1 egg
Pinch salt
1 cup sour milk
1 1/4 cups sugar
1/2 cup shortening
4 tablespoons cocoa
1 teaspoon soda in milk (makes a cake darker in color and does other
    good things to it)
1 1/2 cups flour
Beat in the egg white separately.

Why do I always have to read the recipe? You already got it ready to put in the oven by the time I finish!

Mother: Because that way you learn something about cooking and practice reading out loud; someday you might want to talk in public or make a speech or something and then you would sorta' know what to do. (Changing the subject.)

We're going to the show tonight. There are newsreels about the war. We have to go and look. We might see Fred. (She pours up the cake batter in the three pans; crosses to oven, kitchen-stage, right.)

You didn't light the oven. Don't ever put a cake in a cold oven. The oven's got to be heated first, "350 degrees for thirty minutes," that's what the directions say. Now, we'll have to wait. (She strikes a match, holds it to the opening at the front of the open oven door, waits for the flame to catch and the "whoosh" that signals the catch, and returns to the table.)

Joyce Ann: (Taking bowls and spoons to the sink, also stage right, but not washing them.) We never have seen Uncle Fred yet but we did see Mrs. Jones's boy, Willie, one time, didn't we? There was such a bunch of 'em and all in soldier suits. They all looked alike to me. I don't have any lessons tonight either. We won't do anything at school tomorrow but have our Christmas party. Did you bake the cookies for the party? Mary Jane's mother is supposed to bake a bunch, but you know we won't be able to eat 'em. I hope you made double. Couldn't we skip the movie part and just go in time for the newsreel? I've seen the movie three times. (Comes back to table.)

Mother: No, we have to pay for the movie and not just the newsreel. We'll see all of it or else not get our money's worth. That would be wasteful not to see everything. The oven's hot. Carry one of those pans for me.

(Both go to oven, kitchen-stage right; Mother waits on Joyce Ann to put hers in first, then rearranges the pan to suit herself and puts in the other two pans, making comments such as "don't burn yourself," "put it more on the right side in the back," etc.; both return to table and Joyce Ann sits down.)

Joyce Ann: Tell me the story about when Uncle Fred was home that Thanksgiving and we shot at the ducks and you said I could never go hunting again.

Mother: That's the silliest thing I ever heard of. I wasn't even along on that hunt. You were there. I just heard about it. You tell me, silly. (She closes the cookbook as she speaks and washes off the oilcloth with a wet dishrag.)

Joyce Ann: Yeah, but I was just a little kid and I don't remember how funny it was. Just Fred remembers how funny it was and he isn't here. Mother, is he ever coming home? Is he gonna' get killed? I don't like my birthday or Christmas without him.

Mother: Of course, he's comin' home and he certainly isn't going to die. Wait a minute, let me check the cakes. (She goes to the oven, checks the cake, but continues to speak as she walks back to the table.) Let's see. It was Thanksgiving two years ago just before Fred went away to the Navy. You and him and your daddy went out to Audie Weir's place to hunt. You didn't get a thing, just tramped around all day in the woods picking up pecans. You must have had ten pounds of big ole Burketts for Mama Hartman and me to pick out. I never saw such a bunch of pecans, as if we needed any with a tree right in the backyard here. Well, anyway, the three of you put the guns in the back of the ole truck your daddy fixed up and called the "hoopee." (They both laugh.) Just about the time you got a bit past Audie's big tank, Fred hollered, "Stop, Dave! Stop the truck! There's ducks on the tank!" (Mother stops her story to get a pan with ingredients for the icing which have already been measured out and await cooking. She puts pan on the burner, after lighting it with a match; then turns off the oven, removes the cakes, and stands stirring the mixture.)

Joyce Ann: Tell the rest of it! That's not the funny part. Tell it all.

Mother: Well, he made ya'll get out, told you to be real quiet, and whispered that you all three had to crawl on your hands and knees across the icy ground up to the dam of the tank or else you'd scare the ducks. And you got the guns and . . .

Joyce Ann: (Joyce Ann giggles, puts her hand up to her mouth, and whispers) And—and then we did crawl over the dam and right down to the water and then Uncle Fred jumps up and shouts, (Joyce Ann screams now), "Shoot, Dave, shoot!" And Daddy shot the gun, lost his balance, and fell full face into the tank and the ice cold water. And, and—he didn't hit one duck, not a one!

(Both Mother and Joyce Ann laugh until the tears come. Mother comes to the table with the icing and the cakes, and speaks, with tears still running down her cheeks.)

Mother: Read the directions for the icing, Joyce Ann. And then read me the baking directions and about how to grease the pans and how many it will serve. (She speaks quietly, barely above a whisper.)

Joyce Ann: But, Mother, the directions are always the same. You already cooked the icing.

Mother: Yes, Joyce, it is always the same. Some things always have to be the same, never different, never changed, or else how could we know how to cook or how to make it through—till Fred comes home?

(Lights down on mother and daughter as Joyce Ann takes a tablespoon, scrapes the pan, and licks the spoon.)

Narrator:

CHOCOLATE ICING

2 cups sugar
Pinch salt

"God is great, God is good; Let us thank him for this food." *Courtesy Otha C. Spencer, Commerce.*

228

3/4 cup evaporated milk

Lump of butter, the size of a walnut

As much cocoa as desired

Cook to the soft ball stage. Then drop in butter and vanilla and wait until lukewarm to beat.

BAKING DIRECTIONS FOR THE CAKE

Bake at 350 degrees for 30 minutes. Cake is very light. Makes two layers unless you make three thin layers. Also a good cupcake recipe. Be sure to grease and flour the pans. If the icing gets too thick and tries to set up on you, add more evaporated milk. The icing could be made with cream, if you can afford it. The recipe doesn't call for it, but I would put in a teaspoon of vanilla in batter and icing too.

This recipe was copied from Mother's black notebook-cookbook just the way she wrote it in 1936.

Uncle Fred did come home. He took up his place as the storyteller once more. The scene of My Birthday Cake was repeated with a larger cast. My mother told me a secret about what made the cake batter taste so good, about something that was not in the recipe. She made me promise not to tell, but I'll tell you. Put just a pinch, not a half-teaspoon even, of cinnamon in the cake batter. Just promise not to tell anyone else or she'll know I told the secret. She knows I never could keep my mouth shut about anything.

—Joyce Gibson Roach

"Clean your plate, darlin'!" *Courtesy Otha C. Spencer, Commerce.*

Afterword

Eden's Greens

Eating is one of the basic drives. Every phylum in the animal kingdom, including protozoan, votes aye to eating every time the question comes up. As in many other matters, human beings tamper with their basic drives, try to manipulate, alter, and raise them to the level of artistic and aesthetic. Since man first dropped his victuals in the fire, said, "Oh, oh," and learned to cook, he has aimed for ever better results and responses to his gastronomical urge. In Texas, man has been willing to wage salt wars and fight over the grains of Paradise, peppers, in order to improve the basics.

Verification of man's tampering with eating instincts may be noted in the Bible right up front in Genesis. It was Eve's fault, of course—the problem with food and eating. And the problem began in the Garden over Eden's greens.

"Eve," said Adam, "I'm tired of vegetables. I've eaten collards every way known to mankind—stewed, boiled, fried, and baked. I appreciate the variety of preparations and notice a little change of yellow color in some of the stuff, but, Darlin', I need a new taste. My cholesterol level is completely normal. My triglycerides are manageable. Could you come up with something that tastes—well, different?"

"What do you mean, different, Sweet Thing?" asked Eve.

"Eve, you've hit on something—that Sweet Thing name you call me? Could we find something sweet to eat? You know, there is that tree out yonder. It has red balls on it. God said not to fool around with it, said we shouldn't eat it, but maybe He meant that we ought not eat the tree itself, like we eat the bushes and shrubs. Maybe He wouldn't mind if we tried those red things that look as if they are sweet."

"I don't know, Adam," philosophized Eve. "I have seen Snake hanging around down there. He talks to me now and then, and—frankly, I didn't want to say anything except that you did bring it up—Snake has been suggesting that we ought to do just that, try apples. He says they are an excellent source of Vitamin A, that the peeling is also a source of niacin and the roughage is as dramatic as spinach."

Adam and Eve tried the apple and the rest is history—about how civilization began the Exodus from Nacogdoches out to Midland/Odessa in the Permian Basin where steak and black oil dressing got on the menu. Eden's greens and everything in the garden went by the wayside. So far as this researcher knows, no vestiges of Genesis remain except an eating place in Fort Worth which goes by the name of Eden's Greens. The menu features salad fixings only and vegetables such as potatoes which may be adorned with sour cream, butter, cheese, broccoli, stroganoff, chili, and hot peppers.

The folk history of Texas foods and foodways is well documented and illustrated with recipes and tales in the preceding pages. Examples abound of what happened to food over the years, where it happened, and with whom. It remains only to speak of the historically recent—the full flowering of the Foodway Phenomenon, the Eating Revolution of the 1980s—to complete this volume.

Research pertaining to the evolving ideas about food and food lore cannot be conducted from books. One must go among the folk and be a "folk" in order not only to give a clear picture of foodways but also to demonstrate that "we" and "us'ns" are in the very midst of the fray.

The reformation in foodways—habits, preparation, attitudes, and uses pertaining to edibles—is clearly the fault of women, Eve first, closely followed by Rosie the Riveter who left home to put nuts and bolts in ships during World War II. A woman by the name of Gloria Steinem who, in the seventies, suggested that the womenfolk could "bring home the bacon, fry it up in the pan and never, never let you forget you are a man," left the refrigerator, cabinet, and particularly the oven door completely ajar for good. Since this is a Texas folklore book, there is no need to probe psychologically into the types of women who are to blame for the radical departure from the tradition of eating. Let us press on to the Food Insurrection itself.

In the late seventies and early eighties, the nation of which Texas is more and more often a part, experienced a recession reminiscent of the Great Depression of 1929—complete with double digit inflation and interest rates, little money to spend, poverty and unemployment levels at an all time high. Necessities, food and shelter, were top priorities. Soup lines and temporary housing were set up for the indigent in many cities across the nation and in Texas too, just as the nation had served and sheltered its indigent in the thirties. The Oil Crisis and OPEC manipulations resulted in skyrocketing prices first of gasoline and then of petroleum-related products upon which much of the economy was based. Life was drastically altered.

Logically, predictably, historically, people would have stayed at home more, prepared their food at home, gone back to gardening, canning, and dehydrating foods. Mother or somebody would have returned to the kitchen. Economy and common sense demanded it. Wrong! Wrong! Wrong! While it is true that some predictable results did come about, it is also a modern phenomenon that during the recession of the eighties, food and all businesses related to its serving, preparation, preservation, and sales have in many ways helped restore and stabilize the economy and provide a job market which continues to enlarge and change foodways dramatically and irrevocably. The *Washington Kiplinger Report*, which keeps the public aware of trends, curves, and possibilities of business, continued to advise in the early eighties against all sane reasoning that one of the best investments would be in the foods/sports-recreational/health-related fields. Anyone can testify that tennis shoe stores (excuse me, Sports Footwear Stores) and hospitals (Health Centers) are on every corner. Places to eat are also on every other corner.

No one would exactly say that the food business was a phoenix rising from the ashes, but no one could deny that a redefined bird was about to spread its wings. The bird was Colonel Sanders and it was Kentucky Fried. The Colonel was on the scene long before the eighties, but his offering was among the first to reach national consciousness as a convenient, economical way to get a quick, specialized meal. The Colonel is still around today but behind some others in number of restaurants. There are Dairy Queen, McDonald's, Burger King, Wendy's, Jack-in-the-Box, Long John Silver, Taco Bueno (Rio and Bell), Grandy's, pizza places by a variety of names, and others, less or better known depending on where you live. They too have been around a long time, some twenty years or more. Although each offers a specialty, each also serves a little of the others' offerings. You can get a fajita at Jack-in-the-Box the same as you can get at Taco Bueno. All of them offer Coke/Pepsi/Pepper, potatoes in one form or another, and sweets of some kind. None of the food demands more than a piece of cardboard and plastic in the way of utensils. Most of it can be eaten out of your hand. Everything can be tossed, is disposable. The food is cheap, predictably less than delicious but only rarely bad. Accommodations are available for small or large groups because it is "to go" whether you eat the food there or not. Convenience is crucial and available since most of the Junk Joints, as they are called by mothers and nutritionists, group themselves one after another on the same block. One may direct the family members or the football team with the mere pointing of a finger and opening of a car or bus door.

For those who are, by now, jumping up and down and hollering righteously, "No, no, no! Junk foods aren't healthy, no matter what else you may have to say," I say, "Yes, most fast food is healthy." The chains have had to acknowledge nutrition priorities or get out of business. Consumer groups demand to know. Consequently, the public is informed about calorie count and nutrition: One advertises lower calorie count; fish is fried in unsaturated oil at another; essential food groups are recognized and satisfied on another corner where the customer gets whole wheat buns and fresh undoctored Eden's greens. Some offer "grilled" and "broiled" in addition to fried.

Fish and chicken, thanks perhaps to a million-dollar advertising campaign, are better for your health than beef. Such meat additions have wreaked havoc and not a little consternation in the food-related cattle industry. Cattlemen are grim, fewer than ever, and developing a leaner, taller, non-traditional cow. Fat is out and svelte is in. When fat cattle appear in the show rings of Texas, they are given the gate. Winners are now long-legged, crossbred, tall, attractively trim, and they remind me of short-necked giraffes. But I digress.

It should be remembered and reflected upon as well that many of the fast food favorites are traditionally thought of as folk foods—fried chicken, biscuits and gravy, corn on the cob, cream gravy. One place even employs grandmotherly types to dress in costume and wait tables. One mother was heard to remark, "See, son, that's what a grandmother looks like. That's the way they dress and that's what they do—cook good food, smile at you, and then clean up after you." About that time, the grandmotherly type walked over to the table and said, "Clean your plate, darlin'." After that remark, the mother got up and ate Granny out soundly for suggesting that her boy eat everything on his plate since her pediatrician and the *Ladies Home Journal* had counseled her that to encourage children to clean their plates was to invite obesity. But I digress again.

Nearly every other quickie offers employees in folk dress—Mexican, Italian, even seafaring outfits. Usually there is also folk decor in the restaurants, some of it authentic and tasteful, some not. The message is clear: this place is a lot like your home or somebody's home. Witness the current trend in home decorating which plays on Mexican, Indian, country, or folk decor. I'm not sure that the ideas for such trends did not come from fast food decor rather than from the minds of decorators who have a hard time convincing homemakers to do anything they haven't seen first somewhere else. (I will not say that I have digressed again. Instead, I shall tell you that I am interpreting, according to my understanding, the meaning of my observations. Anybody can digress. Not everybody can interpret. It's a gift.)

Television advertisement deliberately plays on Home and Mother in at least three cultures—Anglo, Hispanic, and black. One of the subliminal messages may well be tolerance for other races. After all, say the ads, all families regardless of race, color, or religious preference share certain warm, genuine, folksy characteristics—they eat out. Magazine ads and radio give the same messages. One new advertising gimmick designed to melt hearts while the cook melts the Jack, Swiss, or Cheddar, is the policy of hiring some past-sixty-five citizens—in other words, grandparents. The messages, through whatever medium, are not subtle, not designed to celebrate cultures or family, but to cause us to gather at the nearest quickie location.

The preponderance of fast food establishments should not leave the impression that there are no other eateries affected by the Food Liberation. Restaurants, not to be confused with cafes, are of two kinds and grades. The first kind of restaurant may be a chain such as Bennigan's, Bay Street, Steak and Ale, Red Lobster, or may be individually owned and called by any number of names. Restaurants are more expensive than fast food places. They, however, get a good share of business. They too are often lined up side by side and offer specialties or mixtures. Many feature glamorized salad bars—Eden's greens again. Because restaurants also had to keep up with the Edibles Expansion, their main feature is well-prepared food, at higher prices, naturally, but plenty of it. Plates are often heaped high. The full plate effect may also be achieved by using small plates, and restaurants do, incidentally, use glass dishes and metal tools. Salad bars do not merely have greens, but also potato salad, pea salad, jello, pudding, macaroni salad, and a whole array of folk relishes such as pickled okra, beets, itty-bitty corn, pickled watermelon, tomatoes, hominy relish, and such. There is often a fancy bread reminiscent of Mama's kitchen—corn bread, cinnamon rolls or whole wheat loaves to slice at the table. Folk decor, even if generally folksy instead of culturally specific, is obvious. All is blended into a tasteful setting to remind us of the supper table somewhere. These restaurants even fry all kinds of vegetables, recognizing that even Mama had to coax the family to get those nasty ole green things down. If they are fried, we will clean our plates of such nonsense as zucchini, mushrooms, and okra. (There is one member of my own family who would gladly eat a dried cow chip if it were dipped in batter and fried.) One other addition should be noted, and that is that nearly all restaurants serve liquor of some kind. Liquor, I must assume, was added merely in order to wash down fried mushrooms or other peculiar menu additions. To choose liquor over iced tea, sweet milk, or buttermilk at table is truly an invention of restaurants and may perhaps convince the population in time that alcohol is an old family tradition that ought not to be denied.

In these times of high prices the public must make adjustments too, since the folk are determined to eat most of their meals out. I can testify from research among my own family that we have taken to what my grandmother used to call "eating and drinking after one another." There is usually plenty on a plate for two at restaurants, or at least all two need to eat when one considers cholesterol, blood sugar, triglycerides, and price. One orders a basket of fried something, say. Somebody else orders a salad. (There must be vegetables still.) Somebody orders a chicken plate. It must be chicken or fish but not you-know-what, for health's sake. Somebody doesn't order anything except something to drink. Then we take the bread plate, slice a piece all around and give the bread plate to the someone who didn't order anything.

Next we all pass our plates around and make our meal. We are not so bad as to "drink after" each other at restaurants. That would be going too far, a real impropriety. Drink-sharing is saved for such gatherings as football games. In more informal settings we are not reluctant to pass round a Coke selling for $1.25 and all take a good swig or several "swallers" each.

In addition to the restaurants which play on large servings, dishes on the table, home specialties, and country decor, there are Restaurants of another kind which deserve capitalization. These Restaurants have been around for many generations and do not rely on "homey," "cute," or "convenient." These places spelled with a capital R charge really high prices, often fifteen dollars a plate and up, serve in specialized and sumptuous locations, offer small helpings of gourmet foods, and feature plenty of help to serve Haute Cuisine. They do not cater to family reunions or football teams and would be offended if the public did come even if they could afford it. They exist to provide a place where one does not partake of ordinary home cooking, but of the exotic, rare, and acquired culinary tastes. Tasteful entertainment and liquor are often included.

Texas, particularly, boasts many quality Restaurants, although other states have some too. Restaurants over the years have not changed much. The surprise is that their numbers still are strong. One of the reasons may be related, although peculiarly, to the Great Recession of the eighties. While most people have less money, a growing number have more money than ever before and can afford the accoutrements of wealth. The number of millionaires has increased and so has the number of billionaires, according to government and IRS statistics.

Only a brief mention of Restaurants—with a capital R—would be necessary if the business did not serve a folk function in the modern world. It is another curiosity, a shift perhaps, that visitation to the Restaurant has now become a rite of passage for some young adults. Primary research among the youth of my own community revealed the following: young people do not go to proms or graduation parties anymore. Instead, they dress up fit to kill in tuxes and dinner gowns, either rented or purchased, and go to a Restaurant, sometimes by way of a limousine which may be rented for an evening for about a hundred dollars. The couple, maybe two couples, head for Dallas from Keller and learn about gentle and gracious dining, living, and manners. Some young people feel that it is good to know of such things as courtesy, gentility, good taste, etiquette; to glimpse good breeding; and most important of all, to learn how to eat off pretty glass dishes, drink from crystal, and use real silverware instead of their hands before one goes out into the world.

Aside from fast fooderies, restaurants, and Restaurants, there are cafes. Cafes are those places, mostly in small towns but also in large ones if you know where to look, where plate lunches and homemade pie are the main staples. Cafes never existed to compete with home cooking or to interfere with the rhythm of home life, and this characteristic puts cafes in the same camp with

Restaurants, although the two places may be worlds apart otherwise. The cafe has always been, in Texas at least, just an extra place to get breakfast now and then, drink coffee and "eat your dinner" although it was merely lunchtime. A cafe is a place where you do not go much past noontime; it is an institution like church and the town square. Cafes have their own folklore and seem somehow suspended in time, an operating foodways museum that shows no sign of disappearing yet and operates relatively untouched by the Food Phenomenon of the eighties. A complete volume ought to be devoted to cafes, the stereotypes of women who serves as waitresses, and the clientele of country people, rednecks, and corporate officers who patronize them and why.

Additionally, there are other kinds of Texas eating places which fall between the cracks, fit no particular category and which, no doubt, have interesting connections to the Food Catastrophe. A few that come to mind are truck stops, cafeterias, West Texas steak houses, catfish huts, health food bars, waffle houses, Oriental restaurants which have increased significantly because of the influx of Eastern immigrants into Texas and under whose influence our Eden's greens are now topped off with bean sprouts and other funny-looking stuff. That's not all. What of shopping mall food, where the smell of chocolate chip cookies fills the air better than expensive perfume and old-fashioned, hand-squeezed lemonade is available to quench the thirst after a hard day of hoeing the Liz Claiborne and Oscar de la Renta rows. There are delicatessens and bakeries and vending machines which spew great varieties of fresh foods instead of just gum and candy. There are now industrial food services which carry hot and cold foods to sites in trucks which open up and look like a version of the Texas chuck wagon. The list goes on and on, and every entry on it promotes distinctive food and folklore.

The Food Connection seems revolutionary, and sometimes revolting, but it has revitalized more than just the food industry. Food marketing has virtually saved gasoline stations—yes, gas stations. In the near past gas stations existed to sell gasoline and such car-related services as lube jobs, repair of tires, motor tune-ups and such. With the oil crisis, once the long lines at the pumps subsided, gas stations began going out of business left and right. Those that did manage to stay afloat offered self-service pumps and nothing much in the way of service. It would be difficult to pinpoint an exact year when the gas station/ grocery/deli (How about Grodelsta?) was born, but in Texas corner lots and entire blocks were bought up to offer gasoline pumps and a convenience store with delicatessen and frozen food offerings complete with microwave ovens, hot dogs rolling along in a rotisserie, coffee in the pot, pop in a machine and frozen gourmet ice cream treats of Barricini and Häagen-Dazs waiting in convenient cases. Sliced meats, fresh sandwiches and cheese are available in a refrigerated glass case. Oh yes, and beer is handy as well. All can be added to your gasoline credit card purchase. Junk? Not on your sweet life. Much of the food is delicious. Every major oil company has similar arrangements in most of their stations and more are going up even as I write. The modern Grodelstas are reminiscent of the country Gro/Ser/Sta which used to be in many small Texas towns, where you could have a cold soda water, candy, watch the Spit and Whittle Club convene, buy a few things for supper. Could it be that the Grodelsta concept is simply the Gro/Ser/Sta reborn and that old-fashioned Texas virtues will return as well?

Is no one taking their meals at home anymore? Yes, but most of those eating at home are doing it differently, even radically. Few are home at the same time to sit down at a table, or coffee bar, or anywhere to eat together. Eating has become an often lonely act, and the floor or a comfortable chair or even the bed may serve as a place to ingest food. Paper products, cardboard, and plastic are big-selling items for both home and party gatherings. Cheap and disposable are first priorities in choosing tableware for the eighties. Whether or not the products are attractive rarely enters into a decision, and yet there is a booming business in matched paper products—cups, plates, napkins, cloth—all in beautifully colored designs. The better offerings are also slick-finished instead of dull matte and of heavier, stiffer quality. My children think of such matched quality as Sunday dishes, or at least that whenever such tableware appears it portends a gathering featuring better food. Their concept of Sunday as opposed to everyday dishes, added to the fact that both know only how to eat with or out of their hands, has caused my mother and me not to will the treasured china and sterling to the children but to leave the valuables to a museum instead. What is being eaten at home is nothing new necessarily. Frozen foods replaced home canning and preserving long ago, but the already-impressive array of frozen foods has escalated and now includes entire dinners, separate entrees, breads, breakfasts, and desserts of gourmet quality. Even Stanley Marcus confirmed in *Quest for the Best* that Sara Lee puts out the best pound cake he's tasted. Calorie and nutritional information appears on some packages. Frozen diet specialties offer meals for under three hundred calories. Microwave cooking removed the final drawback of oven-prepared frozen foods and reduced the time to mere seconds or minutes. Some dishes can even be boiled in a cooking pouch.

Grocery stores are still in business for those who prepare food at home, even if the food is eaten in peculiar settings. Other places such as wholesalers carry food items in industrial size and quantities. Such specialties as Cordon Bleu, stuffed flounder, and lasagna come in large enough quantity to feed a bunch and, incidentally, seem suspiciously reminiscent of selections being served in some restaurants. Traveling meat markets offering steaks, bacon, sausage, chicken, and other selections catch the cook at the beauty shop or even at home and offer their convenient variety. The return of open-air produce stands along highways and even in the big cities reminds customers of times long past. Houseware sections in department stores offer an array of futuristic-looking devices and appliances all designed to make cooking at home better and faster. In addition, these housewares sections carry a fine assortment of matched aprons, napkins, dishes, and pot holders of a folksy design.

Most of the innovations of the Food Phenomenon are designed to attract and tempt the eye. One of the most innovative businesses, however, has to do with smell. The rebirth of burning candles and incense may well have come from the hippie movement of the sixties and still conjures up images of gurus in meditation. Smells of the eighties, however, are surely designed to remind us of old-fashioned home life when the family prepared to gather 'round the table. Mere candles have graduated to little ceramic pots filled with water and—take your pick—peaches and cream, strawberries, vanilla, cinnamon and apples. A small candle underneath causes the pot to simmer and exude its steamy contents. The last home I visited in for more than ten minutes had such a pot. After about fifteen minutes of smelling cinnamon and apples, I wanted to cry because I knew there really would be no dumplings. It was just an aromatic illusion. When the hostess did serve refreshments, it was a slice of fabulous frozen Black Forest bakery cake which I had to lick off a napkin since there were no plastic forks offered.

The idea of cooking odors is not new. Mabel Major, a Southwest literary and scholarly figure in the first half of the century, remembered how her mother would have her hurry to the kitchen and put on a pan of water with cinnamon in it when she caught sight of Father coming up the walk. "He will think supper is on and give me a few minutes to get something started," was her mother's explanation. In modern times, the odor pots are not deliberately designed to make a person hungry. They are used for one of two reasons: to remind us of home where families gathered around a table for a meal, or else to cover up the odor where the dog died under the table and nobody was home long enough to notice until he was two weeks gone.

A survey of the changes in the Food Syndrome at the end of the twentieth century would not be complete without at least brief glimpses into vocabulary, the arts, health, and fashion.

Vocabulary, a sure sign of importance in any time span, demonstrates that food in the eighties is superlative business. Desserts are often called by fabulous names, and even Eden's greens are sometimes dubbed Spinach Delight, Cabbage Surprise, Broccoli Supreme, and Eggplant Extraordinaire. Women, of course, have always figured in food comparisons such as Sweetie Pie and Chocolate Drop, but men are now eligible. Food is the ultimate adjective in this best, if unfamiliar, of all possible worlds where men are known as Hunks, Beefcakes, Sugar Shorts, Honey Lips, and Nice Bananas.

Fashion designers for men, women, and children use food to describe color in terms everyone understands. Whereas mauve or teal leave the customer with no generally agreed upon idea about color, such descriptions as Peach Parfait, Lemon Meringue, Chocolate Chip Brown, Candy Cane Red, Iceberg Lettuce Green not only let purchasers understand exactly the shade they are buying but also prompt them to run by the grocery store before they go home. In my case, I must hurry to the brown-chocolate-chip cookie store for a "hit" before I can drive the toast-colored car home to the cinnamon brick-colored house with the whipped cream trim.

Because of the importance of visual advertising in the tail of the twentieth century, there is literally a category of food art and music. Grocery stores and restaurant television commercials offer the most dazzling array of truly beautiful foods, which incidentally often feature home and family as a background. Music is as important. If we can hum or sing what we have heard, it may prompt us to buy. There are new tunes beautifully orchestrated. School children and teenagers have new folks songs to sing. There is a lovely Campbell ballad, "Soup is good food," a new morning refrain, "Kellogg's in your bowl," and the children's marching song, "I wish I were an Oscar Mayer Weiner," to name a few.

Many would disagree about what I have called by many names—Foodway Phenomenon, Revolution, Connection, Syndrome, Shift, Change, Departure—and insist that I protest too much, that food is still prepared in the traditional way in most homes, that families still do take meals together and that cooking is still an art and act of love which bonds a group together in a folkloric ritual peculiar to mankind not only in Texas but everywhere in the world. The fact that cookbooks are consistent best-sellers in Texas and in the United States must prove that there is no reason for me to rant and rave and stick many of our modern foodways on a satiric skewer. I would not disagree with the disagreers. What I am saying is that a radical change in foodway patterns and foodlore is emerging and that the change will not reverse itself, but instead will evolve into yet another pattern. When food, meals, and eating and the ritual which attends them are no longer connected with home, a special center or area, then the place and what it represents or symbolizes changes too. Whether the departures will result in something of value remains to be seen.

In many Texas homes of the past the pattern focused on one incomparable cook, the one remembered, revered, and to whom all others were compared. That cook nearly always was a mother, was often the repository of the lore, the family saga, the stories, the secrets, and that cook was indeed the keeper of the hearth, with all the warm and attendant meanings attached to that word. Sometimes unspoken in this volume but always underlying the recipes is the memory and suggestion of that person, whoever she was. She was not unlike the medicine woman in the Indian culture; not unlike the Tía for the Mexicans. She bore other labels in other cultures. Not only cooking but healing was in her hands, counseling a part of her familial duties, and ministering like Mary and Martha of the Bible. To her all hearts were known and from her all needs supplied. She was that source of strength acknowledged and proclaimed by young and old, male and female. Not every family contained such a one in each generation. Sometimes there was only one in every three or four generations. Such a person existed in my own family. Her name was Mama Hartman.

One of our favorite topics as grandchild to grandmother was heaven. We talked about it in the kitchen mostly. She spoke of it often and how it would be and who would be there. It seemed such a familiar place by her description that I knew I would want to go when my turn came just because she would be there.

As part of our family lore, I tried to convey to my children the same warmth with the same tactics used by my grandmother. My daughter and I one day had a conversation about Mama Hartman and heaven. She asked me how I visualized the kingdom of heaven and what it would be like for me. I replied that when my time came, Mama Hartman would meet me at the gates. Peter and Gabriel would not be the keepers. None but Mama Hartman would command the entrance. She would demand of angel guardians that they step aside and go and check the oven instead. While I was passing through, she would lay the clean white cloth. I could smell the coffee even before I saw the gate and yea, verily, the table held loaves of hot bread. There would be honey and jelly made from wild plums and grapes. There would be no Eden's greens and no chicken. Cakes and pies and baked goods would abound though. After Mama Hartman put her arms around me she would sing her favorite song: "Break Thou the bread of life, dear Lord to me,/as Thou didst break the loaves beside the sea." My Uncle Fred and all those others who had "passed before me, one by one" would greet this poor, wayfaring stranger.

My daughter Delight was touched by my description. After she had sat thoughtful for a few minutes, I asked her a question. "Delight," I said, "you are a child of the modern world. When you go to heaven someday, what will you look for?" She said, "Why, Mother, for you of course." I was touched to my very core. My child knew I'd be there for her. It was the response I had hoped to hear. "Delight, what will I be doing, and what song will I sing for you?" I waited, sure of her description.

And her reply was surely what I deserved as a modern mother. "Mother, you will meet me with a Burger King sack, and there will be Little Debbie Snack Cakes by the dozen and you will sing the song of my childhood: 'Oh, thank Heaven for 7-11.'"

Oh, how sharper than a serpent's tooth is an ungrateful and realistic child!

The very best part of Texas ever put down on paper may well abide on the pages of this book. Mark it well, and don't say nobody ever told you.

Joyce Gibson Roach

Sources Cited

Abernethy, Francis E. "Hunters Take Delight." *Dallas Times Herald*, 31 March 1985, A46.

Ashley, Carlos. "Saukerkraut." *That Spotted Sow and Other Hill Country Ballads*, 53–54. Austin: Steck, 1949.

Atkins, Daisy. *'Way Back Yonder*. El Paso, Texas: Guynes Printing Co., 1958.

Barker, S. Omar. "Bunkhouse Christmas." *Rawhide Rhymes*, 146. New York: Doubleday, 1968.

Bludworth, G. T. "The Texas Pecan; . . ." *Follow de Drinkin' Gou'd*, 79–80. Publications of the Texas Folklore Society, no. 7. Dallas: Southern Methodist University Press, 1966.

Bourke, John G. "Folk-Foods of the Rio Grande Valley." *Southwestern Lore*, 85–117. Publications of the Texas Folklore Society, no. 9. Dallas: Southern Methodist University Press, 1965 (reprint).

Brooks, Audrey Parker. "Baling Wire and Memories." *Albany News*, 16 April 1987, 6 June 1987, 3 September 1987.

Byrd, James W. "Creeping Ignorance on Poke Sallet." *The Sunny Slopes of Long Ago*, 157–63. Publications of the Texas Folklore Society, no. 33. Dallas: Southern Methodist University Press, 1966.

Cobb, Sally Gates. *Sally's Country Inn*. Covington, Louisiana: n.d.

———. Letter to Ernestine Sewell Linck, 14 September 1987.

Dallas Times Herald, 17 March 1986, *Living*, 1.

Darnton, Robert. *The Great Cat Massacre and Other Episodes in French Cultural History*. New York: Basic Books, 1984.

Dobie, J. Frank. *The Flavor of Texas*. Austin: Jenkins Publishing Co., 1975.

Dunbar, Paul Laurence. "The Party." *Complete Poems of Paul Laurence Dunbar*. New York: Dodd, Mead, 1940.

Everett, Malissa C. Unpublished paper. Carl Coke Rister Collection, Southwest Collection, Texas Tech University.

Ferber, Edna. *Giant*. New York: Doubleday, 1952.

The First Texas Cook Book, 1883. Austin: Eakin Publishing, Inc., 1986 (reprint).

Flach, Vera. *A Yankee in German-America Texas Hill Country*. San Antonio: Naylor, 1973.

Giroux, Mark. *Life in the English Country House*. New Haven: Yale University Press, 1978.

Goyne, Minetta. Letters to Ernestine Sewell Linck, 24 June 1987, 16 November 1987.

Hamner, Laura V. *Light 'n Hitch*. Dallas: American Guild, 1958.

Hittson, Jack H. *The Brazos Broncbuster's Scrapbook*. Mineral Wells, Texas: Brazos Books, 1971.

Huckaby, Esther C. "How Sweet the Sound: A Definition of Sacred Harp Music." Paper presented to the American Studies Association of Texas, November 1986.

Hughes, Stella. *Chuck Wagon Cookin'*. Tucson: University of Arizona Press, 1974.

Hurley, Elizabeth. "Come Buy, Come Buy," 115–138. *Folk Travelers*. Publications of the Texas Folklore Society, no. 25. Dallas: Southern Methodist University Press, 1953.

Hyatt, Gordon. "A Texas Menu." Austin: *Texas National Dispatch*, February 1984, 2.

King, Edward, and J. Wells Champney. *Texas: 1874*. Houston: Cordovan Press, 1974.

Leckie, William H. *The Buffalo Soldiers*. Norman: University of Oklahoma Press, 1967.

Leeper, Faye. "Tall Tales from Down Under: Storm Cellar Wisdom." Paper presented at Texas Folklore Society meeting, 1988.

Lomax, John A. "Cowboy Lingo." *The Sunny Slopes of Long Ago*, 12–25. Publications of the Texas Folklore Society, no. 33. Dallas: Southern Methodist University Press, 1966.

Machann, Clinton, and James Mendl. *Krásna Amérika*. Austin: Eakin Press, 1983.

Marcus, Stanley. *Quest for the Best*. New York: Viking, 1979.

Marcy, Randolph B. *The Prairie Traveler: A Handbook for Overland Expeditions*, 1859. Williamstown, Massachusetts: Corner House, 1968 (reprint).

McDaniels, Mac, and Jalyn Burkett. *Chuck Wagon Cooking*. Fort Worth: Texas Trails Bar-B-Q, 1985.

Olmsted, Frederick Law. *A Journey Through Texas: Or, A Saddle-Trip on the Southwestern Frontier with a Statistical Appendix*, 1857. Austin: University of Texas Press, 1978 (reprint).

Olsen, Palmer. Quoted in the *Dallas Morning News*, August 16, 1987.

Owens, William A. *Tell Me a Story, Sing Me a Song*. Austin: University of Texas Press, 1983.

————. *Three Friends: Bedichek, Dobie, Webb.* New York: Doubleday, 1969.

Piner, Howell Lake. "Let's Go Back to Honey Grove!" *Writers and Writings of Texas*, edited by Davis F. Eagleton. New York: Broadway, 1913.

Russell, L. B. *Granddad's Autobiography.* Comanche, TX: Comanche Publishing Co., n.d.

Smith, Richard. "Richard's Tales," 220–253. *Folk Travelers.* Publications of the Texas Folklore Society, no. 25. Dallas: Southern Methodist University Press, 1953.

Smithwick, Noah. *The Evolution of a State or Recollections of Old Texas Days*, 1900. Austin: University of Texas Press, 1983 (reprint).

Sosa, Mrs. Alonzo (Sylvia). Interview with Ernestine Sewell Linck. 3 August 1987.

Spikes, Nellie Witt. "The Early Days on the South Plains." *Tasty Traditions*, edited by Women's Division of Ralls Chamber of Commerce and Agriculture. Olathe, Kansas: Cookbook Publishers, 1985.

Stilwell, Hart. *Uncovered Wagon*, 1947. Austin: Texas Monthly Press, 1985 (reprint).

Sweet, Alexander. *Alex Sweet's Texas.* Austin: University of Texas Press, 1986.

Templeton, Julia Terry. *By Request—Only the Best.* Charleston, South Carolina: Templeton, 1984.

————. Letter to Ernestine Sewell Linck, 15 November 1987.

Texas Committee for the Humanities. "Juneteenth." The Texas Experience: Texas Sesquicentennial Series. 1985.

Texas Living: Past and Present. Texas Agricultural Extension Service. Dallas: Dallas County Home Economics Resource Commission, 1986.

Thomas, Aileen, and Elkin Thomas. "Homecoming Sunday." Shantih Recordings, Krum, Texas.

Thomas, Marcia. Letter to Ernestine Sewell Linck. 15 July 1987.

Tolbert, Frank X. *A Bowl of Red.* New York: Doubleday, 1972.

Walker, Virginia. "Pie Suppers in East Texas." *Texian Stomping Grounds*, 33–34. Publications of the Texas Folklore Society, no. 17. Austin: Texas Folklore Society, 1941.

Wesley, Howard D. "Ranchero Sayings of the Border." *Puro Mexicano*, 211–220. Publications of the Texas Folklore Society, no. 12. Dallas: Southern Methodist University Press, 1935.

West, John O. Archived Collection, University of Texas at El Paso. Unpublished collection of frontier folk foods and foodways, assembled by Donna Koch, Helen Vaughan, and others.

————. "The Galloping Gourmet, or The Chuck Wagon Cook and His Craft," 215–225. *By Land and By Sea: Studies in the Folklore of Work and Leisure*, edited by Roger D. Abrahams et al. Hatboro, Pennsylvania: Legacy Books, 1985.

Acknowledgments

Grateful acknowledgment is made for permission to use materials from the following:

That Spotted Sow and Other Hill Country Ballads, by Carlos Ashley. Steck, 1949. Reprinted by permission of the author.

Tasty Traditions, by Women's Division of Ralls Chamber of Commerce and Agriculture, 1965. Reprinted by permission of LuAnne Bourland.

"Baling Wire and Memories," by Audrey Parker Brooks. *Albany News*. Reprinted by permission of the author.

Complete Poems of Paul Laurence Dunbar, by Paul Laurence Dunbar. Dodd, Mead, 1949. Reprinted by permission of Dodd, Mead.

"Hunters Take Delight," by Francis E. Abernethy. *Dallas Times Herald*. Reprinted by permission of the author.

Publications of the Texas Folklore Society: no. 33, 1966, "Creeping Ignorance on Poke Sallet," by James W. Byrd, and "Cowboy Lingo," by John A. Lomax; no. 7, 1928, "The Texas Pecan," by G. T. Bludworth; no. 12, 1935, "Ranchero Sayings of the Border," by Howard D. Wesley; no. 9, 1931, "Folk-Foods of the Rio Grande Valley," by John G. Bourke; no. 17, 1941, "Pie Suppers in East Texas," by Virginia Walker; no. 25, 1953, "Richard's Tales," by Richard Smith. All reprinted by permission of Francis E. Abernethy, Texas Folklore Society.

The First Texas Cookbook, 1883. Eakin Publications, 1986. Reprinted by permission of Eakin Publications.

A Yankee in German America Texas Hill Country, by Vera Flach. Naylor, 1973. Reprinted by permission of Jean Wiedenfeld and Ernest K. Flach, Jr.

Mirrors, Mice, and Mustaches, by George Hendricks. Texas Folklore Society, 1966. Reprinted by permission of the author.

The Brazos Bronchbuster's Scrapbook, by Jack Homer Hittson, Sr., 1971. Reprinted by permission of Jack Homer Hittson, Jr.

The Buffalo Soldiers: A Narrative of the Negro Cavalry in the West, by William H. Leckie. University of Oklahoma Press, 1967. Permission granted by University of Oklahoma Press.

Chuck Wagon Cooking, by Mac McDaniels and Jalyn Burkett. Texas Trails Bar-B-Q, 1985. Reprinted by permission of the authors.

Krásna América, by Clinton Machann and James Mendl. Eakin Publications, 1983. Reprinted by permission of the authors.

The Prairie Traveler: A Handbook for Overland Expeditions, 1859. Corner House Publishers, 1968. Reprinted by permission of Corner House Publishers.

Tell Me a Story, Sing Me a Song, by William A. Owens. University of Texas Press, 1983. Reprinted by permission of the author.

Alex Sweet's Texas: The Lighter Side of Lone Star History, by Alexander Edwin Sweet, edited by Virginia Eisenhour. University of Texas Press, 1986. Reprinted by permission of the University of Texas Press.

Texas Living: Past and Present, by the Texas Agricultural Extension Service. Texas Agricultural Extension Service, 1986. Reprinted by permission of Pat Seaman.

"The Texas Experience," in commemoration of the Texas Sesquicentennial. Texas Committee for the Humanities, 1986. Reprinted by permission of Robert O'Connor.

"Homecoming Sunday," by Aileen and Elkin Thomas. Shantih Publishing and Productions, n.d. Reprinted by permission of the authors.

A Bowl of Red, by Frank X. Tolbert. Doubleday, 1953, 1972. Reprinted by permission of the Frank X. Tolbert family, courtesy of Evelyn Oppenheimer.

"The Galloping Gourmet, or the Chuck Wagon Cook and His Craft," by John O. West. *By Land and By Sea*. Legacy Books, 1985. Reprinted by permission of John O. West and Legacy Books.

"A Texas Menu," by Gordon A. Hyatt. *Texas National Dispatch*, February 1984. Reprinted by permission of Mrs. Gordon A. Hyatt.

Uncovered Wagon, by Hart Stilwell. Copyright 1947, 1974 by Hart Stilwell. Reissued in 1985 by Texas Monthly Press. Reprinted by permission of Texas Monthly Press.

The Gilmer Mirror and *The Twentieth Century Club Cook Book*, Gilmer Mirror, 1972. Reprinted by permission of Sarah Greene.

Chuck Wagon Cookin', by Stella Hughes. University of Arizona Press, 1974. Reprinted by permission of the University of Arizona Press.

Life in the English Country House, by Mark Giroux. Yale University Press, 1978. Reprinted by permission of Yale University Press.

Giant, by Edna Ferber. Doubleday, 1952. (Copyright 1952 by Edna Ferber. Copyright 1980 by Harriet F. Pilpel, as executrix.) Reprinted by permission of Harriet F. Pilpel, as executrix and trustee.

Light 'n Hitch, by Laura V. Hamner. American Guild, 1958. Reprinted by permission of Laura V. Hamner estate.

The Great Cat Massacre and Other Episodes in French Cultural History, by Robert Darnton. Basic Books, 1984. Reprinted by permission of Basic Books.

By Request—Only the Best, by Julia Terry Templeton. Copyright 1984 by Julia Terry Templeton. Permission to use by author.

Rawhide Rhymes, by S. Omar Barker. Doubleday, 1969. Reprinted by permission of Elsa Barker.

Flavor of Texas, by J. Frank Dobie. Jenkins Publishing Company, 1985. Reprinted by permission of John Jenkins.

Grandad's Autobiography, by L. B. Russell. Comanche [Texas] Publishing Company, n.d. Reprinted by permission of Dick Tye.

Index

Index to Recipes

Designed and produced by Whitehead & Whitehead
Composed by G & S Typesetters in Goudy Old Style
with display type in Schneidler Light
Printed and bound by Edwards Bros.
Illustrated by Barbara Mathews Whitehead